The Disciplined Online Investor

The Disciplined Online Investor

Steven J. Hendlin, Ph.D.

McGraw-Hill

New York   San Francisco   Washington, D.C.   Auckland Bogotá
Caracas   Lisbon   London   Madrid   Mexico City   Milan
Montreal   New Delhi   San Juan   Singapore
Sydney   Tokyo   Toronto

Library of Congress Cataloging-in-Publication Data

Hendlin, Steven J.
    The disciplined online investor / by Steven J. Hendlin.
    New York : McGraw-Hill, 2000.
        p.   cm.
    ISBN 0-07-135994-X
    1.   Electronic trading of securities.

    HG4515.95.H46 2000   11-926945
    332.64'0285—dc21   CIP

McGraw-Hill

A Division of The **McGraw·Hill** Companies

1 2 3 4 5 6 7 8 9 0 DOC/DOC 0 9 8 7 6 5 4 3 2 1 0

ISBN 0-07-135994-X

The sponsoring editor for this book was Stephen Isaacs, the editing supervisor was Janice Race, and the production supervisor was Charles Annis. It was set in Palatino by Judy Brown.

Printed and bound by R. R. Donnelley & Sons Company.

For permission to reprint the excerpted material by James Cramer in Chapter 5, grateful acknowledgment is given to Thestreet.com

McGraw-Hill books are available at special quantity discounts to use as premiums and sales promotions, or for use in corporate training programs. For more information, please write to the Director of Special Sales, Professional Publishing, McGraw-Hill, Two Penn Plaza, New York, NY 10121-2298. Or contact your local bookstore.

 This book is printed on recycled, acid-free paper containing a minimum of 50% recycled de-inked fiber.

CONTENTS

Now, as we begin a new decade, century, and millennium, there are over 12 million investors with online brokerage accounts. A relatively small number are hyperactive "minute" traders who hold fast-moving stocks literally no longer than a minute or two before selling them. Thousands more are day traders who buy and sell numerous times in a trading session but like to close out the day flat, with all their capital in cash.

Thousands of others are swing or position traders who hold a stock between two and five days. Some hold positions for a few weeks or months. Hundreds of thousands of others are trading a few times a week or a few times a month. And millions more are trading only occasionally but would trade more often if they could only feel more comfortable with themselves and the whole online trading experience.

The Disciplined Online Investor was written with all types of traders in mind, no matter what their style or frequency of investing. And it was written as well for all those contemplating online investing but who want to test the waters without feeling so much apprehension and fear.

As anyone who has done any online trading knows, it is fraught with strong positive and negative emotions. Scary thoughts, doubt thoughts, compulsions, and superstitious trading rituals pervade online trading of all types. This may be verified simply by walking through any day trading room or watching individuals at home trading on their own computers.

Why? Because of the anxiety of having money literally on the line. Excitement, anticipation, exhilaration, and the rush of adrenaline at making profitable trades also are part of the process.

How can we learn to harness these emotions for our own benefit, so that we may make better trading decisions? How can we become more self-aware, more conscious of our behavior? How can we become more disciplined online investors, able to follow through with our intentions?

We will look at important psychological issues that are unique to online trading and how you, with some insight, can use them to your trading advantage.

For many of you, it is not just the desire to strike it rich through trading that motivates your interest. It is also the pride of managing your own finances, of feeling like a "player" like the Wall Street big boys, and the positive feelings of controlling your own financial destiny that draw you to the game.

Ideally, this book will not only be used as a source of basic information on the psychology and discipline of online investing but also as a handy reference when you find yourself in the heat of the trading battle. It may be pulled out and referred to perhaps to calm your nerves after a trade turns against you. Or maybe to help keep emotions in check during the inevitable panic you may feel when the markets go through their typical fierce gyrations. Perhaps it will be of help when you need to block out unwanted distractions while you are trading.

My intent has been to keep *The Disciplined Online Investor* simply written and to make the ideas practical. If you can manage an online brokerage account and learn the methods and techniques of good trading, you will be able to make use of this book.

Armed with psychological insight into your own motives for online trading, and understanding your thoughts and feelings that arise during trading, you will be better mentally equipped to make profitable trades. You will feel more confidence and pride in managing your investments, attend to trading with better focus, and have more enjoyment while doing it.

I also want you to understand something about the psychology of the market. With insight as to the powerful psychological forces that shape the market, and how others tend to react, you will be better able to predict market movements and use them to your advantage.

Realistic or not, most online traders have hopes of striking it rich. Like the days of the old wild west, we want to take responsibility for our own financial destiny. Except, instead of being armed with a six-shooter, a pick, a shovel, and a pan to hunt for gold, trading prospectors are now armed with cable modems or direct access lines, speedy processors, multiple monitors, and all the news, opinion, and real-time stock data that they can possibly digest.

We have discovered the new millennium version of panning for gold. My intention is for *The Disciplined Online Investor* to help you distinguish between fool's gold and the real thing.

Steven Hendlin, Ph.D.
Corona del Mar, California
January 1, 2000
e-mail: golfdoc@home.com

ACKNOWLEDGMENTS

The writing of this book was short and sweet—but intense. The manuscript was completed in four months in one shot, with no drafts or rewrites. During this period, I continued my part-time psychotherapy practice around my writing. The intensity of the writing meant lost sleep, as I averaged four hours per night. My golf game also suffered, as I fell short of my normal quota of practice balls and played little.

This writing was an exercise in what the Buddhists call *one-pointed attention*. Most of my waking hours during these four months were spent either closely watching or reading about the stock market, trading online, writing about trading, or thinking about writing about it. I was enveloped in a delicious bubble of creative flow, relying on very few notes or references to outside sources. Since I did not lean on the word and expertise of others, any errors in describing the factual workings of the securities markets are my own.

I want to thank my editor at McGraw-Hill, Stephen Isaacs, who showed immediate interest in my proposal and allowed me creative license to alter it as I sprinted along the way. He permitted me unbridled freedom in the themes I chose to focus on. This allowed for the consideration of some cognitive processes, such as the role of images, fantasies, and moment-to-moment awareness in trading, that are just never discussed in books on investing or trading. He was also kind enough to preserve my style of writing, as was the editing supervisor, Janice Race.

Thanks also to my literary agent, Jeff Herman, for his enthusiasm and for being a mensch.

Thanks to my mother, Susan Hendlin Phillips, standing behind me, as always, in loving support and encouragement. And thanks to my brothers, Timmy and Ricky, for their lifelong companionship.

My devoted wife and colleague, Deborah, helped formulate the topic for this book, visioning how I might combine my career in clinical psychology and my interest in the market into what I believe is the first book published specifically on the psychology of online investing. Thanks, Deborah, for permitting me to step inside the bubble undisturbed and come out only for food, gourmet coffee, exercise, and a little sleep.

The New Millennium Gold Rush

Referring to online investing as the new millennium gold rush is not hype. Nor is it simply a clever way to indicate our hope of striking it rich. For a growing number of traders and investors it is simply the truth.

The Internet is not only profoundly impacting how we shop, do business, gather information, and communicate, but it is also transforming the way the major stock markets and brokerage industry work. Both are changing more rapidly now than in their whole history. This change is toward catering more than ever before to the individual investor who trades online.

We are moving rapidly toward an electronic environment in which we will have the freedom and convenience to be able to wake up at three in the morning, sit down at the computer, and with a few mouse clicks, trade any stock, commodity, currency, or index anywhere in the world.

While we are not yet able to plug in to such a grand design, ever increasing numbers of us have already gone west (discovered online trading) and have staked a claim (made a deposit) with a discount broker. We then mine individual stocks to find their kernels of gold.

The goal of *The Disciplined Online Investor* is to help you, as an online prospector, manage your thoughts and emotions around the process of trading. By doing so, you will increase your chances of success in hitting the vein of gold. And you will come to know yourself better in the process.

1

Continuing with our new millennium gold rush metaphor, here are some ways the brokerage industry is rushing to accommodate online prospectors.

THE RUSH TO LOWER COMMISSIONS

By the time you read this, the market landscape will be changing in significant ways to favor you, the online trader. For example, Merrill-Lynch, the traditional brokerage house that resisted online trading to protect the income of its brokers, recently announced they are going to become an online presence, joining the more than two dozen others who are already at it.

When you have assets deposited with them over a set amount, they will offer you a flat-fee-per-year trading fee that allows you unlimited trades. Surely, other brokerage houses will jump into the fray with competitive offerings so they will not be left behind.

What is significant about this move by Merrill is that it acknowledges that the old system of paying hundreds of dollars commission for a full-service broker is drastically changing. Full-service brokers are realizing that they must offer customers discounts for online trading or they will lose substantial business.

If your full-service stock broker doesn't have any information that you don't have, and can't get it any faster than you can, what added value is he or she providing you to justify charging up to 10 times higher commission? With all news and analysis immediately available to you on the Internet, all you have to do is know where to find it, take the time to read it, and learn to understand it.

It is quite possible that in the next few years, individual full-service stock brokers will become the dinosaurs of the brokerage industry. And like dinosaurs, they will slowly become extinct. If you think I'm exaggerating, listen to this story for a clue as to where it's going.

A guy in his fifties comes into my office looking and sounding miserably depressed. He is facing the loss of his home, no longer able to make his mortgage payments. He tells me he used to head his own brokerage office where he managed 10 stock brokers, earning a small fortune in commissions.

Because of the explosion in popularity of online trading, in the last two years all of the brokers have left him. They no longer could afford to work for him, struggling to hang on themselves. He had no long-term clients to help him survive economically.

Now relegated to the ranks of working for another firm on commission, he's making almost nothing. He can't afford to pay for counseling treatment. How many other brokers out there are currently facing a similar predicament?

As more investors migrate to the Internet, brokers will be used only by the very well-to-do, who don't care to take the time to manage their own investments, or don't mind paying exorbitant fees for the luxury of having a professional do it for them. Some will keep an account with a traditional brokerage to increase their chances of getting shares of lucrative IPOs.

Full-service brokers will be used by those who simply don't believe they have the knowledge or interest to manage their own investments. And they will act as consultants to provide feedback regarding your own thinking.

Brokers already are forced to compete with financial planners, helping people deal with estate planning, trusts, and retirement issues.

It seems inevitable that the cost for stock trades will steadily go down. This is because competition and increased online trading volume will force online brokerage houses to outdo each other with more and more attractive offerings. They will be trying to win new customers and steal customers from competing houses. Instead of only one online broker offering a fee of $5, we will have many.

Before long, online brokerage houses may even allow you to trade absolutely free, just to get your account, especially if you have a large amount of money to place with them. If you think this just can't happen, wait and see. Increased electronic trading by individuals is going to truly turn the brokerage industry upside down.

Three months after I wrote the preceding paragraph, this piece of news came out: "The chief executive of Lucent Technologies predicted on Tuesday that free stock trades on the Internet will be announced within a year. 'There is no doubt in my mind that within the next 12 months someone of substantial repute will announce they're going to provide trades free online, with the value of you coming to their (Web) site for other services,' Rich McGinn, chief executive of the New Jersey–based telecommunications equipment supplier, said." (*Reuters News*, September 14, 1999)

And then, two months after the previous news item, comes this: American Express announces in a full-page ad that account holders with $100,000 will trade free, up to 3000 shares per trade. Those with at least $25,000 will not pay when placing buy orders online, only to sell. The sell cost is $15. The only catch with this offer is that you can only buy the same stock once per day, or you have to pay commission each time after the first. So day traders won't go for it. But active traders holding for at least a day will find it attractive, especially those with the higher balances. Just an example of where the momentum with commissions is headed.

THE RUSH TO OFFER MORE DATA

What is called Level I data is simply real-time quotes. A real-time quote tells you the best *bid* (the price you can sell at) and *offer* (the best price you can buy at) on any stock for sale at the given time.

It was not all that long ago that getting a free real-time quote was not so easy. Most quotes were delayed, which was OK if you just wanted to get an idea of where a stock stood, but good for nothing if you wanted to trade. A 15-minute-delayed quote is ancient history in the stock market.

To get real-time quotes, you needed to pay for a separate feed through a satellite or cable TV that could cost hundreds of dollars per month. In addition, you had to use special equipment to receive the quotes. In the last two or three years, free real-time quotes have become readily available at dozens of discount brokerage sites and other stock-related sites.

More elaborate research is now available at a number of stock sites. This data includes past performance charts, real-time charting, technical and fundamental analysis, analysts' reports, earnings estimates, legal filings for initial public offerings, and various other useful information to aid investors. In addition to what is available at web sites, special software packages are available from a number of day trading companies which offer everything named above plus additional esoteric data.

It is easy for the average online investor to become overwhelmed with the amount of sophisticated data available, especially for those not trained to interpret it. For those who are interested, this is an area that is best approached slowly and carefully, learning one topic at a time. It is not something we can expect to immediately comprehend. We need to remember that instant access to sophisticated charting and analysis in no way means instant comprehension or application of it!

LEVELS OF ACCESS TO THE GAME

For the active trader, the single most valuable offering is what is called Level II quotes. These quotes are for the NASDAQ computer-traded market only. Packages of real-time charting, news, and Level II quotes are now offered for a fairly steep fee ($250 to $350 or more per month) at a number of online sites aimed at active traders.

This packaged data, however, may be "free" if you make a certain number of trades per month, depending on the provider. In other words, you will most likely pay something over $500 in commissions per month to get the free quotes.

Over the next few years, Level II quotes will become the norm for all online investors, not just serious active traders. And they will drop drastically in cost even to those who don't really need them or care to use them. But once understood, this tool will be appreciated.

Having Level II data puts you in the position to see not just the best price at any moment, but where all the *market makers* (those institutions or individuals who buy and sell shares to the public and "make a market") on a stock stand in relation to each other. You also see what is called *time and sales,* which is a dynamic scrolling list of all transactions and the time they occur.

This data was previously reserved only for market makers or those willing to pay costly monthly fees. It is a speedy and powerful tool that helps level the proverbial playing field for the individual online trader. But you need to get some training to understand it, as it moves very fast. You can get into trouble with it if you don't know what you're doing.

With Level II, you see not only the best current price to buy and sell, you are also privy to everything right behind the current prices. You see the "pressure" that is building at various prices, as market makers line up to buy and sell, and thus you get a better sense of which direction the stock is moving.

One metaphor that describes this is to say that Level II is like flying an airplane with radar guidance, while Level I is like flying by the seat of your pants, with no radar to indicate direction, force, or turbulence.

But the true picture of what is happening in the game is somewhat more complicated. There is another layer of the action. Level II data, while a tremendous advantage over Level I, is still only a part of the whole picture. This is because even with Level II quotes, you are unable to see the buys and sells that the market markers are doing "behind the curtain."

Although altogether irrelevant for the occasional investor, it is quite relevant for the active trader. I mention it only to indicate one of the ways the individual trader, even with Level II, is at a disadvantage compared to the institutional players.

Level III: The Heavy Hitters

Most of the day trader software packages don't include access to the major league where only the heavy hitters are playing, and this layer of the game is taking place on what is called Level III. In this league, the players are trading large amounts of stock to each other on one of the electronic networks, Instinet. And they are doing it for slightly better prices than you will see disseminated on Level II.

The purpose of their using this Level III system is that they are able to buy and sell blocks of stock anonymously. They not only make money on the spread between the bid and the ask that shows up on Level II, they also "scalp" a better price in the stock they buy and sell to each other than the prices that go out to the public. So, they effectively make money two ways. And they do this repeatedly, earning a nice profit along the way.

None of this activity shows up in the Level II screen. It is possible for the individual active trader to passively monitor this Level III activity by paying $200 per month to the exchange. But the cost to be able to actively trade with live Level III is a cool half million dollars. Welcome to the big league, where membership has its privileges.

The Level II screen has different colors to represent the best price, the next best price, the third best price, and so on, both to buy and sell the stock. It identifies the name of each market maker at each price. When the stock is active, the colors change rapidly with each change in price. The colors make it easy for those viewing the screen to quickly assess how fast a stock is moving at each price.

When you watch Level II quotes, it looks something like a fast game of Pac-Man. You see two rows of prices on your screen—one to buy and one to sell a given stock in varying amounts by market makers. As shares are bought by and sold to the public, the lumps of shares are "eaten up," and leave the screen. Each market maker waits in line for his or her turn to offer a lump of shares to be consumed. So, as each market maker's supply of stock is eaten, the next one in line comes to the head of the line.

But the process is never so orderly.

Because what makes the game exciting is this: At any time, a market maker can jump in ahead of others in line simply by being willing to offer a new best price to buy or sell the stock. Decisions about changes in price by market makers are made very quickly. Remember, this is all being done electronically. There is a lot of quick strategizing that goes on between them in jockeying for position to buy and sell.

Like a game of poker, players keep their electronic hands close to their cyberchests, not wanting any of the others to know their moves until literally the last second. Also like poker, there is a certain amount of bluffing and "head fakes" that take place. All of this makes up the microworld of determining moment-to-moment prices. While crucial for the serious active trader, it is but a mere curiosity for long-term investors. They don't really care whether they pay a quarter point more or less, since they have a long-term perspective.

But even for online investors whose style is to buy and hold, it is fascinating and instructive to simply sit and watch a Level II screen to learn how electronic trading actually occurs. You may do this by visiting a day trading room in your area or by downloading a trial version of software (usually 15 minutes delayed) at web sites that offer it (for example, *Tradescape.com*).

I have found watching Level II data useful in deciphering some of the strategy employed by market makers. You begin to realize how these people are able to manipulate a stock up or down when it is to their advantage. And, of course, it is *always* to their advantage.

It is because of this perceived (and actual) power to manipulate stock prices that market makers have become the target of scorn and contempt by active traders and serious investors. This may be witnessed by reading a sample of the online bulletin board posts anytime a stock moves unpredictably for reasons that are largely unknown. The first and easiest target for blame are the market makers. Justified or not, in the stock trading world, they are the wretched group that everyone loves to hate.

When watching Level II, it takes a while to understand the flow patterns of a stock. But after days of close watching, you come away with a pretty clear picture of how things work on the NASDAQ market. You begin to be able to predict which way the market is going to move just by watching the action. This is a tremendous advantage compared to having no idea which way it is going with Level I data. And Level II is electronic trading at its most pure level.

Of course, wallowing in this kind of minutiae is not for everybody. You must be willing to narrow your focus to changing colors on a screen without getting bored at watching flashing numbers. I found the flow of numbers captivating, especially as I began to understand more of what they meant.

For those who are more active traders and need to be on a par with other traders, it is crucial to have this information. If you don't, you will be at a huge disadvantage, since most other serious day and swing traders will be monitoring Level II quotes closely.

In the game of day trading or active position trading, you need to have all the data available to compete. You need, in some ways, to think like a long-term investor. You need to know the sector of the company you are trading and the particular stock inside and out. You need to know every bit of news about it, the fundamentals and technicals, and its daily patterns.

You need to become an expert in that one stock and make it such a part of your psyche that you even dream about it at night! You can be sure the market makers are doing nothing less than this. And if you're going to compete against them, you have to take it as seriously as they do. Anything less, and you are likely to lose your shirt. And even with this dedication, you will still be at least a step behind the big-league professionals. If you don't believe this, you are fooling yourself.

Good day traders, in this way, are thinking like long-term investors. They are doing the research they need to do. They are becoming more professional in their approach. We will get into this theme of what "investor's-mind" has to offer traders in Chapter 9. The days of 20-somethings playing momentum stocks they don't even know the names of are coming to an end. It may work for a while in a fast market but, over time, the market will rob them of their money and slit their emotional throats.

So trying to compete against the market with anything less than Level II is impossible. Viewing Level II is like being able to see what's coming around the bend before it actually appears. Because you can see how many market makers are lining up at what prices (and with how much stock) to buy and sell, you have a window on exactly which way the stock is headed.

One simple way to use this information is when I can comfortably put in a market order to buy at a certain price and can see that there is plenty of stock for sale at that price. In other words, I see that there are a number of market makers lined up offering stock at my price.

Otherwise, I have to pay a little more for a *limit* order (an order to buy the stock only when it reaches a limit I have specified), not knowing whether the price I want to pay will still be available by the time my order is processed. But even this is changing, as at least one company is now offering limit orders at $5, the same as for market orders (*rjt.com*).

Online investors simply don't know where the stock is going to be in a minute without Level II information. And when you're trying to get the best possible prices, a minute into the future translates into a big advantage.

As we become more sophisticated online investors, we will all want the advantage that comes with Level II. When it is offered for very low cost or even free, all serious investors, even those who only trade a few times a year, will want the very best prices in getting in and out of a stock. They will no longer be as tolerant as they are now of giving such a big advantage to the market makers. In this way, longer-term investors are going to think more like day traders. In Chapter 10, we explore this thoroughly.

THE RUSH TO INCREASE TRADING HOURS

For some time now, you have been able to trade after normal market hours. Two online brokerages, Dreyfus and Discover, began the new wave, joining forces with an after-hours market site (*www.marketxt.com*), initiating extended trading for the online investor. And many other online brokerages have jumped in to offer the same advantage. This means that those on the east coast who have accounts can trade from Monday through Thursday from 6 to 8 P.M.

Perhaps more significantly, those on the west coast can enjoy trading from 3 to 6 P.M. in the afternoon, during what are still normal afternoon business hours. My prediction: Within no longer than six months after this book is published, some form of trading will be available 24 hours per day.

This new development is important because it means you can trade on news at the close of the market rather than be forced to wait until the next morning. This is one more way the individual online investor gains more equal status compared to professional traders, who have enjoyed this privilege for some time.

Although there may be some problems related to fair bid and offer spreads (the difference between buy and sell prices are too far apart) and a possible lack of volume in the after-market, these issues will be resolved as more traders and investors become more comfortable with trading outside normal market hours.

And it doesn't stop there. By the time you read this, the NASDAQ market will have extended afternoon hours just to cater to online investors.

If that's not enough, the NASDAQ itself is planning to sell shares of itself to its members, and perhaps later, to the public. What the NASDAQ does will be followed by the New York Stock Exchange—because nobody wants to be left out of the game. Nobody wants to lose the orders that will be put through by individual investors sitting at their own computers. The reason for lengthening trading hours by the exchanges is not only as a convenience to online traders. It's mainly because of the pressure not to lose business to independent electronic trading networks, discussed later in this chapter.

In this country, we are heading for nothing less than one large electronic stock exchange that will operate around the clock. This may very well mean that the New York Stock Exchange becomes entirely electronics, and the floor trading system as we know it will cease to exist. As the following news items indicate, this will ultimately turn into one gigantic worldwide exchange. Every new computer sold will include built-in software that immediately gives you access to this worldwide exchange. Just as we may now connect to web sites all over the world, the world's markets will offer us the same mouse-click-away convenience. It's all coming right around the bend.

> **Item (*The New York Times*, November 5, 1999, p. C2):**
> On November 5, 1999, NASDAQ announced plans to open an Internet-based exchange that will list shares of companies based in Europe.

This is part of its effort to build a global stock exchange that offers nonstop securities trading in all parts of the world. They also announced plans to set up a virtual stock exchange in Japan as well. NASDAQ officials hope to begin operations in Europe and Japan in the final three months of 2000.

> **Item (*Los Angeles Times*, November 6, 1999, p. C1):**
> Under pressure from upstart computerized markets, the New York Stock Exchange plans to break with centuries of tradition by creating its own electronic trading system, Chairman Richard Grasso announced Friday. The proposed system would allow trades of 1000 or fewer shares to be executed

automatically, bypassing the "specialists"—traders on the Big Board floor who hold the franchise for dealing in specific NYSE-listed stocks.

The plan is seen by some analysts as a key step toward an eventual all-electronic market. The NYSE has long maintained that its system for filtering all trades through 480 specialists provides better prices and market stability for investors. But critics, including many of the NYSE member broker-dealers, are pushing the Big Board to emulate the competition—namely such quick and low-cost electronic trading networks or ECNs, as Instinet, Island, and Primax Trading, which automatically match buyers and sellers with no intermediary involved.

THE RUSH TO OFFER ALTERNATIVE TRADING SYSTEMS

As indicated earlier, another important development is the ability of individual traders to place trades with independent electronic networks, so that you may be able to eliminate your present brokerage house altogether. These are already commonly used by day trading firms, handling millions of stock trades per day.

These alternative systems line up buy and sell orders from brokerages and match them automatically. This eliminates the role of dealers and stock exchanges. These alternative systems are currently available to a small number of individual investors who pay for the privilege to use them.

These systems have come about because of the new computer technology and customer pressure for low costs and fast trading. They have taken business away from exchanges by offering cheap trade execution during regular market hours and after hours. It is because of these systems that both the NASDAQ and the New York Stock Exchange have been forced to lengthen their hours of trading.

Before long, these electronic systems will be available to all of us who are trading online. By eliminating the middle role that your brokerage house plays, you will pay less in commissions and be able to make immediate trades with other traders directly, guaranteeing yourself the best possible prices.

The gold rush has really just begun. Thousands are joining the prospecting game every week. And as a growing number have money to invest, online trading will continue to grow. This is not a passing fad—anymore than the Internet itself is. And that leads us to why we need this book—the first to explore the psychology of this exploding phenomenon of online investing.

WHY THE PSYCHOLOGY OF ONLINE INVESTING?

Some might be wondering what the value is of a book on the psychology of Internet trading. Isn't it just as simple as pushing buttons and hoping the trade goes our way? Do we really need to understand how our own thinking and emotions affect our trading habits?

Of course we do!

Without understanding how our thinking and emotions influence our trading behavior, *we will tend to unconsciously repeat the same mistakes over and over again*. Whether you are a day trader or a long-term investor, your thinking and emotions will affect your decision making, your money management, and your overall investment outcomes.

From my perspective as a psychologist, this is obvious. But it is not so obvious to those who have never really considered their own habitual ways of dealing with money. By the time you finish this book, it will be obvious to you, too.

Here are some simple examples: Feeling fearful of making the wrong decision may block us from taking decisive action. Or: The tendency to be overly conservative may make us take profits too quickly on a rising stock. Or: Not considering carefully enough some of the factors affecting current trading conditions may prompt us to leap prematurely. Any of these things may happen to us occasionally. But it is the repeated mistake that we need to identify and understand, so that we may change our behavior.

WHOM IS *THE DISCIPLINED ONLINE INVESTOR* FOR?

This book will be most useful for those of you who already know how to push the right keys to trade on the computer. It is for all online traders and investors. It doesn't matter whether you are a "minute trader," who trades dozens of times per day, or just a few times per year.

I will be using the word *trading* in this book simply to indicate buying or selling a stock—a stock transaction. Online investors, then, make trades when they execute a buy or sell, even if they are investing over the long term.

But when we think of the difference between approaches to the market, we need to remember that *investing* over the longer term is a bet that a company or an industry will improve its profitability or market share over time. *Trading* is a bet a stock will rise or fall in the next 10 minutes or other short-term period of time. Investments can lead to real gains for all shareholders as the market rises, while trades require someone to lose a dollar for every dollar you gain.

If you trade online, you will find that the topics I present will be relevant to you. Those who are more active online traders (at least a few times per month or more) and who follow the markets closely, will find that many of the issues will be especially relevant to their trading frequency.

Technical trading strategies, trading systems, and analyzing stock fundamentals will not be our focus. So it is best if you already know how to gather this information. Since there are hundreds of web sites, books, and newsletters offering systems and strategies, you should have no problem finding what you are looking for. As a starting point, a comprehensive and well-organized web site with links to virtually any topic in the investment arena is *www.investormap.com*.

As I did earlier, I will mention a few choice sites along the way that I have found very useful. I will also identify some basic facts about market behavior that everyone needs to be aware of, and how you can use them to your advantage. So some strategic moves, as they relate to psychology, will be considered.

There are also a number of manuals on the mechanical aspects of electronic trading, including the basics of moving around on the computer. Since anyone who is computer-literate can, with some practice, learn the mechanics of online trading, inability to perform the simple tasks should not be an issue. But even here we find emotions come into the picture.

Emotions and the Mistaken Trade

For example, in a "fast market," when stocks are moving very quickly (big, heavily traded stocks are *always* moving quickly but sometimes they move *very* quickly during panic buying or selling) and you must execute trades decisively, it is common for some—especially beginners—to get anxious and hit the wrong keys.

From this we get the horror stories of inexperienced traders inserting a price into the trading box different than the one they intended. Or they put in the wrong number of shares, or the wrong type of trade—all of these errors often resulting in frustrating losses. All this just for hitting the wrong keys. I have seen these mistakes occur both with those trying to learn day trading in professional trading rooms and by individuals trading on their own.

For example, a very experienced trader who teaches beginning traders revealed that he had recently not only hit the wrong key once but then went ahead and did exactly the same thing again! He was used to hitting the "buy" key, as he usually went long on a stock. But this time he was selling it short, that is selling the stock first, hoping it would go down, and then buying it back if it did. Out of habit, he hit the "buy" key and realized that he was supposed to hit the "sell" key, as he was going short. He had 1000 shares of the stock and it was going down quickly!

He again puts in an order for 1000 and again hits the "buy" key and begins to panic. He had to take one hand and hold the other hand and guide it to the "sell" to bail out of both positions, losing $750 in a matter of seconds. This is a good example of how even the most experienced traders can have a mental lapse, where habit kicks in and they make the wrong, costly move.

In the trading rooms, initially it can be quite intimidating just to learn how to use the souped-up computer systems they have available. There is a large amount of data flashing at you continuously and multiple open windows filling every corner of your screen.

Often, you are trying to monitor more than one screen at a time. So, you may have all the data flashing on one main screen in front of you and off to the side will be a smaller screen tracking the Standard & Poor's (S&P) futures index. Closely monitoring the futures is common practice by day traders and a good idea, since it gives you a slight jump on which way the stock market is headed.

Of course, it doesn't really give you a jump on other traders, because they are doing the same thing. There is a direct positive correlation between the direction of the futures index and the broader market. This is why some say, if you are a day or minute trader, never buy a stock unless the futures index is moving up. It is also why one of the first things they teach you at a trading firm is to always keep an eye on the futures index.

In any case, the apprehension that goes with having your money on the line, and the need to speedily execute trades, makes it ripe for mistakes to occur. And of course, once the error is made, you have no recourse. If the trade goes through, you have to live with your mistake. Good luck in getting your brokerage firm to make allowances because you pushed the wrong keys!

However, it's not impossible for them to be understanding, and here's a personal example of this. (It helps if you have a long-standing account with your brokerage and at least a modest amount on deposit.)

Before I had *dynamic* (quotes that update continuously by themselves as prices change) real-time quotes, I would use my on-line brokerage to get real-time quotes. The only way I could do this was by entering a trade on an initial screen, getting the quote, and then voiding the trade after previewing it, but before it was actually sent through for execution.

Once, a few minutes before the market closed, I entered a trade for a stock just to get a quote. But I unconsciously pushed the "place trade" button when I meant to push "void." After the market closed, feeling a bit flustered, I called and told the brokerage firm I had made a mistake.

How would they know if I really hit the wrong button by mistake? They wouldn't. Maybe I'm just trying to undo a bad trade that went against me, like so many of the others who must call them and try the same tactic.

Amazingly, they were very understanding, maybe because I had held a retirement account with them for over a decade. They did not charge me a commission for getting out of the trade the next morning. In fact, they allowed me a couple of hours to sell the position when I wanted, and ironically, I actually ended up making a small profit from my accident.

Of course, most who tell stories of mistaken trades are not so fortunate.

This was my one and only "get out of jail free" card. I would not ask them to be understanding like this with me ever again—at least, not on a mistaken trade.

Although most traders at home or at their offices don't have the sophisticated systems of the institutions and professional day trading rooms, still they have to contend with the anxiety of putting their money on the line. In each case, it takes time to get comfortable with the motions of trading.

So, part of containing your emotions while trading is to be able to coordinate your eye-hand movements and your brain without letting anxiety get the best of you. Later, we will look at some tips for preventing this from happening.

THE EXCITEMENT OF ONLINE TRADING

If you already trade online, you know the feelings of power and excitement that go with the trading experience. You know how watching your portfolio may become a frequent interest, if not an obsession.

It is likely that you have already decided not to use a full-service broker because of cost. Rather than hand your money over to a broker to manage, you believe you can do just as well or even better yourself.

Perhaps you have been influenced by the numerous ads on financial TV channels that encourage you to take your own financial future into your hands and trade for yourself. These ads have whet your appetite for quick riches through trading. We watch others strike the vein of gold through trading volatile, fast-moving stocks and we want some of the easy money ourselves.

The Disciplined Online Investor is the first book aimed at helping online traders understand their own thoughts and feelings while they are trading. It will address the psychological forces that affect you, the individual trader, as you sit at your computer and go through the process of making a trade. And it will help you gain insight into the psychology of the market, so that you may better understand, predict, and anticipate the moves of others.

"MIND MOVES THE MARKET"

From my perspective, it is not the economy, interest rates, company earnings, stock stories, business cycles, political maneuverings, astrologic, atmospheric, or seasonal influences that dictate the ups and downs of the market. While some or all of these factors definitely play a part in short-, medium-, and long-term market swings, they are not the most basic ingredient.

The most crucial factor is this: How individual and institutional traders *interpret* all of these different forces in the various markets *and their actions based on their interpretations.*

This is what determines why a change in a company's future prospects, a change in federal fund rates, a change in earnings, a stock split—or any number of other small or large changes—are (or are not) taken seriously. When what traders *tell themselves* about these events changes quickly and drastically, you can bet that the market will move with these perceptions.

The answer, then, to the question as to why we must value psychology is simple. We value the psychology of you, the individual trader, and the psychology of the "market" (or the mass of other traders) because it is psychology that shapes and moves the market. This is why understanding our own thoughts and feelings while trading online and having some sense of the psychology of others is so important.

Again: Psychology is the most powerful force that moves markets. My shortcut, sound-bite way to say this is: "Mind moves the market."

It is our *belief* about what is happening right now that shapes our immediate actions, *not necessarily what is actually happening.*

And it is how we *imagine* the future will be (based on the past and the present) that also shapes our actions—not necessarily how the future actually turns out to be.

DEFINING THE TOPICS

We will look at the following basic psychological issues that are relevant to online traders:

- Identifying what type of investor you are. Do you have the personality type and temperament that can tolerate watching market swings very closely? What is your approach to online trading? How frequently and with what scope do you want to trade?
- Balancing the opposite forces of greed (reaching out, risk taking, letting gains run) and fear (withdrawing or staying neutral, defensive, taking profits, cutting losses). Finding the balance that is right for you.
- Balancing the isolation of trading on your own at home or the office with the large amount of information available through the media. How to trust your own analysis when so many sources of information want to shape your opinion and your actions. How to use the available information without becoming overwhelmed by it.
- Balancing *active* and *yielding* forms of self-control, and understanding how to apply each of them, according to your needs and the market conditions.
- Confronting the fear of taking decisive action; dealing with trader's block. Or: "Don't just sit there, do something!"
- Confronting the fear of doing nothing. Knowing when it's time to sit back and watch, taking no action. Or: "Don't just do something, sit there!"
- Understanding and applying the difference between perfectionistic thinking and trading excellence.
- Balancing short-, medium-, and long-term thinking and developing a frame of reference to understand your own trading moves. Understanding the concepts of how short-term

traders can learn from some of the thinking of long-term investors and, conversely, how long-term investors can learn from some of the thinking and tools of short-term traders.

- An overall investing philosophy that allows for the ups and downs in the market and your own portfolio. How to manage catastrophic "all or nothing" thinking when it comes to your trading fortunes.

DEFINING THE APPROACH

Our approach to the issues we will focus on will be one of balancing opposites. We will not assume there is just one right answer to solve a problem or one right stance to take each time the same problem arises. Instead, we will adopt a balanced way of thinking that allows us to respond to each new situation in a flexible manner. We will assume that being right will be defined by the particular situation in which we find ourselves.

In fact, it is the tendency to do the same thing repeatedly, no matter what the situation calls for, that gets us in trouble when trading. It accounts for many of the habitual conscious and unconscious choices we make that lead to bad trades.

For example, let's say you are a *position* trader (or speculator) who likes to hold a stock for a few hours, days, weeks, or even months and then capitalize on a special situation. (This, by the way, is my own style of trading, combined with some long-term holds).

Your thinking is not the same as the day trader, who does not care about these situations except as they relate to the minute-to-minute momentum of the stock. Nor do you necessarily care about the long-term fate of the stock like the buy and hold investor. Instead, you want to take advantage of a specific event related to the stock.

Maybe there is a stock split coming. Or news about the company that you believe will make the stock jump. If you are not very trusting of making your own decision about whether to buy this stock, you may find that you are on the stock bulletin boards, seeking confirmation from others that your thinking is correct.

Some who are unsure of their own thinking have great difficulty making the decision to buy without this confirmation from others. They become quite dependent on it. And often, they are trusting the opinion of people whom they don't even know and whom may not know any more about the stock than they do .

They are not able to trust their own due diligence and then make up their minds as to how to proceed. This inability to trust their own judgment can make for arbitrary decisions, unreasonable risk taking, or becoming paralyzed and unable to take action in a timely manner. And it may happen again and again.

So, a particular personality weakness, in this case the inability to trust your own analysis, judgment, and decision making, forces you to seek the approval of others before taking action. And yet you may not actually realize this is what you are doing!

Here's another example. If you happen to have the kind of heavy risk-taking personality that likes to always be in the action, you will tend to err on the side of making too many trades. You will go about your merry way as a day trader without any awareness that being in the action and feeling the flow of adrenaline rushing through your body is what the trading is all about for you.

Yes, you will say you are doing it to make some money. And consciously, that is true. But the thrill is in making the trade, and it is this that unconsciously pulls you. If you have no awareness that this tendency is operating, you will make hundreds of trades and often have little or nothing to show for it. In fact, it is clear from studies that track the trading records of day traders that the greater percentage lose a good deal of their initial stake. And they lose not only their initial stake, but continue to lose even as they become more experienced.

For example, a study just released by the North American Securities Administrators Association concluded that only 11 percent of All-Tech traders (a large day trading firm) make money consistently.

My point is that you need to know something about your own personality tendencies and how they affect your trading behavior. So, with this in mind, let's now turn to some broad types of investing and the personalities that go with them.

2

What Kind of
Investor Are You?

Do all online investors have the same trading style? Or have the same personality? Of course not. Then why do we so easily overlook how these different personality styles may affect the outcome of our trading?

It is exactly these personality styles, with their strengths and weaknesses, that are responsible for our repeatedly making the same kinds of good or bad trading judgments. And yet understanding our basic style of trading is often disregarded or taken for granted.

We may think, "That's just how I am," and so we don't really question whether "how we are" may be getting in our way of being more effective online traders. This is where some personal insight as to our style is useful. Because when we are aware of our own tendencies to lean one way more than another, we can consciously take them into account and compensate for them if we choose.

HOW DO WE LEARN A TRADING TYPE?

The following trading styles are based partially on character traits that develop from childhood. While there may be a genetic component to the early shaping of our character, it is largely learned from parents and shaped by the early environment.

A trading style is also shaped by our early experiences with money and the meaning money has played in our lives. Trading *decisions* resulting from these styles are influenced by how secure we feel in the present, where we are in our lives financially, how we imagine our future to be, and our short- and long-term investment goals.

We need not delve into the past here to analyze the foundation of personality traits. For our purposes, we shall simply identify the trading styles shaped by it.

Remember that favoring one trading style over another doesn't preclude changing our style. For some, it just may be more difficult, because it means fighting our natural ways of thinking and behaving. But it is never impossible, just as changing habits in other areas of our lives is never impossible.

We will see that each of these styles seems to fit best with a particular type of trading—whether it be active trading, short-term position trading, or occasional trading with an intermediate- or long-term orientation.

If we wanted to create the "perfect" balanced trader, however, it may be that a *combination* of behaviors from differing styles is most desirable for a particular kind of trading. I believe this is actually the case, especially for those interested in active trading. But, as we said, because those with one style of trading tend not to easily acquire traits from another style, it is tough for anyone to have the all-inclusive, balanced traits that may prove to be ideal.

For example, those who are cautious, conservative, and tend to be disciplined investors have trouble developing the required chunk of the *gambling-impulsive* style, which would make them better able to take risks and more comfortably execute short-term trades. Or gambling types may have trouble learning the necessary discipline to make reasonable, well-thought-out, intermediate-term trades.

To repeat, the important point here is this: When there is a mismatch (for example, long-term investor types want to start active trading), they need to realize they will have a tougher time than if they have the personality traits that are suited for day trading. They will have to fight against what is their basic inclination.

People whose trading style is opposite the traits required for a different approach usually aren't interested in that style. For example, those who hate being focused on a computer screen watching quotes go by for long periods of time simply won't entertain the idea of being frequent traders. If they do trade a lot, they refuse to watch quotes and just put in *limit* orders to buy and sell at set prices. They realize they can't tolerate the "boredom" of watching numbers for any length of time.

Another example: some have an interest in the flashing quotes, but are too hounded by anxiety to sit for very long and watch how much money they may be losing. Those who tend to be highly anxious don't do well even when the market is rising. They tend to see doom right around the corner. They are not very successful at climbing the proverbial "wall of worry" that the market erects. Like the soldier in training who tries to scale the obstacle wall but flops back, they just can't seem to make it over the wall of worry.

They often err in selling their positions prematurely when they have made some profit, rather than risk losing it. What they give up, of course, is the chance to make even greater profits should the stock keep rising.

DIFFERENT HORSES FOR DIFFERENT COURSES

In the trading types described here, the first word indicates the personality *style*, while the second word points to the *trading behavior* that typically accompanies it. In making these generalizations, please remember that I am not giving absolute types. If you identify some characteristics that feel true for you, don't expect all of them to be. These descriptions are offered solely to help you identify your trading style, not to categorize you in a limiting fashion.

Trading Style: Obsessive-Disciplined

To be obsessed is to have irresistible ideas or feelings or both. They need not be bothersome or unwanted. For our purposes, we're not using this word in a clinical, negative way. I mean it to be a general label to indicate a certain way of thinking and behaving. Some like to refer to this type as your garden variety anal or anal-compulsive personality.

Personality

Obsessives are able to dig in and become very involved and focused when something grabs their interest. They pay close attention to detail—a very desirable trait to have when it comes to trading stocks. They like their life in order. Because they pay attention to detail, they sometimes overlook the big picture because the detail is more enthralling.

Their time is used efficiently, except when they procrastinate about projects they aren't sure about. Otherwise, they disdain wasting time and have little regard for those who engage in what they consider to be frivolous pursuits. They get anxious when they or others are late for appointments, even when time is not of the essence.

Their style of dress, work, personal grooming, surroundings, and care for personal possessions all reflect a rather orderly mind that likes things put in their place. They may have perfectionistic tendencies.

They don't like most of what they can't control. They like to steer clear of surprise. Their idea of a surprise is something positive that comes a little sooner than they expected. They don't like to take unreasonable risks with their physical safety or their money. The more predictable the world is, the more comfortable they tend to feel.

They expect a lot from themselves and are motivated to succeed in much of what they do. They have high expectations of others as well, and are critical of them when they do not measure up to their expectations.

They are willing to practice something that they want to improve in and may even become zealous about a hobby or sport that really grabs their interest. Their competitive feelings are easily aroused.

Their minds are curious and not afraid to probe for meaning. They become easily absorbed reading something new that interests them and are not afraid to explore new topics to see where they may lead. They are aware of the nuances of things.

Obsessive-Disciplined: Money Management/Trading Style

Obsessives like to save money. They make sure they have a safe amount of cash on hand for emergencies, no matter how hot the stock market may be. They keep close tabs on their finances, are comfortable with budgets, and like their checkbook balanced. They like to pay their taxes and other bills promptly and are not comfortable owing money to credit card companies. They are careful in buying on margin, if they use it at all.

In their wallet, money clip, or purse they like cash to be filed by denominations—never scattered loosely or crumpled up in their pants. Oddly enough (and with the knowledge that comes from writing a book on perfectionism), I believe this simple behavior is such a telling sign of the obsessive-disciplined style that if someone routinely crumples bills in his pants or her purse and is careless with the placement of money, he or she almost certainly is *not* this person-ality type.

Obsessives get a certain satisfaction in tracking their invest-ments and following the stock market. Even if they are not frequent traders, they may become compulsive checkers of their online port-folios, especially if they spend a lot of time on the computer.

Conservative Style

They tend to be rather conservative in their investment style. They began thinking and saving for retirement long before their friends, who are not so concerned about the future. But they aren't afraid to take thought-out, reasonable risks and will routinely perform the due diligence required to feel fully informed before putting their money on the line.

They are comfortable with mutual funds that are balanced, not too heavily oriented toward aggressive-growth stocks. They tend to pay attention to asset allocation models that tell them not to place too much weight on any one risk category.

For example, they appreciate the concept of including "boring" bonds in their portfolios and are not past considering CDs that pay little interest but let them sleep at night. They think of their home as a secure, appreciating investment that diversifies their portfolio of stock holdings.

Anything too volatile, like high-flying Internet stocks, sends chills down their spines. They think people who go after them will ultimately get skinned. But that doesn't stop them from reading about the companies and wanting some of the fast money that comes with the big moves when they are hot.

If they designate a small portion of their investment capital for high-risk plays, they may even take a chance and buy some of the lat-est "dot com" that has hit the market. But then they watch it like a hawk and may very well exit it prematurely when they can't handle the volatility. Options trading is too risky for them, unless they re-search them thoroughly and then dabble very sparingly. They be-lieve it is best to leave options to the professionals.

Because they tend to be conservative and methodical in their investing style, they will not be tempted to overtrade online. Nor are they comfortable trading on margin (money loaned by the broker-age that allows you to gain leverage, buying more stock than you otherwise could).

Margin is secured by stock and cash positions, and the stock may be sold by the brokerage if you get too far in debt and are unable to come up with added cash to secure your positions. If this type uses margin at all, it is only for short periods of time. They are most comfortable using margin to give themselves a short-term loan.

This trading type will value a discount broker who offers service as much as speed of execution or the lowest cost, since they are not likely to be attracted to active trading. They will also like a discount broker who offers research reports and tools to analyze their portfolio, as this kind of stuff is enjoyable to them. For a respected web site that offers objective, in-depth comparison reports between discount brokers for the whole spectrum of online investors, visit *www.sonic.net/donaldj*.

When it comes to individual stock selection, they often feel most comfortable picking well-known, large-cap companies that are solid performers. They like to think of themselves investing in companies, not just stocks. In fact, they are among those who may become married to a stock, never wanting to give it up.

Some of those with this investment style become what are called *chartists*. These people like to analyze the technical aspects of stocks. When the market is closed, they plot the daily price movement of stocks and pore over the charts to determine entry and exit points, based on the stock's history. Of course, what used to be done painstakingly by hand may now be found at numerous online discount brokerage and stock analysis web sites.

Much like looking at constellations of stars in the sky, chartists find all kinds of patterns in the charts that are deemed to be meaningful. The whole market of custom charting software has them in mind. Online, when the market is open, technicians like to monitor intraday price movement graphs, volume, ratio of new highs to new lows, and various other technical data.

The obsessive-disciplined investor who spends a lot of time online loves to stay up to the minute on all breaking news and how it may affect his or her stocks. Some like to know the quarterly earnings results of a stock just as they are released and then stick around to listen in on the company's conference call.

Obsessive-disciplined investors also enjoy participating in some of the many online stock message boards, closely following the conversation "thread" related to one of their favorite stocks. In fact, they often become part of the core of regulars who are valued contributors to these boards.

Obsessives tend not to be lurkers who sit back, read others' posts, but never "come out of the closet" and actively participate. This is because they have opinions and like to get involved with other posters. Their enthusiasm for the stock and their obsessive nature makes them tend toward attachment when they find the right mix of contributors.

Just as can happen with anything else in cyberspace, some even become overly attached to these boards, spending large amounts of time in dialogue. When forced to stay off the boards, they may experience withdrawal symptoms in the forms of agitation, mild anxiety, and feelings of loss. The stock bulletin boards may serve the same function for them as do social chat rooms for others. Yes, it's easy to want to say to the most dedicated, "Get a life." But they would tell you how well they get to know other posters, how friendly they become, and how sometimes they even end up getting together in the "real" world for face-to-face interaction.

Because they are thorough and attentive to detail, if they have a strong interest in the market, they might make good active traders, perhaps position or speculative traders. Short term for them is a few days, weeks, or even months.

But to become a position trader, they would have to overcome some anxiety that is common for obsessives to feel when taking short-term positions. By their nature, obsessives are prone to worry too much about the risks they take.

The Obsessive as Position Trader

Position traders try to take advantage of specific events related to a stock, like a stock split or other important news that affects the price. They wish to capitalize on the short-term position and then exit. When anxiety is in check, disciplined traders like this kind of trading because it allows them to take advantage of their skill for doing research and staying up with the latest news.

To *speculate* does not mean to gamble wildly without any idea of what you are doing. Speculative or position traders go in fully informed and take the risk that their assessment of the information available will move the stock price within a specific period of time.

For example, knowing there is usually a run-up in price a week before Dell announces its earnings each quarter, speculators might buy Dell shares for just that period. Further, knowing that there is typically a drop in price after the earnings announcement, speculators may sell their shares just before the earnings release. Or, if they are a little more risky, take a chance that the earnings are good enough to further propel the stock. But the bet is for the short-term situation.

Because obsessive-disciplined investors keep close tabs on news of their stocks and learn their typical patterns, they are well-suited to be position traders, assuming they have the interest and the willingness to take higher risk. They have done research, which gives them the confidence to strike when the time is right.

The Obsessive as Longer-Term Investor

In terms of time horizon and trading frequency, the typical obsessive-disciplined type, who is not highly interested in the market *or willing to face some anxiety*, is ideally suited for intermediate- to longer-term trading. This means from months to years into the future. They don't get too upset at the daily or weekly movements of the market, because their focus is on the long haul. Their patience serves them well in this regard.

The reality is that most who are obsessive-disciplined traders are most comfortable and have the most success when they do what they do best. And that is to carefully analyze stocks and, when ready, take positions and hold them for the long term. If you are a typical obsessive-disciplined type, clearly you are a horse who prefers a medium- to long-term course.

The Obsessive as Day Trader

Those who are pure obsessive types are clearly *not* the best candidates for super-speedy minute trading or day trading, at least as it is done by professional day traders.

Why? Because the unpredictability of it and quick decisions required make them just too anxious and uncomfortable. It just goes too much against their grain. And if they do trade more frequently, they prefer to do it in the comfort of their own office or home. They will not adjust well to the tense environment of a day trading room with dozens of other anxious people around them.

If they want to do more frequent trading, say, many trades per week, they will also have to overcome some of their basic conservative orientation. If they want to be day traders, they're in for some serious jolts to their typical style.

They would have to learn to handle the anxiety and unpredictability that goes with it. And they would have to tolerate processing large amounts of data very quickly without being able to carefully analyze it, as is their preference. Then they would have to learn to make buy and sell decisions based on this data.

Along with these alterations to their style, they would also have to adopt at least a bit of the risk-taking, go-for-broke mentality that is the stuff of the skilled day trader. The successful day trader must be nimble, able to make decisions very quickly. They don't have time to carefully consider their moves. They must react instinctively and be able to change directions on a dime. This is not an easy thing for the obsessive-disciplined type to learn. Most don't even want to try.

Some can make the transition and are able to use their ability to show restraint positively in limiting the number of trades they make. They also have a good grasp on when to cut their losses and are less likely to lose their entire investment capital.

Another strength is that often they are quick learners. So, while going against their personality is tough, it is easy for them to learn the mechanics of day trading as well as the technical aspects. For example, they may learn a few stocks inside and out, knowing the typical daily patterns, trading ranges, and stay up on all the news of the company.

They may become specialists in trading only one or two stocks, achieving a measure of comfort and knowledge that allows them to dart in and out without too much anxiety. I ran into a number of obsessive types who did exactly this. As long as they did not venture beyond the one or two stocks, they were able to manage their anxiety.

COMBINATION OF TRADING STYLES: EXAMPLE

I believe some of the best professional traders actually combine traits of the obsessive-disciplined style with the gambling-emotional style, described later in this chapter.

For example, James J. Cramer is a professional trader who manages a hedge fund (a fund that holds stocks that try to balance each other whether the market is up or down), and writes three or four short columns daily for the online stock web site "The Street.com," of which he is a founder.

A frequent past guest host on CNBC's *Squawk Box*, until his own site began a show on cable television, he often expressed his views passionately. In the stuffy Wall Street world of self-conscious, conservative, and often self-serving stock commentators, Cramer provides a breath of fresh air. He is not afraid to tell it as he sees it, even when he knows his views may be unpopular.

In his columns, Cramer often shares with readers his trading moves and his thinking behind them. He is offering readers lessons in money management through the mind of one professional trader.

Cramer appears to be a healthy blend of the obsessive-disciplined and what I call the *gambler-impulsive* trading types. He is an experienced trader who has learned to "smell" moves in the market either before or as they occur (or at least faster than most traders).

He is not afraid to take reasonable chances, sometimes acting by instinct and educated hunch, when time is of the essence. And he is not afraid to let readers know when he is wrong. Yet he tempers his gambler-impulsive trading style with the disciplined mind that comes with earning both undergraduate and law degrees from Harvard.

With the help of his partner and staff, he does all the research he can before making big moves, including calling companies at the last minute to find out if there is any news that may affect his trade.

As an example of the compulsive style, when I e-mailed Cramer my assessment of his combination obsessive-disciplined and gambler-impulsive trading styles, within 10 minutes, he shot back this response: "Shoe fits."

What better example of an obsessive-disciplined personality than a guy who is hooked up to his laptop computer continuously throughout the day and who reads and responds immediately to e-mail? In addition, he carries a beeper for any late-breaking news when out of the office and surfs the message boards at his site late into the evening, posting messages when the mood strikes him. No surprise to find out he suffers from insomnia, a common symptom with perfectionistic personalities.

Trading Style: Doubter-Timid

They are skeptics and, often, worriers. Much of what others may take for granted they are not so sure about. They like to question what they hear and read and are not afraid to disagree with others. They like to have intellectual arguments with others, challenging their viewpoints.

Personality

They pride themselves on their critical thinking. Like obsessives, they aren't afraid to go deeply into an area that captures their interest. They tend to be conservative in their politics, clothing, and the risks they will generally take in life, including how they invest their money. They have a healthy dose of mistrust for government and other institutions.

Kept in check, their healthy skepticism prevents them from being taken advantage of by salespeople, advertisers, con artists, and the mass media. But when taken too far, they may become overly suspicious or even paranoid, thinking others are out to take something from them or hurt them in some way.

Some with this doubting orientation become independent, creative thinkers. They are unafraid to think of things in a new light, and like to apply their insights to creative problem solving. They may become writers, artists, or musicians. Some may do innovative research, or develop new technologies.

Those who are the doubter-timid type tend to be cautious with strangers, and warm up to others slowly. They may make others repeatedly prove themselves before they let themselves trust them. They may prefer mental activities over physical ones.

When it comes to personal safety, they are careful not to take unnecessary chances. They are not the adventurous, risk-taking type.

Sky-diving, parachuting, bungee-jumping, and flying in small airplanes and extreme sports of all kinds are out of the question.

For them, adventure means risking getting lost by taking a new route to work. For amusement, it means sliding down a shoot feet first at a water park. They think they're living on the wild side when they try a new restaurant without first reading any reviews of it.

Doubter-Timid: Money Management/Trading Style

They like to think independently of the crowd. Because of this, when they trade online, they are prime candidates to be contrarian investors.

They manage their money as (if not more) conservatively than the obsessive-disciplined type.

But what they have in common with the obsessive type is the compulsion to build a sizable savings account to protect themselves in case of emergency. And when they sometimes focus on the negative, that emergency is seen as just around the corner.

Their cautious nature means they might be overly weighted in risk-free vehicles, such as a money market cash account, bank CD, or a safe bond fund. When everybody else laughs at the idea of owning gold, they consider buying some. Or at least a gold fund.

They are not easily swayed by online bulletin board hype, online newsletters, or tips from friends or colleagues. They would rather pass up an opportunity than jump at something that they haven't researched carefully. They are slow to commit to an investment. They know there's always another hot stock if this one gets away.

Likewise, they are not among those who favor getting advice from investment professionals, so a full-service broker is not their cup of tea. Above all, their cautious orientation means they favor the intermediate term (three to six months or more) and the long term in their investment style.

Infrequent Trading

They probably will not make more than one or two trades online every couple of months. And, to be comfortable and consistent with their trading personality, that is probably all they *should* make. Mutual funds may be a better vehicle for them than individual stocks, at least for the greater percentage of their investment capital.

If they decide they want to become a more active online trader, they will need to alter their bias toward the negative, becoming more assertive and less timid. Doubting and timidity have little place in the world of fast-paced trading.

When it comes to trading execution, timidity and caution turn into fear when it comes time to pull the trading trigger. Their orientation biases them toward seeing all investments as inherently more risky than they actually are. They also have the tendency to be inflexible once they have made a trade.

So, they will tend to hold a position longer than may be wise, as it is tough for them to make the decision to cut their losses. Like the obsessive type, they are horses basically bred to run the intermediate- and long-term course, plodding slowly but surely.

Trading Style: Gambler-Impulsive

This trading type likes to be where the action is. They tend to be emotionally driven, following their impulses and passions more than their thinking. Because of this, sometimes they exercise poor judgment, letting their desires of the moment lead them into hasty action.

Personality

They view the world as a glittering playground, with all things new and shiny competing to attract their attention. They are the proverbial kids in the candy store. When something does attract them, they may be passionate in following it. This may lead to overindulgence, or at worst, dependence or addiction. But kept in check, it just keeps them passionate about their interests.

Because they are impulsive, they make more than their share of poor choices. Often they may later feel sorry about the consequences of these choices. But interest and passion—not clear thinking—tend to pull them along.

So, for example, the color and speed of a car they see on the road make them want to buy it, while the obsessive carefully studies *Consumer Reports* and various car magazines. At the races, the jockey's colors or the name of the horse make them want to bet on it, while the obsessive is analyzing the horse's past performance from the daily racing form.

They are more interested in hunches, good luck, tips, and random coincidences than the other trading styles. They tend to focus on the surface of things rather than take the time to discover the deeper essence. Why? Because, getting bored easily, they don't have the patience or interest to hang around long enough to dig deeper.

Possible Addictive Problems

They may have (or have had) addictive problems in their lives, either to work, food, sex, drugs, alcohol, or sports betting. They regret many of the impulsive risks they take when they don't turn out as they hoped. Usually, however, not quite enough to actually change their behavior, unless pressured by others or by catastrophic downfall.

They are the most willing of all the trading types to take chances with their physical and relationship safety, enjoying the adrenaline rush that comes with high risk. They feel most alive when danger and intrigue are part of the equation. They may challenge themselves by driving fast on a race track, climbing high and rugged mountains, or skiing down the advanced run to prove their skill.

In relationships, marital infidelity is more common with the gambling type. Because impulses are so powerful in guiding their behavior, it is more difficult for them to listen to the voice of reason, morals, and self-restraint. Of course, this does *not* mean all gambler trading types are this way—only more likely to be involved in marital infidelity than other trading types.

For this type, the distinction between reasonable risk that is adventurous and crossing over the line into foolhardy indulgence is often lost. In fact, they will misperceive and mislabel foolhardy risks as reasonable. And then they will believe their misperception.

In other words, they do the opposite of the doubter-timid type—they err in *underestimating* the actual risk involved in following their impulses, as well as the severity of the consequences.

Having a gambling-impulsive trading style is simply a reflection of their view of life itself as the Big Gamble.

"Anything can happen at any time—I might as well follow my tastes, preferences, and go for all the gusto I can!" Or: "You're gonna die of something anyhow—I might as well enjoy it while I'm here." That is how they might describe their philosophy of life. By God, nobody's going to tell them whether to smoke, eat steak, or to have a dessert after dinner!

On the positive side, they are open to a wider variety of experiences than the more conservative types. From different foods, to foreign travel, to multiple viewpoints, they tend to be more accommodating to the novel and strange. This makes for flexibility to change and openness to new experiences. Often this type is flamboyant, charismatic, and enjoys a measure of popularity with others.

Because of their risk-taking nature, they may strike it rich through a start-up business or willingness to take a chance on a new venture that promises big returns. They are open to adventure and while this means some exciting experiences in their lives, it also means a higher chance of catastrophe.

These people are often colorful, exciting to be around, and occupy the role of exotic parrots in the menagerie compared to the typical, everyday human birds.

Gambler-Impulsive: Money Management/Trading Style

The phrase that best describes the gambler's money management style is "fast and loose." Money tends to come in fast and go out even faster. And it is cared for loosely. These types like to spend on themselves and may also be quite generous with friends and families.

They also are prone to play fast and loose with the ethics of business as well as with the law. This type of personality is often found behind those who start illegal, fast-buck telemarketing scams, and various other kinds of questionable business practices, including accounting practices and income taxes.

Despite loving the pleasure that money can buy, there is often a disrespect or disdain for money itself. Cash may be crumpled into balls and stuffed in the pants or purse. It may be strewn around the house without regard to whether its resting place will be remembered.

Money is always being found that they didn't even know they had. For the more organized gambling type, rolls of bills may be stuffed into a money clip, which may be conspicuously shown off in public.

Security needs are not highly valued compared to immediate, impulsive satisfaction of desires. Untempered by some of the cautiousness of the obsessive or doubter types, the gambling type is the big spender who gets gratification out of showing off his or her ability to earn large amounts of money and then spending it lavishly.

Life is here and now for this type, the future too far away and too vague to be given much concern. You know: "Here today, gone to Maui."

Not so surprisingly, planning for retirement is often neglected. Checking accounts tend to get overdrawn and bills may be placed aside and forgotten. How can paying a bill tomorrow bring anywhere near the same satisfaction as buying a new pair of fancy shoes right now? Credit card companies and casinos love this type, because charge cards and credit tend to get maxed to the limit.

Day Trader as Gambling Type

At least a measure of this trading type is the predominant style found in the day trading firms, as well as those who are day traders at home on their own. They like the anxious edge of urgency that goes with quick-paced trading. They feel stimulated by all the data coming at them on the computer monitors and by the thrill of making quick decisions based on limited analysis. To the degree that day trading is an intuitive, moment-to-moment crap shoot, the gambler-impulsive trader wants his or her money on the table.

Just as the dedicated crap shooter likes to have a bet down on every roll of the dice, the day trader loves jumping in and out of dozens of trades. If too much time goes by without "placing a bet," the gambler-impulsive style tends to get bored simply watching the quotes flash by. They begin to feel they're missing out on something.

Quite the opposite of the obsessive-disciplined and the doubter-timid types, the gambler just doesn't like the spectator role. Nor does he or she usually want to be bothered with learning about companies, fundamentals, or performance charts. All that matters for the day trader is *momentum*. If the stock is moving, there is money to be made. What else do they need to know?

In learning about the day trading scene, one morning in 1997 I was watching some day traders at a local trading firm enter and exit the same stock repeatedly through the morning.

Finally, I asked one 20-something with long, flowing hair what company he was trading. I was surprised to find out he had no idea what company the stock symbol stood for. All he knew (and needed to know for his purposes) was that it moved fast, so it was a good trading stock.

If life is a Big Gamble, this trading type is looking for the edge that will win the bet. They aren't afraid to put large amounts of money on the line. Nor are they concerned about using margin to leverage their bets. Margin for this type is just another name for a "marker" and leveraging their bets with the house's money. When things are going well, they are the most likely type to make big returns with their big risks.

Often, serious day traders like betting on the horses, blackjack, the lottery, or sports teams. They love Las Vegas and enjoy more than casual betting on the golf course, just to "make things more interesting." Not so surprisingly, a number of present-day top-notch stock and bond traders have come from a past of serious Las Vegas gambling and horse betting. I have had nationally recognized stock and bond traders sit in my office and tell me how they went from casino gambling to playing the markets.

WHEN ACTIVE TRADING BECOMES ADDICTIVE

Since the gambling-impulsive trading type is the most likely to become the "minute" or day trader, he or she is also most likely to take the whole thing too far and end up with a form of gambling dependence. How do we know when online trading—done either in a trading firm with others or in the privacy of one's own home or office—

goes beyond being a form of earning a living and crosses over into becoming a serious problem?

First, we need to distinguish between overtrading and dependent-addictive trading. Overtrading is simply poor money management. It is trading too often to be able to make any money because too much is being racked up in commissions.

Overtrading is what happens with minute traders, who literally are in and out of a position within a minute or two and who do this up to a hundred times or more in a trading session. They are a comparatively small group of hypertraders who push the outside limits of day trading. Sooner or later, they realize they are not making enough profit on their hypertrading to make the costs worthwhile.

Hypertraders may or may not end up dependent, in the sense that they can't stop trading without noticeable symptoms of psychological withdrawal. Even if it may not be the smartest approach to active trading, minute trading may simply be a style of trading that does not necessarily lead to dependence.

Here are the signs of a gambling addiction that have been slightly altered to apply to active trading. They may serve as guidelines as to when traders may have gone too far.

Five or more of these signs taken together mean the gambling is bad enough to be considered meeting the criteria for the diagnosis of "pathological gambling" in the manual used by mental health professionals to determine mental, emotional, and behavioral disorders.

Signs of Trading Addiction

1. Is preoccupied with trading (reliving past trading experiences, planning the next trading experience, or thinking of ways to get money with which to trade).
2. Needs to trade with increasing amounts of money and in increasing numbers of shares to achieve the desired excitement.
3. Has repeated unsuccessful attempts to control, cut back, or stop trading (for example, chases losses when heavily in debt, borrowing on margin).
4. Is restless or irritable when attempting to cut down or stop trading.
5. Takes trading losses out on family and friends through outbursts of anger, irritation, or physical violence.

6. Becomes depressed for days on end after a series of trading losses. Unable to emotionally recover from bad days.
7. Trades as a way of escaping from problems or of relieving a depressed mood.
8. Lies to family members or others to conceal the extent of involvement with trading (for example, how much in debt due to trading on margin).
9. Has committed illegal acts such as forgery, fraud, theft, or embezzlement to finance trading.
10. Has jeopardized or lost a significant relationship, job, or education or career opportunity because of trading.
11. Relies on others to provide money to relieve a desperate financial situation caused by trading.

Some of these indicators are not going to be so relevant in trying to determine when trading has become addictive. And some are very relevant. For example, preoccupation with thinking about trading may be a sign of trouble or may just be an indication that a trader is taking his or her work seriously.

Someone needing to trade with increasing amounts of money to achieve the desired excitement can be a good indicator of addictive trading. But we need to be careful, because it may also simply indicate that a trader is experienced and comfortable enough to take higher risks.

And, of course, unsuccessful attempts to control or cut back is a good indicator. But most traders don't try to control or cut back trading until they have already acknowledged there is a problem.

The excitement derived from active trading definitely provides an adrenaline rush that may help combat depression. But it is highly unlikely anyone is going to become a day trader simply as a way to deal with depression. There are easier and less expensive ways!

The last four items are clearly relevant in determining trading addiction. Any one of them indicates the need to examine the place trading has taken in the trader's life and how it may have become out of control.

Trading Style: Optimist-Gullible

Optimist-gullible investors are pleasant people to be around. They basically sees things positively and have a good attitude for managing the ups and downs of life, including the stock market and online trading. They view the glass as half full. They tend to be friendly, trusting of others, and light-hearted. This type likes to get along with others, avoids arguments, and sometimes yields his or her own interests for the preferences of others.

The optimist likes to smile a lot, enjoys socializing, and prefers the company of others rather than spending time alone. He or she has made a conscious or unconscious decision to accept the difficulties in life without spending undue time focusing on or worrying about them. Disappointments are taken in stride.

This type likes to work with other people and is a good team player. They like to fill their free time with activities and enjoy keeping busy, not spending too much time in self-reflection. When upset, the optimist is more likely to react with anxiety rather than moodiness or depression. The anxiety often revolves around fear of losing the approval of significant others.

The optimist often appears on the outside to be emotionally balanced. He or she doesn't like to show outward signs of disappointment with others. When they do allow themselves to feel down, their preferred style of coping is to keep it to themselves.

They express warmth and caring for others easily and cherish friends and family. They basically believe people are good and that life provides numerous simple satisfactions.

They often like to fantasize about the future and all the wonderful things they hope will be a part of it. They are upbeat to be around and others enjoy their company. To put it simply, they have said, "yes" to life.

Optimist-Gullible: Money Management/Trading Style

Optimists are not the most careful or prudent in their money management. They may be overly trustful of others and therefore are among those who get taken by get-rich-quick schemes that promise unrealistic returns.

They naively assume others will not take advantage of their optimistic personality. So they are gullible, which leads to buying products they don't need and making investments that are not always thought out carefully enough.

Of the different investor types, the optimist has the best attitude to handle the ups and downs of the market. They are able to get through the down periods by staying in touch with a basic positive and hopeful view of the future. While this certainly isn't a bad bias to have in the living of one's life, it can make for some rather tough adjustments when things do not turn out as rosy as expected.

Because they are thinking the future will be as good or better than the present, they may not take adequate precautions to protect themselves in times of major market corrections. Nor do they always think about saving for emergencies or financial reversals.

The gullibility of the optimist is based on the false and naïve belief that others will be as caring, thoughtful, and honest as they are. This makes them open for manipulation and exploitation by others through online bulletin boards, where optimists may follow stock tips given by people they don't know but are too quick to trust.

Camaraderie on the Boards

Repeated posting to online boards tends to make investors feel a camaraderie that leads to thinking they know people better than they actually do. In addition, the underlying desire to please others coupled with a tendency toward compliance may lead to blindly following tips and advice without exercising sufficient critical judgment.

The optimist is always in danger of overlooking other people's less-than-honorable intentions. When more aware of this basic bias, the optimist can learn to stay positive but try and eliminate the gullibility that tends to accompany this trading style.

This type is more common among senior investors as well as very young and naive investors who are susceptible to sales pitches, penny stock scams by telephone, and various other con games that revolve around gaining their trust and playing on the desire for quick and easy riches.

On the positive side, when the optimist becomes a more educated and sophisticated investor, he or she, given an "injection" of the gambler-disciplined trait, has a good attitude for the long haul should he or she try active trading.

They are not easily disappointed by day-to-day losses. They will *not* be the ones who fly into angry rages, shouting or pounding the desk, when a trade goes against them. They expect the next trade to go their way. They have learned to take short-term or long-term financial loss in stride.

This type of investor will be biased toward stocks always going higher, companies always improving their earnings, and the future always looking rosy. This means they will tend to hold losing positions too long, always thinking the stock will move back up.

Naiveté and Real-World Risk

The more naive optimist who has not learned the necessary lessons of real-world risk needs to be careful before committing money to individual stocks. The safest way for them to invest is by buying mutual funds online. They will often overlook all the warning signs that a company may not be good, or a situation may not be what the optimist thinks it is.

It is best for optimists to have a trusted and knowledgeable partner with whom to discuss investments. This may act as an important reality check to counterbalance their own overly optimistic bias.

The positive thing with this type is that it is not that difficult to take a confirmed optimist and temper (or "harden") him or her with the grim realities of deception and exploitation that are rampant in the investing arena.

When forced to face these realities, they may hold their basic positive nature but also learn to lose the naiveté and gullibility that naturally go with it. One of the behaviors that must be altered is the need to gain universal approval. As the need for approval is reduced, this type feels more able to say "no," think more independently, and be less concerned about the judgments of others.

Trading Type: Victim-Blamer

Of the various trading styles, this type is the most immature emotionally and psychologically. The gambler type always appears happier being alive than does the victim-blamer.

Victim-blamers interpret anything in life that does not go their way as aimed against them, believing somebody or something is working against their welfare. It may be another person, like a boss or girlfriend, or an entity, like a company or the government. It may even be outside forces, such as "bad luck," "nature," an "evil force," or even their conception of God.

The victim-blamers need to find someone outside themselves to blame for things not working out or misfortune that is beyond their control. They have never learned to assume personal responsibility for their own actions rather than to blame others.

Taking the role of the victim allows them to feel sorry for themselves and have a ready-made excuse for things not going the way they think they should. It also means not having to change their own behavior—nothing is ever admitted to being their fault, so nothing needs changing.

This type feels they have been cheated of their rightful place in life. They adopt what is known as a "poor me" stance to the world. They think they deserve attention, approval, admiration, and status. But they don't get it. And rather than try and understand why, it is much easier for them to see the cold, cruel world as denying them what they think they deserve.

Often, they have, in fact, had a hard life. Either little opportunity, poor education, a physical or mental disability, childhood deaths in the family, or deep love disappointment may be part of the personal history. Unlike other, more psychologically hardy and resilient people, they never seem to recover from early trauma or disappointments. For example, some of the Vietnam vets of my generation became victims and could never overcome their traumatic war experiences.

Because they are carrying a grudge, the victim-blamer often appears to others to have a "chip" on his or her shoulder. They are easily irritated or annoyed with others and quick to express it. Because of this, they often have trouble working cooperatively with others.

Some victim-blamers are chronically angry and depressed. Finding it so difficult to form trusting relationships, they may be rather isolated in their lives. When they turn their anger toward themselves, they appear withdrawn and depressed. When they externalize and actively blame others, they appear angry and even rageful.

They tend to *project* onto others their own desire to exploit and victimize. This means that rather than admit their own interest in making other people objects of whom they can take advantage, they deny this and instead see others as having the very same motive toward them.

This is what it means to project one's own motives onto another. When held in control, it may surface as suspicion and caution with others. When taken to an extreme, it results in paranoid thinking and delusions of persecution.

Victim-Blamer: Money Management/Trading Style

Victims err by not understanding their own part in creating their fortune and misfortune, always seeing the outside world as the cause.

They tend to be watchful over their money, are mistrusting of large institutions, brokers, or anyone who may use them or take advantage of them.

Often suspicious of banks and other institutions, this type may keep their money outside of institutions altogether, preferring to invest in real estate or collectibles. They may also choose to keep their money in a home safe or other such hideout that provides them with the ultimate safety, even if their money earns no interest.

For those of this type who may invest online, handling losses of capital well is not their strong point. They tend to be moderate to conservative investors, do not make a lot of trades, and are very suspicious of taking investment advice from online web sites.

Those with a strain of the gambler mentality may try active trading. They are the ones you may see explode into rage in a day trading firm, throwing things, pounding keyboards, or yelling at their computer or "the market" when trades go against them.

The Victim-Blamer Type at Its Worst

The shocking case of Mark Barton, the day trader in Atlanta who walked into his two trading firms in the summer of 1999 and killed people because of his large losses, is the epitome of what may happen when the victim-blamer loses all control. The killer blamed the trading firm for his losses. In fact, it was when firm managers finally stepped in and took a responsible stand by refusing to allow him to trade any longer that he finally exploded.

This type should not trade online, as they simply are unable to assume the necessary responsibility for their actions. It would be better for them to deposit their money in a bank or put it in a brokerage money-mart account. The alternative would be to have a financial planner, accountant, or other money manager do their investing for them. In this way, they may feel entitled to blame the consultant if they end up unhappy with the return on the consultant's choices. And, of course, they can always get psychological help to learn to grow up and assume their place as mature adults in the world.

CREATING A BALANCED TRADING STYLE

Using the suggestive descriptions of the trading styles presented in this chapter, you might have found that one type was easier to identify with than the others. Assuming this is true, now answer the following questions:

1.   How does your present style of online trading seem consistent with what you read? What specifically did you identify with?
2.   Was there anything you read in the trading type you most identify with that was very different than your own trading behavior?
3.   What traits would you like to develop from trading types other than the one with which you most closely identify?
4.   How might your style of trading change if you acquired these other traits?
5.   How frequently would you like to trade?
6.   Does your personality and present trading style accommodate this desired frequency?
7.   If not, what efforts are you willing to make to acquire these other traits if they go against your basic personality and trading style?
8.   Do you have any interest in combining trading styles? For example, mixing a core of long-term positions with short-term "trading shares"?
9.   What do you know about your own personality and investment style that would make some of these trading styles undesirable or impossible for you?
10.   How much time do you want to devote to trading?
11.   How much money are you willing to spend to acquire the software, hardware, and training to learn active trading, if that is your interest?
12.   How much time are you willing to devote to staying informed? For example, reading research on and off line, studying charts, keeping up on news of your stocks, reading about economic and company news, etc.?

In answering these questions, you ought to become more clear on how satisfied you are with your present trading style or how much you might like to alter it in some fashion.

Having a balanced trading/investing style means knowing how to call on the behavior needed for the situation and being able to exhibit it. It means knowing, as the song says, "when to hold 'em and when to fold 'em." Learning this only comes with self-insight, a disciplined mind, emotional control, and a wide behavioral repertoire. And it doesn't come overnight.

SUMMARY

In this chapter, we have identified a number of investor types, giving examples of the common personality traits and investing behaviors that go with each of them. We made the point that it is important to understand our own investing biases so that we may take them into consideration when we trade online. With awareness, we may choose to compensate for these "built-in" biases.

We said that when we choose to ignore the effects of our personality on our investing choices, we are going to repeat the same mistakes over and over. And, of course, we will not know *why* we are making these repeated mistakes.

I suggested that the most complete and balanced online investor—our "perfect" investor—would have a combination of traits derived from the various trader types.

So, for example, he or she would have a healthy measure of the obsessive-disciplined type, a dash of the gambler-impulsive, one part optimist (without the naiveté), and one part of the doubter-timid (to know when to err on the side of being conservative). There is, however, no place in the mentally healthy online trader for any part of the victim-blamer type.

Finally, questions were asked to help you begin to think about your present identification with a trading type and how you might like to develop other traits and behaviors so as to become a more balanced trader/investor.

In the next chapter, we will tackle the major psychological emotions of greed and fear with the first chapter in our trilogy. We will continue to look at ways we may find balance.

The Fear and Greed
Trilogy, Part I: Fear

Fear and greed are the yin and yang of Wall Street. They are the primary opposite and competing forces influencing investors. Yet, each also complements the other, creating a necessary balance that makes the market hum. They swirl inside each of us in an exquisite dance, playing upon the larger unfolding market drama.

We declared that "mind moves the market." It is what we *tell ourselves* and *what we feel* related to the story we tell ourselves about interest rates, the economy, news events, or anything else influencing the market that sway us to be bullish or bearish, buy or sell.

With the typical gyrations of today's market, what we feel are varying degrees of fear and greed intertwined. Sometimes in the background, other times much more obvious but, to some degree, they are always operating. And, of course, it's not only today's markets that are ruled by fear and greed—the history of all trading and investing of any kind reveals the same psychological story.

With the easy money investors have made from the raging bull market of the last decade, expectations of return on investment have gone up. Anything less than a 20 percent return per year is viewed as inadequate. These higher expectations are a form of greed. And, as our collective greed has become stronger, so has our fear of losing what has been gained. When there is more money on the line, both fear and greed increase in strength.

The initial public offerings of Internet companies the last few years brought the frenzy to a head. Stratospheric gains were made, virtually overnight, on the new "dot-com" companies, the likes of which the market had never before seen.

Witnessing moves of 30, 40, or 50 or more points up in one day in a single stock simply was mind-blowing to everyone on Wall Street. Growing numbers of investors wanted to mine for gold themselves, as they heard friends and associates boast of their newly earned riches.

These volatile stocks are still the day trader's delight. It is not so surprising to learn that up to 80 percent of day trading volume is centered on Internet stocks. The "mo-mo" contingent (momentum traders) couldn't live without them. Interestingly, it is the at-home day trader who most favors these stocks, as many day traders at trading firms tend to be more conservative, favoring "old-tech" stocks like Dell and Cisco.

One of the tasks of the online investor is to come to grips with—and even try to master—this interplay of personal fear and greed. Sometimes we may experience them very closely linked, along with their associated thoughts. At other times, sucked into the vortex of one force or the other, we experience them as worlds apart.

ON THE EDGE: FEAR, LOSS, AND IDENTITY

We usually experience fear more powerfully than we do greed. Fear shakes our financial security and scares the hell out of us. At its most powerful, it even jars our sense of personal security in the world. Here's an example.

In the movie, *The Game*, Michael Douglas plays a merger and acquisitions big shot. He gets caught in what becomes a very real game that tests his survival strength when his wealth, possessions, identity, and normal insulations from the everyday world are suddenly stripped away from him. He wakes up in a trash dumpster in Mexico, battered and disoriented, with no money.

He is forced to use his wits to get home to San Francisco when he can no longer rely upon the usual support of others he has come to take for granted in his life of luxury. He feels a primal level of fear that he has not experienced since childhood, when he witnessed his father's suicide by leaping headfirst off a building.

He learns he is capable of surviving hardship and physical danger even when he is not insulated by the trappings of wealth. And, as it turns out, the purpose of the game was to teach him exactly this. He realized a perspective that he may not have been able to gain in any other, less radical way.

My point in using this example is this: If we mistakenly equate the core of our identity with our financial success, when dramatic financial reversals occur, this core identity may be drastically undermined. It feels like the carpet of who we know ourselves to be has been suddenly and violently pulled out from under us. If these things are what we are taught define our identity, who are we without them?

Questions of Risk Tolerance

How are these psychological questions relevant to online investing? In dealing with fear, traders and investors need to know how rattled their sense of identity will be should they lose a portion of their investment capital.

How much loss can you tolerate before having to confront this primal level of fear? Think about times in your life when you had your carpet of personal security pulled out from under you. How did you recover?

If you have never had your limits tested, should a big loss occur, how will you know you can reach deeply enough into yourself to find a sense of identity that transcends your financial status? Or are you just a 30 percent loss of capital away from feeling like a "failure" and ending up in my psychotherapy consulting room?

This is why I argue for knowing your own personality tendencies and seriously considering them in your online investment decision making. If you already *know* that the terrible anxiety of financial loss would be more than you can mentally and emotionally tolerate, this concern must be weighed heavily in the risks you take.

Your focus needs to be on large-cap, stable companies that are traded in heavy volume and are less likely to test you beyond your tolerance level. These companies will minimize your risk but most likely will minimize possible reward. Of course, if you happen to choose large technology companies, your risk may still be unacceptably high. For those who do not like to monitor their holdings closely, mutual funds are still the best bet.

To respect your own personality type, it is best for those who want to avoid this anxiety to err on the conservative side. You must let mild anxiety and caution stay in the foreground in investment decision making. And you must keep in control of greed, remembering that you would always prefer to be safe than sorry.

But let us now focus on fear as it is experienced in its most common, garden-variety forms for the investor, not just at its identity-disrupting extreme.

THE CLARITY OF FEAR

Fear is a very clear, raw emotion. It is not something we can lie to ourselves about and pretend we don't feel. When watching a stock plummet, or the bottom of the market falling out, we know very directly how strong fear may be. And, of course, our fear may be compounded by the fear of others, which is what creates mass panic reactions that jolt the market.

Even relatively more hardened professional institutional traders are not immune to frenzied buying and panic selling reactions. But they have usually learned how to cope with them better than individual investors. They are less likely to become frozen with fear and more likely to jump into action as a way of coping with both fear and the greed that mounts during a frothy market. They thrive on the action.

One of the reasons fear is so clear is that we experience physical symptoms that we have learned to identify and label as "fear." These include: accelerated heartbeat, increase in blood pressure, perspiration, shakiness, stomach pains (knot), muscle tightness, headache, numbness of the extremities, ringing in the ears, blurred vision, and dryness of the mouth.

Along with these physical symptoms, we also may experience either nervousness and physical agitation or a sense of being frozen in our tracks, where we can't move. I have seen traders at a day trading firm stare at their monitors with their eyes bugging out and mouths hanging open, unable to move, as they watched their stocks plummet.

Because some day traders are commonly buying in 1000-share lots, each fractional move is significant. To be unable to move quickly enough to get out in a rapid slide can be very costly. They simply do not have the luxury of becoming frozen with fear, even for a minute. Of course, if you're not trading for "teenies" (1/16 of a point), you need not worry so much about immediate fear reactions.

FEAR AND PANIC THOUGHTS

Fear thoughts tend to increase physical symptoms and symptoms tend to increase further negative thinking. Any attempt at clear thinking gets smothered by our emotional reaction.

Our experience of time changes during panic. Time seems to speed up. There is no future—only the urgency of the moment. Each minute rushing into the next stands for further loss. The future spells utter doom; we try to prevent it.

When we feel strong fear and panic, we are psychologically trying to stop the future from occurring. When we feel mild anxiety, we are trying to delay it. Read those two lines again and think about them.

Negativity and fear are often characterized by *all-or-nothing* thinking. We only think of the extremes of what may occur, nothing in between. This is also called "catastrophic" thinking. All we can see is the very worst possible outcome, and our fear is reinforced by focusing on this worst-case scenario.

Examples of Catastrophic Thinking

All kinds of negative thoughts about the present and the future take over:

- "I'm going to lose all of my profit!"
- "I'm going to lose a big chunk of my investment capital."
- "Months (minutes, weeks, or years) of steady gains are now going down the drain."
- "This will only accelerate—I need to get out now!"
- "My vacation (new car, house deposit, new computer, big screen TV, etc.) money is evaporating. I can't sit here and watch this!"
- "My hard-earned retirement funds are losing value big time. I'll end up unable to retire when I had planned. We'll be poor and have to live in a trailer park in the Ozarks."
- "My kids' college funds won't have enough when they need it. They'll be forced to go to some terrible junior college."

FANTASYLAND: THE POWER OF THE DAYDREAM

One aspect of all-or-nothing thinking that we use to scare ourselves with is taking what is a *process* and turning it into a *final and irrevocable outcome.*

This is most often done by a combination of conscious and unconscious thought. The conscious aspect is simply freezing a moment

in time and taking it to be an end state. The more powerful unconscious aspect is the role of fantasy intruding upon conscious, intentional thought. Our minds are very skillful at weaving elaborate fantasies out of the barest of mental threads.

*What is the single most powerful and unappreciated fact of mental
life? No contest: It is the considerable amount of time spent totally lost in
waking fantasy. And most often, not even knowing it!*

By fantasy, I mean a daydream, a fictional story made up of
fleeting pictures along with a story line and associated feelings that
we may take to be temporarily or enduringly real. Or fleeting images
that we can barely even notice as we close our eyes for a moment.
The reason we are unaware of much of the fantasy in our waking life
is because it pops up quickly and we are not trained to be conscious
enough to catch the images as they float by.

We tend to create fantasies to accompany many of the actual
events of our lives. One small thought, one slight incident—that's all
it takes for us to spin off into fantasyland. And these daydreams can
be very intense—both in the clarity of their images and strength of
feelings—and seem very real. They may be quick fantasies that last a
few seconds to more complicated ones that last for minutes. In some
ways, they are much like dreams we have while sleeping. The main
difference would be that dreams while asleep do not have the partly
conscious aspect that makes up daydreams.

Fantasy and the Market

Much of how we interpret the world in general, and scare ourselves
in particular, is based on inner fantasy—not the actual events of our
lives. From the wonderfully positive, hopeful, and uplifting to the
dismal, catastrophic, and perverted—all concoctions of our own active imagination.

The outcome of a fantasy may be viewed as a real and final state.
We forget that we have created this inner story. And we don't realize
that we have made something concrete that is a actually a process.

These fantasies may be especially painful and frustrating when
we focus on our investments because our artificially constructed and
irrevocable end states do not acknowledge the obvious dynamic,
fluid nature of the market.

So, the process of the stock price going down is immediately
viewed as a final end state. We think it will fall and stay down rather
than go down temporarily and climb back up again.

It is interesting to watch this process of thought and emotion in oneself when there is a sudden and violent drop in a stock. Or a protracted correction in the market for days or weeks at a time.

It is equally interesting (and much more enjoyable) to witness the fantasies which arise as our stocks are making money. All kinds of fantasies of how we might spend our profits may fleetingly pass through our minds as we calculate how much money we are making. Clearly, one of the psychological payoffs to online trading is the time spent lost in this delicious reverie. But here is an example of a fantasy which goes the other way.

A Roller Coaster Ride Through Hell

One morning in the summer of 1999 I sat in front of my monitor and watched in near shock as one of my holdings, CMGI, a very volatile Internet stock, dropped nine points in an hour and a half in early trading.

I was getting pretty squirmy in my chair, wondering how far down it would go. I had decided when I bought this stock that, because of its volatility, it was best to view it as a trading stock, not a long-term hold. It was moving down too fast.

To add to my torture, I opened my *portfolio evaluator* window which showed me, down tick by down tick, exactly how much money I was losing as it plummeted. The loss was mounting up. Shock was replaced by anger. I knew this stock moved sharply but this was disturbing.

In the course of this ride down, I began to berate myself for getting involved with such a wild stock. I had traded this stock a few times over the months and had done pretty well, holding it for a few days or weeks at a time. Each time I had made a healthy profit. But right now I couldn't think about how much I had made taking advantage of this very same volatility.

It felt like I was going through a miniversion of financial hell. This fantasy hell is an easy state to get into when you are watching a plunging stock very closely like this. I had negative fleeting images, negative thoughts, imagined catastrophic losses, along with and an industrial strength measure of fear.

After an hour and a half, lo and behold, the stock reaches some kind of bottom, and slowly begins climbing back up. And keeps climbing. Even faster than it had been brought down, it was now bouncing back up. I couldn't believe what I was seeing. There was no explanation for the quick bounce.

Within a half hour of reaching its bottom, the stock was up six points. From its bottom, the stock had gone up 15 points in a half hour. And it finished up for the day.

At the time, I had never seen any stock recover this far and this fast. The following months would provide many occasions to see other fast-moving Internet-related stocks make similar reversal moves. But this one was striking to me. From inner hell, suddenly the sun came out and everything looked good again. A roller coaster ride past the shadow of death and now back out to roses and lollipops. And all just by watching a stock graph!

The moral of the story is twofold: *(1) don't take the process for the outcome and (2) be aware of and learn to control the influence of fantasy on your disciplined decision making.*

Discipline and the Mind's Productions

Crucial for the disciplined online investor is the ability to control the fantasies produced by the mind. It's not that we can normally control what passes through out minds. For the most part, we can't.

Unless we have had a lot of meditation experience, stopping this flow of thought just can't be done. Thoughts, fleeting images, associated feelings—all will jump forward into awareness on their own. This is simply what the mind produces.

If you don't believe this, it is simple enough to test it for yourself. Sit for 15 minutes quietly in a chair and close your eyes. Simply pay attention to the thoughts and images that come up. One of the astounding discoveries that anyone makes who tries this exercise in good faith is how truly out of control our normal thought process really is.

Thoughts, images, and feelings may rush forward, begging to be taken seriously and to be acted upon. It is our job not to be taken in by this deluge of material. We must realize that it is in our power to refuse to take a fantasy seriously. Or to stop the emotion of fear from dictating our behavior.

Since weighing the various factors that go into decision making is hard enough, for online investors, making rational decisions without the interference of confounding emotion will normally be to their advantage.

THE DEMAND TO ACT

As my example of being swept into negative thinking indicates, fear may be magnified when we're watching a volatile market too closely and begin to spin off into fantasy. While day traders need to be disciplined to stay focused on the numbers when they are trading, the greater majority of online investors do not need to watch the tape from minute to minute. They simply aren't doing enough trading to warrant this kind of close scrutiny.

Avoiding panic reactions means learning when it is not in our best interest to watch the tape too closely. And when it is best to turn off the sound of the TV and not be further whipped into a frenzy by analysts and commentators.

In psychology research studies, this pressure we feel to take action is referred to as a *demand* characteristic. It is a behavior evoked just by being in a particular situation. So, just by the act of closely watching the market drop drastically, we may feel a demand to respond to the data by taking some action.

We feel the need to do something *now* and this impulse gets stronger the longer we watch. We think that if we take some kind of action, we are more in control, and if we don't, we are passively allowing the market to control us.

This is a stronger influence than we may think. We may not even be aware how powerfully the situation is demanding that we respond. We know we are afraid but may not realize how automatically our fear pushes us to take action.

When we are not aware of a psychological motivator like this, it is easy to blindly step into the trap. Awareness of the demand, then, can help keep our foot out of the trap.

STEPPING OUT OF THE TRAP

How can we respond to this pressure, this demand? When we notice the impulse to trade based on strong fear, it is usually best to literally step out of the trap by stepping out of the situation.

We need to get up, walk away from the computer and television, take a walk, get a diet soda, go outside and water the plants, or do anything else that will move us out of the fear/panic mode.

Don't return to the computer until you have managed to achieve some emotional control over your fear/panic reaction. If you can't get a grip on your fear, then don't come back that day.

Most likely you will find that even if you keep thinking about the miserable market conditions while you water the plants, simply getting away from the keyboard and monitor is enough to make a difference. It removes the demand to take action and gives you the mental space to gain perspective and let go of your knee-jerk sell reaction.

Only after you've had a chance to get out of the situation and shift your attention should you even consider taking any action in the form of a trade. Often, when you return to the computer, you will have lost the panic reaction and be more ready to think clearly about what you want to do.

Almost all trades done in panic mode will be regretted once you have calmed down and rationality has returned.

The 1 percent done in panic mode that works out to your advantage will be the result of luck, not good decision making.

Think about this and see if it's not true for trades you've made out of strong fear or panic. We're not talking here about mild anxiety, which is a common reaction to having your money on the line. So, it is important to learn how to get away physically and mentally when we begin to notice the panic mentality taking over.

This need to get away when we feel too much pressure to *do something* is one of the reasons I favor doing one's online trading at home or at the office rather than at a professional trading firm. At a firm, the demand characteristic is easily magnified by the dozens of others around you, feeling the same fear and panic.

When I would hang around the local trading firm, I noticed that during normal market conditions, almost no one ever left the trading floor for a break. Hours would pass, but no one ever walked out of the large room.

The windows were darkened so traders could not see out. Some would periodically walk around the floor, use the bathroom, or stop by a table for a cup of coffee or donut. But they didn't take what I believe to be the necessary breaks by *stepping out of the situation.*

Since no one is trading continuously over the many hours the market is open, there is no good excuse for not taking breaks by walking outside into the sun. But no one did it. *I consider this a psychological error in judgment.*

They felt a demand to stay glued to the computer monitors in case they might miss something important—maybe a news flash or sudden change in the S&P futures. The flurry of rapid, continual activity creates a sense that you just can't take your eyes off the numbers for very long.

But it's not true. The market is not going anywhere! There is always another trading opportunity and another day. While this is obvious on one level, too often when caught in the anxious moment, we "forget" this truth.

All online traders and investors who are not day trading 1000-share lots (or more) and looking to gain a quick eighth or quarter of a point have the luxury to step away from the monitor and shake off fear and panic.

Even under everyday, nonpanic conditions, periodic breaks away from the monitor over the course of a market session are crucial. Not only do they give you a chance to stretch your body and refocus your eyes on something besides a monitor, they also give you the necessary mental break.

Catching Fear from the Media

I'm just going to mention the media now since we are on the topic of fear. We will come back to considering its influence in Chapter 6.

As an example of how real-time commentary may aggravate your stability, you need only watch CNBC during a market correction. Personal fear is intensified when we hear numerous "experts" on CNBC tell us how terrible things are.

As the gloom and doom is passed around, we find ourselves being infected by it. This may lead to premature decision making to sell positions rather than ride out the rough period. Many viewers are influenced by what these experts say, even if these commentators have no real idea where things are headed. This is one of the effects of taking market experts too seriously.

Taking Advantage of Overreaction

If we understand that both individual traders and the market as a whole predictably overreact to news events, we can use this fact to make money. Much of the short-term (from minutes to hours to days) action of stock prices may be accounted for by this overreaction. Most of these events are not very significant to the longer-range movement of any given stock.

Timing is of utmost importance in determining who makes money from these short-term overreactions and who is left frightened and sitting frozen. When there is general market anxiety or even panic, one way you can control your own emotions enough to jump in and take advantage of lower prices is by adopting an intermediate- or long-range attitude.

Reframing

In other words, you think about the intermediate term or long term just as everyone else is getting caught in the short term. If you think about the intermediate term by asking, "What is likely to happen to this stock if I buy it now at this reduced price and hold it for two or three months?" anxiety is lessened.

You can also ask yourself, "Have the fundamentals of this stock changed at all so it is no longer worth owning?" One common trap when we are anxious is that we tend to get caught in overvaluing stock price alone. We forget why we bought a stock in the first place.

The psychological term for this shift is *reframing*. It is to take something out of one mental framework and shift it to another one. In this case, we extract ourselves from the short-term anxiety of the news by reframing the stock in the context of the future.

And yes, it is possible to buy too early and watch the price go down even further. Traders like to refer to this as, "catching a falling knife." This is where due diligence comes in.

Catching a Falling Knife

If you have been closely following a stock and know good entry points based on past performance, you can jump in when there is "blood in the street" and feel more confident that you have bought at a good price. You price the possibility of a further drop into your thinking, so that you will not feel you made a mistake or "caught a falling knife" if in fact it goes lower.

Some traders suggest "getting your feet wet" by coming back into the market with a partial position so you can buy more should the stock drop any further.

It is easy to talk about being a contrarian and going against the crowd when everything is nice and secure. The test is being able to pull the trigger when everyone else is caught in anxiety and panic. But you must know the stock well, or your chances are not as good at being confident of your position.

One of the ways you can tell more seasoned investors is that they are less caught in the emotional whirlpool of short-term anxiety. They have been through it, to various degrees, many times before. They are therefore more able to pounce on dips in price and see them for the good buying opportunities that they are.

The less experienced investor adopts scared thinking and asks, "Who knows how far down it can go? How can I trust when it is safe to jump in without risking buying too early?"

While the professional says, "I follow this stock closely. I know everything there is to know about its performance. I know it has hit a good price. Time to buy it, no matter what the scared money is doing."

The Double-Edged Sword

Online trading is a double-edged sword. Real-time quotes, news web sites, CNBC talking heads, chat room message boards, and real-time stock sites feeding us up-to-the-minute analysis and commentary—all provide what we need to trade effectively.

Yet, this same nowness of data also makes for more anxiety, fear, and potential negative thinking when things turn against us.

Even when it's smooth sailing and the market is doing well, the advantage offered by everything being real time makes for a quality of *immediacy* and *urgency* that can be disconcerting. This immediacy can be exciting and keeps us on the edge. But it may just as easily turn into anxiety if we fall off that edge and feel only urgency.

Stepping into the Trading Room

For a period of months, I periodically spent a number of hours per day in a day trading firm for individual traders. My interest was strictly to learn something about the scene.

I didn't go in thinking I would open an account and become a day trader. And, it didn't take long before realizing that the scene was just too frantic and risky for me. So, it was with my psychologist's hat on that I entered the trading floor, not a trader's hat.

I hoped to get a sense of what kind of people became traders and how they approached their work. I also wanted to learn about how the superfast hardware and software worked, including Level II quotes. I needed to learn "trader speak," the lingo of the profession. And, lastly, I wanted to find out what personality traits might typify various traders who I would observe and chat with.

I noticed that even when traders were doing well with their trades, the market was moving, and they had plenty of momentum to trade on, I rarely got the sense they were enjoying the action. Instead, many seemed anxious, tense, and unable to sit still in front of their computers. They had nervous habits, like biting their fingernails, kicking their legs rapidly under the table. I noticed a lot of squirming in chairs and too many cups of coffee.

Feeling nervous and agitated is not so surprising. Having large amounts of money on the line, needing to pay very close attention to each change in the quotes, and needing to make quick decisions as to when to pull the trigger would make anyone nervous.

Add to this the fact that some traders are drinking numerous cups of coffee and eating sugary donuts beginning before the market opens and continuing through the trading day. This jacks them up even further. It makes for a tense and intense scene. Its not an easy-going work environment.

And how could it be? Unlike the chips in Las Vegas that allow seasoned gamblers to "forget" that they are playing for real money, having your profit or loss continually flashing before your eyes never lets you forget what is at stake.

SLOUCHING TOWARD WALL STREET

Why, besides having money on the line, does being thrust into the here and now while trading make us so uncomfortable?

What happens is that coming into and *staying in* the present is inherently an anxiety-provoking event for us. We are just not sure how to get fully comfortable in the present, how to really settle into it easily and gracefully.

Whether it's trying to stay fully present with another person in an intimate conversation or focusing on a computer screen to write these words, there is a subtle avoidance to feeling the full force of the present. Any activity that pushes us into the present and *keeps us there* is usually tinged with some tension.

Pay attention to your own experience right now. Stop reading for a moment and notice what happens when you look around your physical space. Use your ears and eyes to notice what is happening right here and right now.

Notice any thoughts, feelings, or sensations that may arise and just stay with them, not trying to avoid, change, or push away anything you notice.

What happens when you fully enter into the present? Do you notice an impulse to want to distract yourself from feeling its full weight? For most, it is not easy to stay present-centered for very long. Why?

Because we encounter an ever-present, subtle tension that nudges us into the next moment. It's as if we're always *slouching into the future.*

See if this is not true when you try and stay fully focused in the present. It is very easy to do all kinds of things to distract yourself from staying right here and now. The reason why: It is the natural human tendency to *lean* into the next moment. It is just part of our natural, subjective experience of moving through time.

Here's one way this leaning into the future relates to the market: Watching streaming, dynamically updating stock quotes, along with real-time charts, for more than a few minutes sucks us into the present and compels us to stay focused from moment to moment.

At the same time, the quotes are always flowing into the future. Watching them will tend to bring us into a state where we are more aware of this leaning into the next moment. What is between the present moment and the next moment is this tension of *leaning*.

This is especially evident when we are talking about a fast-moving process like the stock market. Everything about it is focused on speediness, on getting the jump on the next guy. Speed of obtaining information and of execution become paramount in being on top versus being left in the dust.

The most obvious example symbolizing the ongoing movement is the ticker tape. When you watch it for a while, does it not tend to beckon you to enter the urgency of the moment?

As an online investor, you need to be aware of how both the urgency of the market and this "slouching into the future" personally affect you. If you don't adjust well to them, you need to limit the frequency and length of your online sessions so that you stop before you get too tense.

There is a group of online investors who just can't watch too closely without getting too anxious. Some obsessive and timid types are like this. They want to enjoy the low commissions that online discount brokerages offer. They want to make an occasional trade. But they will never be able to sit for very long and watch their portfolio rise and fall with each swing in the market.

Psychologically, we can think of it like this: Anything that is based on speed is always going to put us at least a little on the edge. *And the edge is where both excitement and anxiety reside.* When we stay on this side of the razor's edge, we feel excitement—the kind of excitement that active traders thrive on and that keeps them coming back for more and more.

But if we fall off the edge and plop into anxiety and even panic, suddenly it is a whole different experience. Keep this edge in mind when you are trading. Notice how it is tinged for you and how it changes from one to the other.

SPEED AND TRADE EXECUTION

When it comes to day trading, those who make the most money are institutional professionals who get the news two minutes (or more) before you or I do. They pay $1500 per month to have a wire service feed them the news the moment it is released.

If that isn't enough, they have direct access to call company management when they need to get specific information. They also have guys who sit around and do nothing but analyze stocks in every way imaginable using very expensive software programs.

In addition, they evaluate and decide faster than you or I. And, finally, they execute their trades faster than we can because they are not having to go through a discount broker. Their trades are executed directly and instantaneously through independent networks.

This speed of information and execution is available to day traders using super-speedy computers in day trading firms. It is one of the benefits they have to offer. Unlike online traders at home, most of whom are going through discount brokers, they are trading directly with market makers through electronic networks. So, in terms of speed, they are on a par with the big institutional traders.

What they don't have available to them that the institutional establishments have are sophisticated programmed trading software programs that help them buy and sell automatically in huge volume. These programs use mathematical formulas to try and determine stocks that are undervalued. When they kick in, stock prices may be affected quickly and powerfully.

There are now web sites that offer speedy execution for the online day trader at home. To take advantage of these sites, you must have the necessary hardware and software: a speedy computer, a cable modem or fast digital subscriber line (DSL), and the required configuration of browser and software.

At the end of 1999, these day trading sites were still costly and not really worth the price unless you planned to do a lot of trading. If you did, they would give you "free" access for the equivalent of approximately 50 trades per month.

Remember that when it comes to short-term trading, every dollar that is lost in a trade is going to someone else. If approximately 88 percent of retail day traders are losing money, who is making all that money? The institutional day traders are making it, that's who!

Individual day traders have their work cut out for them if they think they can compete successfully on a *long-term basis* against the likes of Goldman Sachs, Morgan Stanley, and the other large players or even smaller firms made up of seasoned professionals.

The fact that the odds are against retail day traders is not likely to stop growing numbers from trying. Only a significant and prolonged market slump would cut down the numbers of traders. And even then, as soon as the market recovered, many would return to try again.

FEAR-BASED TRADING ERRORS

The following few errors are made primarily out of fear. While lack of investment sophistication and personality traits may enter the picture with these issues, it is fear that is most prominent in causing the problem.

- *Too much analysis before buying.* For some online investors, especially among the obsessive-disciplined and doubter-timid types, the basic fear of committing funds to the market is the first hurdle that is tough to clear.

The fear of being wrong is exhibited through procrastination. Too much analysis may be displayed as the need for just one more piece of information, one more trial period to track the stock on paper, one more earnings report, or anything else that may be used to put off committing to purchase the stock.

This felt need for more information may be played out indefinitely on the Internet, where there are so many online stock sites that offer detailed company analysis and commentary.

Procrastination often has a way of backfiring: It ends up leading to exactly the assessment of having made a mistake that investors are most trying to avoid. This occurs because investors wait too long and miss the greater amount of upside movement of a stock.

If they buy toward the top of a run-up, they are often disappointed when they don't make the profit they hoped for. And, unfortunately, this tends to reinforce their thinking that they don't have good judgment in terms of when to buy a stock. For those who repeatedly notice that they enter a position too late, this fear of commitment to a position is often operating.

■ *Afraid to pull the trigger.* This is related to the first problem. But sometimes investors know they want to buy and have done their analysis but still have problems actually entering the trade. I mean, of course, that while they know what menus to click on, they can't bring themselves to go ahead and take the final step and "pull the trigger" by entering the trade.

This difficulty was made into a humorous commercial by the discount broker E-Trade. A rather young investor sits in front of his computer monitor with his index finger shaking over the mouse, but is unable to click it to enter the trade. He paces back and forth across his room, does jumping jacks to deal with his anxiety, and makes a number of premature passes in front of his monitor before he finally works up the courage to press the mouse button. The tag line is, "Be not afraid."

I like this commercial mainly because it is the first one by a discount broker to address a common problem of online investing rather than just enticing everyone with the riches to be made.

While the fear of execution is fairly common for many beginners to online investing, it is not really discussed. This piece acknowledges directly that emotions and, indirectly, investor personality and temperament, are part of the online trading experience.

■ *Afraid to sell when trade goes sour.* According to popular stock market lore, this is the single biggest problem for investors in general. This includes online traders who hold positions as day traders and short-term position traders, as well as longer-term investors.

Selling a losing position requires admitting that we have made a mistaken judgment. Since this is tough for many of us to admit, we hold the position too long and lose more and more money, as we ride the position down to the depths of hell.

I, like almost all investors at one time or another, am guilty of committing this error myself, and continue to hold a couple of "dead money" losing positions that I let get out of hand years ago. One of them, Pairgain Technology, my wife won't let me forget, reminding me with every new moon how much I have lost in this stock. The interesting thing about my continuing to hold this loser is that part of my rationalization for doing so is based on remembering it as a real winner. The other part of my excuse for stubbornly holding on is my firm belief that the company will most likely sooner, rather than later, be swallowed up by a larger company, in which case I ought to recoup my initial investment.

While the prospects for this ultimately taking place are quite good, who knows how much I may be simply telling myself a story to justify going down with the ship? And I won't even mention the lost *opportunity cost*—how else my remaining capital could be working for me.

Update: I was right! In February 2000, Pairgain agreed to be acquired by ADC Telecom. Recovering my investment and maybe even making a profit now appear quite promising.

■ *Afraid to assault the ego.* The psychological theory for needing to reconcile information that is inconsistent with our self-concept is called *cognitive dissonance*. This theory maintains that we want to reduce any dissonant information that clashes with a positive belief we hold about ourselves.

So, the acceptance that I made a poor judgment by holding the stock too long is dissonant with my belief that I am a good stock picker. I reduce this dissonance by telling myself it will turn out all right, that I didn't really make such a lousy decision. But, of course, I did, at least in regard to holding too long. Reducing dissonance, then, is a way we can accept the information that is inconsistent *without* having to change the positive belief or end up pulling our hair out.

Regarding the first part of the rationalization (previously seeing the stock as a winner), I traded Pairgain numerous times in the mid-1990s, when it was a high-flying tech stock that enjoyed popular analyst appeal, good momentum, and the future for the company's technology looked bright.

Once, with perfect timing around a positive news report and holding only a few hundred shares, I made $3000 in two days. I have made what for me is a good deal of money in both short- and medium-term trades of this stock. In fact, in terms of profits made, it ranks in the top five stocks of everything I have ever traded.

Because I felt a certain affinity for the company, which happens to be headquartered very close to my office, I didn't let go when management began to make some poor decisions, the stock lost favor, and the price began to shrivel.

One of the benefits for those who try day trading is that, if they are to survive, they *must* learn how to enter and exit positions quickly. They are forced to learn to sell a trade that has gone against them before it costs them too much money. They can then apply this ability to let go of a position quickly should they decide to hold stocks for longer periods of time. It is a skill that all online investors need to learn to preserve their capital. We will discuss more about ego getting in the way elsewhere in this book.

■ *Afraid to let profits run.* This appears to be a rather common error. It is based on an overly conservative approach to profit taking. We are happy to settle for a little profit rather than take a chance we may lose it.

For conservative investors who know their limits of risk, this is not a bad error to make. Especially if they have a preset amount (or percentage) of profit and they reach this goal, it is good discipline to take the profit and be content. This is the idea behind the self-evident dictum that, "You can't make a bad trade when you take a profit."

But how good a profit do we want it to be? The problem arises when we begin to scare ourselves after making a relatively small profit. In Las Vegas, this would be called, "playing with scared money."

If we see repeatedly that a stock keeps rising after we have sold it, it is a good idea to consider taking the risk to let profits ride, setting our limits at a higher dollar value or percentage. In this way, we can challenge our self-imposed limit based on fear that a little profit is more than enough.

Another way to deal with the fear of losing our profit is to sell a percentage of it and let the remainder stay in play. This is a common strategy of the institutional traders, who are trading in such large blocks of stock that they still have plenty riding even when they take some profit.

The balance or compromise here is to sell a third or a half once it reaches your prearranged gain and leave the rest for further gain. If the stock does not continue to go up, at least part of your gain has been preserved.

We will return to other aspects of fear later. Now let us look at the other face of the yin-yang polarity: greed.

The Fear and Greed
Trilogy, Part II: Greed

At the close of the market on Monday, April 12, 1999, the Dow finished up 166 points for the day, reaching a record high of 10,339. On the same day, Pfizer Pharmaceutical hit 150.

I had picked up 200 shares in mid-January and added another 200 in early February. In less than three months, taking a ride on the Viagra express, I had made a decent return of over 25 percent. While it wasn't exactly the kind of astounding return some of the Internet stocks were providing, the actual dollar amount earned was plump, and I was feeling pretty good about it. Pfizer was looking as stable as the Rock of Gibraltar.

When I put my ear to the ground, I should have picked up the distant vibration of galloping hoofs headed toward me. I should have realized the run-up was a little too frothy not to be more cautious.

Now, when it hit 150, I remember thinking, "It's come up pretty fast. You've got a nice return over a fairly short period. The last time a stock profit reached this point, you sold and were satisfied. Earnings are coming up. Why not take your profit now? You can always buy it back later."

But I didn't act on what I was thinking. I didn't put in a stop-limit order to sell, locking in my profit. Nor did I set a mental stop. Had I followed my thinking, I would have sold at the exact top. But no, I was going to squeeze just a little more juice out of it. Greed reared its head, opened its ugly mouth, exposed its sharp teeth, and bit me hard.

The next day the stock went down about a point. No big deal. The following day it dropped another 4 3/4. These were the "smart money" early birds not taking any chances on the upcoming earnings report. I should have been one of them: $2000 of my profit gone in one day. But it was what happened the next day that threw me for a loop.

"PIGS GET SLAUGHTERED"

A favorite little broker cliché about getting greedy goes like this: "Bulls make money and bears make money but pigs get slaughtered."

The earnings report for Pfizer came out the next morning. Everyone was expecting a good quarter based on the previous quarter's Viagra profits. Many investors were wishfully thinking that the drug would take off beyond its intended clinical use and become a recreational drug for all men to improve sexual endurance. It was an elegant if overly simplistic notion: As the number of men benefiting from Viagra went up, so would the value of the stock. At the least, they were expecting an improvement in earnings over the previous quarter.

No such luck. The earnings came in less than the previous quarter, sending institutional and individual investors rushing for the exit gate. The stock was, as they say, taken out to the woodshed and thrashed mercilessly, sliding 14 1/2 points. It was the single largest one-day drop in Pfizer's history. The following day, Friday, it dropped another three points. By this time, my profit was oozing out of every pore.

At no point during this miserable free fall did I sell, thinking the stock would recover after the earnings disappointment wore off. Here I am, still kneeling with my ear to the ground, listening for the coming Indians, while their arrows are already being zinged fiercely into my back!

Because the stock had been on such a steady upward climb for months, I couldn't (wouldn't) change my thinking fast enough to accommodate what was happening.

Monday of the following week brought more emotional uproar. After soaring 250 points at one point, the Dow finished down 56 points. Not to be outdone, the NASDAQ had its second worst day ever, closing down 138. To add insult to injury, Pfizer finished off its punishing meltdown by dropping another nine points to put me back where I started.

I had managed to lose all my profit in one miserable week as a result of a disappointing earnings report and a general market melt-down. Unable to erect itself again following the strong rise it got from Viagra, Pfizer has not recovered its luster since this episode.

My greed to increase my profit to 30 percent had been my downfall. That, and not being mentally nimble enough to respond immediately to what was clearly a change in the short-term stock story and the general market psychology.

I should have known better. I had committed one of the mortal sins of investing: I had allowed my profit to be wiped out. I have vowed never again to build up that kind of profit without having a stop-loss in place to protect me from down-side risk. While the merits and disadvantages of using stop-loss orders can be debated, in this case it would have saved me a healthy profit.

As well, I will be more careful about letting all profit ride. This is not the craps table in Las Vegas, where you can talk yourself into believing you're playing with the house's money. The object of the game is to make money, not take undue risks just because you're ahead.

Next time, I will sell at least a portion of my position to lock in part of my gain. There are times when the dictum of "let your profits run" needs to be tempered to a more conservative position like: "Take some profit off the table and let *part* of your profit run."

In this case, taking even part of my profit would have meant letting the Viagra Express zip us back to Lake Como in Italy. Since I continue to think about this loss of profit with Pfizer many months later, it appears that I may have learned an important lesson from this error based on greed.

THE NATURE OF GREED

Greed is not nearly so clear to us as fear. It is often realized only indirectly, after the fact, or not at all. This is because greed is not really a feeling but a combination of *thinking* and *behavior*.

While it may be all right to admit to ourselves, and sometimes even to others, that we are feeling fear over something, it is less acceptable for us to admit to being greedy. Think about your own reaction to this statement. Is it true for you? Are you more willing to admit to feeling some fear, at least in relation to making an investment, than you are to acknowledge your greedy actions?

I know from two and a half decades of clinical practice that men typically dread having to admit feeling afraid of anything, especially to another man. Some are so out of touch with fear that they can be shaking in their loafers but not label what they're feeling as fear. Our John Wayne culture doesn't encourage men to be aware of, or admit to, fear. It teaches the opposite—to deny it and block it out.

Once they let down their defenses and become more in touch with themselves, men begin to acknowledge this primal and powerful emotion. Admitting to feeling fear is tough enough. But it's nothing compared to admitting to greed. Nobody admits to thinking or acting in a greedy way, except Gordon Gecko in the movie that defined the 1980s, *Wall Street*.

Although Michael Douglas proclaims eloquently that "greed is good," we do not typically view greediness as a desirable personality feature. Those in the business and financial worlds are perhaps more direct than those who aren't with their desire to make as much money as possible. Only those related to the Wall Street world have the gall to walk around wearing a tie with $100 bills printed on it or suspenders with stock quotes on them.

But even those who are very direct in their avaricious intentions to accumulate wealth and impressive possessions shy away from thinking of or describing themselves as greedy.

Because greed is inferred from our actions, it is not so easy to examine our behavior after the fact, especially when we have a suspicion we're not going to like what we see. When we compare a behavior like greed, which is outside of us in the sense that we act upon the world in a greedy fashion, to the immediate recognition of fear, which is felt inside us, it becomes clear why one is somewhat easier to decipher than the other.

Just to make the point more simply: Have you ever heard anyone say, "I'm feeling really greedy today"? Probably not. What they will say is that they feel a hunger, craving, or an excitement to have more.

What they feel is an intense *desire* for possessions and wealth. Then they take certain actions that appear to be greedy, like holding out for just a bit more profit, buying more of something that they really don't need, or not being able to stop overworking for more money even when their personal relationships may suffer.

TO THINE OWN SELF BE TRUTHFUL

We might tell ourselves or others we are ambitious rather than greedy. Or we might think of our desire to make a lot of money as fulfilling our security needs. We may feel excited as we're making increasing amounts of money. Why ruin our excitement by labeling it greed? Can't we just say we have a healthy interest in earning as much in income and investments as possible? Sure, we can label it anything we like.

But for our purposes of balancing fear and greed and understanding how these motives affect our trading behavior, we must be ruthlessly truthful with ourselves. We want to understand how greed, or the desire for more, can push us to make poor decisions when we're investing online. We need to be able to identify our own thoughts and feelings of *never enough*, of yearning for more, and not call them something more innocent or flattering.

In the example I gave of my own holding back from taking a profit with Pfizer, it certainly would have been easier for me to attribute my behavior to something more benign. I could have tried to convince myself that it really wasn't greed operating but simply a lack of understanding of how dependent the stock price was on the expectations of Viagra.

Or, I could have tried to convince myself that Viagra is just one drug among many that Pfizer sells and that this company is far too large to rest its hopes on any one drug, no matter how popular it may have become. And there is truth to each of these assertions. But they aren't why I didn't sell when it hit 150. I didn't sell because I wanted to see it hit 160. And that is what greed is all about: *Squeezing a little more juice out of the orange.*

Is there anyone reading this who doesn't know the feeling of well-being and exhilaration upon watching a stock go up very quickly? And how hard it can be to take profits when one hopes the stock will move even higher? This feeling of *never enough* or wanting more profit, that no matter how much we've made, we want just a little more—this is the face of greed. And, as we said earlier, it has been a part of the human financial story in one form or another since the earliest exchange economies.

Even with all the fancy technology, real-time news, and everything else available, we never really have all the information that would be desirable about a company or what moves its stock price in helping us make our investing decisions. We are always being forced to use our best judgment to evaluate and make decisions, knowing we don't have all the pieces, that we are operating on limited data. Of course, this is true not only with our investment decisions but in the rest of our lives as well. This is pretty self-evident, isn't it?

Unless you are sitting on the board of directors of a company or have the CEO whispering in your ear, you really aren't privy to all the details that are relevant to a company's current condition and future prospects and how this information may affect its stock price. Even then, as we all know, a company's actual condition may not be accurately reflected in its stock price, which is simply its perceived relative value at any given time.

A company may have stellar earnings, solid fundamentals, technical indicators looking good, great prospects, and a CEO who knows how to charm the pants off the analysts and the press. And yet still the company may be out of favor with traders and investors for no apparent reason.

This is where my dictum, *mind moves the market* helps make sense of what is at first glance tough to comprehend. If the way people *interpret* all the data about a company is not in line with the actual facts, you have a discrepancy that shows up in the stock price. Sometimes, all the good things about a stock are already priced into it. Then the least perception that the company is not outdoing itself each quarter leads to a sell-off.

Dell is perhaps the best example of this. The company was growing at such an astounding rate that when it began to cool off just a little, the stock got hit hard. Nothing had changed with the fundamentals of the company. In fact, it continued to gain more market share. The company's prospects looked bright. But the expectations had become very high to justify the high premium attached to the stock. When it beat, but did not "blow out" its earnings number for a couple of quarters, the sell-off was severe.

So many variables related to the market are out of our control. Because of this, it is important for us to be truthful to ourselves, since our own emotions, thoughts, and motives are at least one domain of the investment game that we may know and within which we may exert a measure of self-control. We'll talk more about self-control later in Chapter 7.

Why an Increase in Greed?

The bull market of the last decade is certainly partially responsible for an increase in greedy thinking and behavior. We watch others make a lot of quick money on high-tech stocks like Dell, Cisco, and Intel by being in at the right time.

We hear colleagues and friends boast about their huge profits with Internet stocks that head for the stratosphere. We start salivating. We want our share of the wealth and we want it fast and easy. That's greed.

The bull market and the explosion of easy online trading have made it seem like anyone not cashing in on the bonanza was not getting their fair share of the easy wealth just waiting to be made.

We make 20 percent a year return owning mutual funds when things are good. But it feels like it's not enough compared to the 60, 80, or 100 percent returns made by the guy who had the guts to take a chance with AOL, Amazon.com, Yahoo, Inktomi, CMGI, or any one of two dozen other Internet stocks as they were getting going. When the NASDAQ returns 86 percent for the year, as it did for 1999, obviously our expectations go up.

As another example, it's tough to be satisfied with a 20 percent return once you've had the thrill of a 150 percent profit in a few hours by "flipping" a hot initial public offering. If you're lucky enough to get in at the offering price before it begins selling on the market, it is an exciting and no-risk way of making a fast profit. And, what's more, there's a nice ego boost in feeling special, having been among those selected to get in on a sure thing.

When our expectations go up, it tends to push our behavior more toward greed and risk-taking rather than fear and caution. This will undoubtedly swing back to fear and caution when a prolonged bear market shakes up our security.

There are a number of issues related to money that we need to identify to understand why greed exerts the influence it does on our thinking and behavior. Then we may begin to see how the *never enough* mentality works to push us to reach for more.

THE MULTIPLE MEANINGS OF MONEY

Money signifies a number of psychological and emotional needs for us that go beyond its use as a medium of valuable exchange. Think of your own personal associations to money. What does money mean to you? If you had just one word to describe it, what would it be? Here are some of the common meanings we attach to money:

- *Financial security.* Money providing the security to not only economically survive in the real world but to afford the lifestyle we choose given our skills, ability, education, social status, affiliations, motivation, and good fortune; the desire to gracefully meet and exceed material needs without continual worry about the cost of living.

- *Sense of identity.* Money as helping to define our sense of who we are; how it builds and fortifies ego strength, contributing to a mental and emotional stability in daily life that helps weather difficulties; the "safety net" function it may serve in stabilizing assaults to the ego.

- *Success.* Money as one yardstick of success, having "made it" in the world, feeling competent, enhancing self-worth; enjoying respect from others, being recognized for one's contribution; and being perceived as a desirable "catch" in the social world.

- *Freedom.* Money as the means to create personal and financial independence, to have time to spend the way one wishes rather than tied to a rigid work schedule; to break away from the crowd and enjoy life through hobbies, family, interests, travel, and possessions.

- *Power.* Money as a means to exert influence over others; to get one's way in the world; to have the clout to get things done; to attain position and influence in the business world, social and political organizations; to be able to join clubs that one wishes; to be accorded special favor and recognized by others; to distinguish oneself from the crowd.

- *Retirement and leisure.* To be able to retire when one wishes rather than work for a lifetime; to afford a leisure lifestyle to the degree one wishes; to spend time with hobbies, interests, sports rather than feel financially compelled to work full time; to have discretionary income or savings so as not to have to worry about old age, medical or life insurance; to have something to look forward to.

THE REAL COST OF LOSING MONEY

Listing the previous associations to money helps us to realize that our activities of earning, accumulating, spending, and investing money all carry with them the particular values and meanings associated to it that we have developed through our lives.

When money means some or all of these things to us, we can see how both fear and greed slip into the picture—we have more riding than just earning a little profit. We can also begin to glimpse how all of these associations are online with us unconsciously when we are trading.

Since we are attaching personal meanings to money, it follows that when we lose money on a trade or longer-term investment, we are losing more than just our capital. We are also losing part of the meaning we associate to the money. Psychologically, we are losing a feeling of success, freedom, power, security, independence, or whatever other value we have equated to money.

When we see how losing money means losing the values we associate to it, we can more easily understand the common behavior of letting losses mount up. Logically, it doesn't make sense to hold a losing position until it buries us. But if we can preserve our sense of identity, freedom, security, power, independence, and hopes for the future, what's a monetary loss compared to these important values? *As long as we don't sell, we have preserved the associated value.*

The next time you find yourself stubbornly resisting selling a losing position, ask yourself what else is psychologically being lost if you sell. Sometimes, simply in bringing to awareness what we are really risking, we are freed to go ahead and take the necessary action.

Just because we don't consciously think about these meanings of money doesn't mean they aren't affecting us when we're trading. They are always lurking, even if unconsciously, in the background. To the degree we make them conscious, we may take them into consideration as part of our personality makeup when we formulate an approach and style of trading.

And we can free ourselves to execute trades more decisively. This is an element in helping us become more disciplined investors.

OBSESSION WITH KEEPING SCORE

One of the common errors made by beginning day traders, position traders, and long-term investors alike is spending an inordinate amount of time thinking about and tracking gains and losses before, during, and after trades. Because money is on the line, our decision making is overly conditioned by the fear and greed that accompany this score-keeping fixation.

While we obviously need to monitor our gains and losses, the difficulty comes in when our flexibility to respond is compromised by never being able to get the tally of profit and loss out of our minds.

Being obsessed with keeping score does not appear to be the optimal approach to working with fear and greed.

So, the question that arises is this: At what times is it useful to consider the score and at what times should it be the furthest thing from our minds? Take a moment before reading on and answer this question for yourself. Can you allow for the idea that score-keeping sometimes is best kept out of your mind? Or do you think this is impossible to do?

If we're constantly thinking about preserving our capital, we will be overly cautious, fearful, and unable to take calculated risks at just those times when we need to strike. The fear of jumping in to buy when a stock has dropped fast but a floor, or resistance point, has not been firmly established is one example of this fixation. Traders say that "scared money never wins." And money that is being counted up too often tends to become scared rather easily.

On the other side of the coin, using margin to greedily trade in larger share lots than we can really afford because of some arbitrary amount we want to make is another example. In both instances, being too concerned with the score dictates our actions. Emotions—fear and craving—rather than disciplined thinking, prevail.

So, one way we can try to balance both fear and greed is to diminish their strength through the persistent application of clear, rational thought. With clear thinking, emotional swings between fear and greed become less frequent and less intense when they do occur.

It is not that we expect to wipe away all emotion—that would not even be desirable if it were possible. Because knowing how we feel is important as one piece of data to be weighed in our decision making. We just don't want emotion to be what we prematurely base our trading decisions on. And we sure don't want momentary impulses causing foolish, snap decisions.

THE TRADING GAME PARADOX

The obsession with keeping score suggests an interesting paradox: While the whole game of equity trading is focused on earning a solid return, limiting losses, and preserving capital, at the same time being too fixated on keeping score hampers our ability to treat trading more as the serious game that it is.

This is exacerbated by online trading program screens, where we may view an ongoing, real-time tally of our bottom line at any minute. Nice to have it when you want it—but also a built-in recipe for fixation.

An obsession with keeping score blocks finding ways to creatively play the game—ways that might very well result in exactly what we're trying to accomplish. So, how is it possible to be surrounded by continually flashing numbers that represent real money being made and lost but not treat our actions as if real money is on the line?

I use the word *game* in the following senses: that there is an amusing, exciting, playlike aspect to electronic trading that encourages a lighter, rather than heavier, hand on the keyboard; that we are, despite all the discipline we can muster, still engaging in an activity of some chance to gain something of value; and in the sense of *showing no fear* when faced with something difficult, dangerous, or unknown.

It is this last meaning of the word *game* that is most relevant to balancing greed and fear. To the degree we can think and act *as if* we're playing a game, fear and greed may be diminished and at least kept in check. How might you include an aspect of playfulness into your trading that would make it less of a grind? It will be different for everyone. What might it be for you?

Playing with the Paradox: Personal Examples

Sometimes to keep things from getting too heavy, I will watch the flashing quotes and make some guesses as to what's going to happen next in the movement of a stock or the market as a whole. Or I will guess what the effect of a piece of news hitting the market will have on the indices.

I do this without taking a position in the stock, only to play with my hunches as to the way things are moving. This keeps me interested, alert, and often leads to an inner chuckle when I predict correctly, and to a mental shrug of "oh well" when I don't. It helps me stay balanced, keeping in mind that the impact of no one piece of news, economic report, analyst downgrade, or anything else is going to last forever.

Of course, there is something more going on here. I am playfully trying to understand the movement of the stock, learning broad rhythms of movement as I make my casual guesses. I begin to see daily cycles that certain stocks repeat at certain times of the session.

The objective is to get to the point where I can feel the same playfulness when money is on the line as I do when it isn't. While I can do this reasonably well when things are going my way, it is unquestionably more challenging when the stock is heading in the wrong direction.

If you've worked long and hard to accumulate your investing capital, you're not going to find it easy to be lighthearted about money that has taken so much effort to earn. From a psychological standpoint, that's what makes the paradox of the trading game interesting. And especially as it relates to trying to balance fear and greed. We have so much of value riding on the line (and online) and yet we need to act is if we don't.

Another way I try to stay balanced while scanning the monitor is to sometimes turn on music or watch a bit of a light-hearted TV show. I want just enough distracting input from other sources to maintain my mental equilibrium so that I don't fall into the black hole of constant score-keeping. In addition, as mentioned earlier, I get up from the computer and take periodic breaks to stretch and refocus my vision and attention.

I also use these intended distractions to help ensure I'm not unduly influenced by the talking heads on CNBC, whom I listen to during selected segments and mute the rest of the time. I have not found that distracting myself in these ways gets in the way of attending to the numbers when I need to.

I should be clear that my style of trading is not that of scalping fractions of a point with dozens of trades per day. That said, I still spend as much time watching quotes and doing market analysis as would a conscientious day trader—and much more than those traders who don't do research.

I'm at the computer every morning from 5:30 A.M., one hour before the market opens on the west coast, to market close, unless I'm seeing patients, in which case it's only for five hours in the morning. I conduct my psychotherapy practice at a separate office from my home study. I don't have a computer at my office, for the most part keeping the activities of following the market and writing separate from clinical practice. I do, however, carry a laptop to the office when I may need to respond urgently to e-mail IPO confirmation requests.

While I follow the market closely enough to be an active trader, I actually don't do anywhere near the same number of trades as most day or position traders do. Many days go by successively when I make no trades at all. So, I give myself the freedom to turn away from the quotes and other data any time I wish.

I spend time in the evening reading online market analysis and company-related news, managing my portfolio, writing and answering e-mail, researching stocks, and reading and sometimes posting to online stock-related bulletin boards. Off-line, I read a number of market-related magazines that I subscribe to, in addition to psychological journals.

When unsuspecting people find out that I watch the market so closely, spending ungodly amounts of time looking at streaming quotes, they look at me incredulously. Some ask why I spend so much time watching quotes flickering by and doing research when I don't really do all that much trading. I answer, "So I can manage my portfolio skillfully."

But the truth is that I began doing it because I was interested in knowing more about this whole new game of online investing. And when I become really interested in something, I tend to thoroughly explore it. My interest led to the discovery that there were many important psychological and emotional issues related to this new technology of investing that no one had as yet discussed.

Reframing It into a Game

Those who seem best able to reframe trading into more of a game to be won or lost, without getting so caught up in the fear or greed attached to money, come in a few different forms.

One group that appears to be successful at going beyond overconcern with actual dollar amounts are institutional money managers, trading large blocks of stock for mutual funds and other accounts. This group would include all those professionals who trade for their own account as well as institutional accounts; floor traders; market makers; and specialists.

Professionals who daily trade tremendous amounts of money know how to pull the trigger without a lot of apprehension. If they don't, they simply won't last doing this kind of work. They get comfortable with the rhythms of the market and learn to trust their instincts so that they may "play the market rather than the market playing them."

These money managers trading for large funds are usually not risking their own capital. If they lose a few hundred thousand dollars in a bad trade, it is not coming from their own personal accounts.

But they are, ultimately, risking their jobs. Since receiving bonuses based on performance is a significant part of their income, the trades they make have consequences.

A second group are young day traders in their twenties who are capitalized by others and who wear golf caps that read, "No Fear." They may be found in trading firms as well as on their own trading from home. Because they have usually not had to work to earn the capital they are risking, they are not afraid to jump head first into trading with large share lots on the line. These traders attack the market and electronic trading with a vengeance, taking no prisoners in their efforts to win the game.

Having grown up on a diet of video games, they seem poised at transferring the gaming mentality to the serious game of electronic trading. The technical aspects of learning to push the right keys and understanding how to interpret the data coming at them is not threatening to them, as it is for those not so conversant with computers. They love the action and enjoy the adrenaline rush that trading provides.

Some of this contingent are likely to be found among the ranks of the rather small group of microtraders, who hyperactively trade dozens of times per hour, at the extreme racking up between 500 and 800 trades per day.

A third group that seems to have an easier time of it are those who are already independently wealthy. I'm not referring to all the midlife baby boomers of my generation who can handle a loss of $25,000 to $50,000 of capital without jumping off a bridge. I'm talking about really wealthy people who don't need to worry about anything related to money. They know they can lose a chunk of their investing capital and not have it adversely affect their lifestyle or future security. They can let go of $100,000 in the way I let go of $100.

Most of these people have traditionally put their money in the hands of professional money managers. But the convenience and thrill of online investing has now piqued the interest of some to test their own stock-picking skills. They are more able than the average investor to adopt a spirit of play and excitement, where the score-keeping aspect of the game is incidental.

For example, we learn that Barbra Streisand butters up the head honchos of a hot technology company on the eve of its initial public offering. She wants to get some shares at the offering price. She says, "pretty please," sending congratulatory flowers and six bottles of champagne for the coming-out party. And, of course, she gets her shares. Who's going to say no to her?

Does Barbra Streisand really need to go through this dance just to be allocated a few hundred shares of a hot IPO so she can make a fast profit? Of course not—she doesn't need the money. But the word is that she has done very well with her investments—not hard to believe if she is able to capitalize on a few juicy IPOs.

So, there must be another motive besides the money. Perhaps it's feeling like a savvy "player" who knows what's worth getting in on. The financial payoff is obviously secondary to receiving the special treatment accorded a celebrity and being *in the game*. Here we see one of the associated meanings of money in play.

BRINGING OUR FINANCIAL PAST TO OUR TRADING

Just as we bring our values and associated meanings of money with us when we trade, so do we bring our past experiences related to it. Anything we have learned about money from childhood and into adulthood is consciously and unconsciously brought into the present.

Greedy thinking and behavior—and its polar opposite of reacting from fear—may be introduced to our online trading approach as a result of being shaped by any of the following :

- *Early experiences of poverty, hardship, and material deprivation* as a child that may have had a scarring effect on self-esteem and self-worth, leading to insecurity and fear, or compensation in the form of greed; the impact of living through a depression or recessions; early loss of parental financial support through divorce or death; being adopted, in foster homes, brought up by relatives, or blended families that affected money flow or ways of relating to money.
- *Experiences of shame, humiliation, and ridicule* in elementary, high school, or college due to having less money, less fashionable clothes, less social status than classmates; parental programs taught regarding socioeconomic status; racial or ethnic mores taught regarding money.
- *Family of origin patterns of fiscal irresponsibility*, such as heavy gambling losses; bankruptcies; reversals in fortune that changed lifestyle; parents unable to provide for family adequately; frequent job losses or loss of business; family modeling regarding savings and investment.
- *Personal inheritances and windfall gains* from relatives or friends that changed lifestyle, allowing for up-leveling

lifestyle; lottery wins, scholarships, gifts, other windfalls and their effect on spending habits and investment patterns.

- *Feelings about past and present earnings,* that is, recognition achieved or status attained through career; effects of career disappointments; loss of dreams, desires relating to money; unfulfilled parental expectations for earning power; resentments toward bosses and other authority figures; failure in entrepreneurial ventures, loss of a business, being "burned" in previous investments; trust or lack of it for banks, institutions.

- *Personal gambling history,* that is, horse racing, Las Vegas, sports betting, golf course betting, etc.; how has past gambling behavior influenced trading and investing thinking? how much is nonmonetary gambling or risk taking a part of one's life? how much is thrill seeking a part of one's life? how much excitement in life does one crave?

- *Attitudes regarding living beyond one's means*; use of credit cards, bank loans, mortgage equity loans, car loans, loans from relatives; debts owed on taxes; overall credit history; how extended can one be and not have it become a major concern? how deeply can one go into margin to buy stocks and still sleep at night?

EGO AS FRIEND; FALSE PRIDE AS HINDRANCE

Pride is the reasonable or justified sense of one's own worth, based on the attainment of one's values. But we also create a false image of ourselves, a grandiose image that we try to live up to, and false pride is what we feel when we try to live up to this false image. False pride is the tenuous feeling of worth based on fooling ourselves into believing we have attained our values. It is neither reasonable nor justified.

When our feeling of false pride is challenged, it fights back and says, "You're not going to get the best of me!" When it is attacked and beaten down by the irrefutable facts of reality, it is injured, having to admit defeat or loss.

I'm now using the term *false pride* as most people use the term *ego*. Common knowledge in the trading world (and the world at large) suggests that ego, used in everyday parlance to mean an inflated or grandiose sense of self, gets in the way and pushes us to commit foolish actions. These include getting even, refusing to admit defeat or loss, not letting the market or market makers get the best of us, and other defensive gestures that protect ego from being assaulted.

But this is not really a problem based on ego, at least as it is viewed in the world of psychology. It is, more accurately, a problem of false pride. The everyday mind confuses what is actually false pride with ego. Let me explain.

To put it simply, psychologists view the ego as a healthy and necessary core organizing part of our mental structure that helps us maintain a sense of stability and continuity in our daily lives. Its prime function is the perception of reality and adaptation to it, to make sure we don't get too far out in fantasyland or too caught in arising desires.

Metaphorically, the ego is like a good executive secretary who keeps control of the office. The various tasks of the ego include perception, including self-perception and self-awareness; motor control (action); adaptation to reality; and keeping us in touch with our thought processes so as to temper our impulses.

My point in distinguishing the term *ego* from false pride is that the everyday use of the word tends to be negative, seeing ego as a hindrance, as in. "Look at him trading in 2000-share lots—he's just on an ego trip." Ego is viewed as grandiosity, overexuberance of self, and something that needs to be controlled and even beaten down to size.

This is supported, incidentally, by the layperson's belief that the work of psychologists is to "shrink" the ego, thus the common slang term for us is "shrinks." Behind the use of this term is the idea that those involved in psychotherapy will have their large egos reduced to a manageable size. Because various forms of irrational thinking and behavior are confronted in psychotherapy, it may initially seem to the patient as if something is being taken away from them and that ego is being diminished, as they begin to shape a new sense of self. But nothing could be further from the truth of what really takes place. It is exactly the opposite: The ego is strengthened through skillful psychotherapy, not reduced by it.

Actually, *ego is exactly what the disciplined online investor is trying to strengthen.* We want the strongest possible ego we can develop. A strong ego is *always* the friend, *never* the enemy. Please read these last three sentences again and let them sink in before reading on.

The stronger the ego, the more we feel in control. The more self-control we feel, the more able we are to strictly follow a trading plan, and the more confident and secure we are in our in decision making.

The stronger the ego, the less likely we are to be overwhelmed by emotions of the moment and therefore make decisions based on fear or greed. This is what disciplined investing is all about. And anyone who tells you differently about ego being the enemy simply doesn't have the psychological sophistication to know what this term really means.

Here is one example of how the confusion over the meaning of the term "ego" is evident. You will hear psychologically untrained market pundits talk about how "overconfidence" leads to making poor decisions, and how it is the "big ego" that causes this feeling of overconfidence.

Let's be very clear: Feeling overconfident is not a matter of having too strong of an ego. It arises from a laziness and complacency that sneaks into our thinking and behavior. We stop questioning or taking in new information that might challenge our established view.

We stay firm and unyielding in our present positions and may proclaim how sure we are of our own beliefs and actions. This looks deceptively like "overconfidence." But it is not a matter of confidence or of having too big of an ego. It is much more a matter of the "hardening of the mental arteries," of refusing to let fresh information flow into the mind. And, if anything, it is the insecure ego that needs to be always right—not the strong ego—that blocks the mental arteries from taking in the new information.

Confirmation Bias

The natural mental inclination is not to question our judgments that have already been made and acted on. We tend to look for information which confirms what we already believe to be true. This mental habit is called a *confirmation bias*. In regard to our stock positions, the confirmation bias works such that we look for all data which allows us to confirm our present beliefs and the associated actions we have already taken. At the same time, we tend to ignore or discount data which does not confirm our present thinking and behavior.

For example, the difficulty I had in realizing that the stock story of Pfizer had changed when Viagra revenues could no longer be counted on was partly conditioned by the confirmation bias I held. This bias oriented me to only seeing the positives of the stock and made it tough to swiftly shift gears when new information needed to be grasped and acted on.

One answer to the question of how we can find a balance between the yin of fear and the yang of greed is to let our strong egos temper both ends of the polarity through clear, rational, discerning, and highly focused thinking, which leads to thorough evaluation and better decision making. Then, when emotion comes in, it will work to enhance the process instead of impeding it. We will continue to examine methods to balance fear and greed in Chapter 5, the final part of the fear and greed trilogy.

Example of Overreaction: From Fear to Greed

To end this chapter, I want to give an example of how market overreaction to initially perceived scary news may be quickly turned around, leading to frenzied buying, as traders leap in to take advantage of the panic selling. This is an example of how the further the market moves to one extreme out of fear, the more likely it is to swing back in the other direction out of greed.

On May 1, 1999, only a half hour after the market opened, a panic reaction ensued to the impending news that Robert Rubin was resigning as secretary of the treasury. The Dow was already down 200 points at the time the news actually broke and for a few minutes after.

Within one hour (8 A.M. PST) of the newsbreak of Rubin's resignation, the NASDAQ was up and the Dow had cut its loss from –200 to –60. Traders began to reconsider what the resignation would mean to the market beyond the immediate knee-jerk reaction of change to the administration.

A cooler assessment was that perhaps it didn't matter much who was in Rubin's position and that his leaving the job would not appreciably affect the daily psychology or functioning of the market.

The "market mind" changed from fear and panic to a dash to get back in. By 8:50 A.M., the Dow was down –36 and the NASDAQ was up 27. By 11:20 A.M., the Dow was down only 16 and the NASDAQ was up 32. By noon, the Dow was unchanged and the NASDAQ was up 35.

Up until 20 minutes before the close the Dow was a couple of points in the plus column and the NASDAQ was up 41. A sell-off the last few minutes left the Dow down 25 for the day and the NASDAQ finished up 37. All this on a day when the market was initially down 200 points due to the Rubin resignation.

5

The Fear and Greed Trilogy, Part III: Hugging the Emotional Flatline

We have examined the nature of both fear and greed, calling them the yin and yang of investing. Presenting the context from which these investment pressures arise, we maintained that they have been operating since the earliest economies were set in motion by the first exchange of goods.

In this final chapter of the trilogy, we now focus on how investors may balance these conflicting motivations. Keep in mind, however, that we are actually talking about a larger perspective than just how these forces play out in the investment arena. We are working with two emotions—fear and desire—that encompass so many other aspects of our lives as well.

THE LARGER CONTEXT

To varying degrees, we all face fear in life. And we must also come to grips with our desires—be they in the form of greed or any other contour. In fact, if we reflect for a moment, we realize that no day goes by without some form of both fear and desire arising.

Fear may not necessarily come in the form of anxiety, panic, or a quickened heartbeat. It is often far more subtle, visiting us in the form of aversion (turning off) and avoidance (turning away). We turn off and away from something because we're not sure we know what to do with it or how to solve a problem.

For example, at a certain point in this writing, if I am not sure how to best express an idea, I may temporarily distract myself with any number of things that grab my attention. This turning away may give me the necessary pause to organize my thoughts so that I may come back to the keyboard and continue writing. But whether or not my temporary turning away and avoiding is useful, it is a subtle form of fear nonetheless. In this case, the fear of not knowing exactly what to do next.

We are not in the habit of labeling these kind of avoidances fear. But after working with people for over two decades in psychotherapy, it is pretty clear to me that behind much of our turning off and turning away we discover a basic fear of facing something we're unsure about.

Moments of aversion and avoidance are popping up for us on a daily basis. They may be experienced as momentarily blanking out, anxiety, confusion, or feeling "spaced out." But the ground of these reactions is a subtle fear.

In the same way, desires big and small are continually popping up during the day, some just teasing us and others begging for immediate satisfaction. When we watch the mental process of desire arising during the day, we notice how much of our existence is made up of one desire after another arising and falling away. They may be physical, mental, emotional, or material. They may be attended to, like eating when hungry or sleeping when tired. Or they may be ignored, like not following the impulse to buy something we see and like in the store window. But the point here is that desire comes in many shades, as does fear.

When we begin to see how we deal with fear and desire in the larger context of our lives, we may then apply what we notice and learn about our reactions to them when they arise while trading. Conversely, when we present methods of thinking and practical tools, these ideas may be extended to any sphere of life that involves the same emotions.

THE BIPOLARITY OF FEAR AND GREED

What do we mean by a bipolarity? When we think of a polarity, a simple example is a pair of two *apparent* opposites, like love and hate. In what is called "either/or" thinking, where the mind thinks things must be either one way or the other, black or white, all or nothing, we think of love and hate as having nothing to do with each other, as being total opposites.

This is not, however, an accurate conception of how these emotions are related to each other. The psychological reality is that love and hate are closer to each other than to any midpoint between them. This is because they share *a common emotional intensity* that intimately connects them.

Instead of thinking of them as complete opposites—as far apart from each other as they could possibly be—we begin to see that when we love someone, it is easy at times to feel hatred toward him or her. If we don't care about someone, we don't feel strongly enough to love or hate him or her. So indifference is the midpoint between love and hate.

Look at Figure 5-1 to see this graphically. With true polar opposites, the middle point **C** is closer to both **A** and **B** than **A** is to **B**. Just as true polar opposites should be, **A** (west) and **B** (east) are as far away from each other as they can possibly be.

But in Figure 5.2 **A** (love) and **B** (hate) collapse or bend back toward each other when one point is stretched to its limit. The midpoint **C** is the furthest point from both **A** and **B**.

It is the common denominator of strong emotion that ties these apparent opposites together. The fact that one emotion (hate) is intense dislike and the other (love) is intense liking is not as psychologically meaningful as their common intensity. We are feeling something that moves us strongly with both love and hate.

So, when girlfriends hear that a friend has strong feelings, even "hates" the new man she is dating, they tell her, "Watch out you don't fall in love with him." They intuitively understand that strong emotion can move from positive to negative and back again, that it is not stuck on one side of the bipolarity.

Another common example is that children will get the attention they crave from their parents by misbehaving if they are unable to get it in more positive ways. While they would certainly prefer it come in a positive form, they understand that, in the end, it is the attention that matters most—not what they have done for it or the form in which they receive it.

A third example that drives home the point is how in the middle of a bitter divorce and custody battle each partner can say and do bitter, resentful, and vicious things toward the other. They often will use their children as pawns in a deceitful and manipulative game aimed at vindictively hurting the other party.

This hurtful turning against the other is the most powerful way they have to deal with feelings of rejection and injured false pride.

F I G U R E 5-1

"True" Polarities

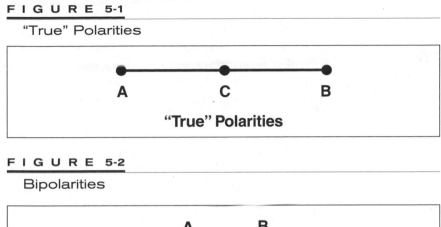

"True" Polarities

F I G U R E 5-2

Bipolarities

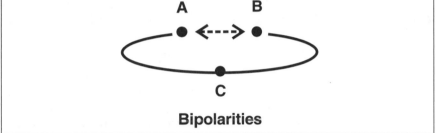

Bipolarities

Source: From Steven J. Hendlin, Ph.D., *The Discriminating Mind: A Guide to Deepening Insight and Clarifying Outlook*, London: Unwin Hyman, 1989. Used with permission.

Here love and hate are very close, and the same energy that had gone into loving behavior can turn and viciously take the form of hate. Often, even while in the middle of these emotional battles, there is a conscious or unconscious hope that the other will come back and desire to love them again.

Rather than *either/or* thinking, these bipolar emotions fit more easily into what we call *both/and* thinking. We can both love and hate our partner, depending on what they may evoke from us.

The concept here is simply that many pairs of emotions that may first appear to be total opposites, when examined more closely, end up being intimately related because of the emotional energy they share. They approach each other because of this common intensity of energy but don't become each other. The flavor of love certainly isn't the same as hate and never will be.

How is this concept of bipolarity relevant for balancing fear and greed?

The feeling of fear of loss that we feel when we make a trade is not far from the desire we feel for wealth and possessions.

Here is the relationship I would like you to consider: That the more fear we feel of losing our money, the more underlying desire we have to accumulate more, which may or may not result in greedy behavior. This desire may be conscious or unconscious.

When I scratch the surface with investors who are telling me about how afraid they are at risking money on a trade, I see they often harbor strong desires for more than they have. These desires are not all that deep and hidden. They are simply blocked by fear from ever being acted on. Often, they are revealed when investors talk about their dreams and fantasies for the future. Or how they have gone without certain possessions they would really like to have.

But the fact that they may not be acted upon does not mean they are not *unconsciously* motivating the investor. This is what makes the bipolarity of fear and greed so powerful. They feed off of each other in what for some becomes a vicious cycle.

Conversely, when someone exhibits greedy behavior and is very upfront about the desire for wealth and possessions, beneath the surface he or she harbors fears of loss of wealth, material possessions, and what is believed will be the accompanying loss of respect of others. Again, this may not be conscious to him or her, as false pride may get in the way of admitting fear.

For some, it may not be the fear of directly losing their wealth but of losing their health, a marriage partner, or coping with getting older and losing some of their strength and power. The point is, there is fear of loss of something that is deemed of the utmost value.

Greed, then, is fueled by the fear of never having enough. It is a psychological stance of insecurity in the world and an attempt to provide security through the insulation of wealth. This is often why it seems that those who have so much material wealth continue to push themselves to keep making more money and accumulating more possessions. They are afraid that feelings of emptiness and loss are just around the corner. This underlying insecurity it also why wealth and possessions do not necessarily make us happy.

This insecurity is not just on the material or personal levels, however. It is also related to the basic insecurity we all face simply being in the world, confronted with continual change and never knowing exactly what may happen to us. This is called *existential* insecurity, as it is a fact of our existence, and therefore must be faced by everyone.

A simple demonstration of this dynamic at work as it relates to the material level may be witnessed when we see people who have been poor or who went through a depression when they were young. No matter how successful and wealthy they may become, they fear losing what they have, never feeling that they are secure, and that enough is enough. The poverty can always happen again, they think. They are operating out of an unconscious fear, which propels them to want more and more. And this, of course, is exactly the original face of greed.

All of this is simply to point out that *greed and fear are intimately connected*, not such total opposites as we might like to believe. This is what makes them the yin and yang of investing, the two parts of the whole where each needs the other for its existence.

Always the person on the other end of your panic sale is licking his or her chops, looking for a killing out of your moment of panic. And always someone is on the other end, gladly selling you his or her stock, taking advantage of your fear of being left out, when that person thinks it's gone high enough to get out.

Market makers know how to play on the greed and fear of the investor because they know something about how these forces work within themselves. They know what you are thinking and feeling and they do their best to take advantage of it. That is how they make their living.

It is the rhythm of greed and fear, forever locked in a struggle both within the individual and played out in the market as a whole, that makes for part of the mystery of market direction. While many aspects of market movement may be analyzed and conjectured upon, no one knows for sure exactly how the market forces of greed and fear will be played out on any given day or even in any given hour.

GETTING IN TOUCH WITH FEAR AND GREED

If it is indeed true that fear and greed are closer to each other than we think, and that behind greedy trading actions lies fear and conversely, behind fear lies a barely concealed desire for wealth, what is the practical implication?

Simply this: That as investors we must be aware of both of these parts in ourselves. Tempered fear is caution. Tempered greed is assertive action to take decisive action despite never having total information. Both are necessary for the disciplined online investor.

We cannot deny our fear of losing money, nor can we deny our desire to make as much as possible. If we don't accept both of these motivations as operating within us, we will be out of touch with ourselves when we take actions based upon one force or the other. We will not hear the inner voices of fear or greed that push us to take action. It is for this reason that it is necessary to be comfortable with each of these inner voices.

But being comfortable with these parts of ourselves is only the first step. We must also have them on speaking terms, working cooperatively rather than against each other.

Perhaps you've noticed what I have done in redefining the conventional view of greed. I have taken the concept and put it into its larger context of desire, with which all traders and investors can identify. In framing greed in a larger context, I am trying to make it easier for you as an investor to identify with how it comes up for you.

If you don't want to admit that you are greedy, because this is such an undesirable trait, at least you can admit that you have desires. I am offering you a more acceptable context that allows you to own up to your desire to make as much money as possible. A little greed pushes us to hold out for greater profits and to take some reasonable risks that we might not otherwise take. So, the more comfortable we are with this part of ourselves, the more sense some of our investing behavior will make.

On Speaking Terms: Giving Voice
to the Inner Dialogue

We said that if we are going to balance greed and fear, we need to be on speaking terms with these parts of ourselves. One way to do this is to hear the inner voice of each distinctly. Here is an example of how these two voices may come up in the course of watching the market.

As you read the following example, notice that:

1.   Both parts have a distinctive identity.
2.   Both parts have a part or role they are playing and each wants its voice to be heard and taken seriously.
3.   When the part feels heard and its role appreciated, the threat to its survival is lessened.
4.   Dialogue is the key to this appreciation.
5.   When no longer feeling their existence is threatened, both parts may begin to find common ground by compromising

their all-or-nothing positions to benefit the common good of the total self.

Fear: I'm the fearful part of you. I come up and give you a jolt whenever you are about to do something I believe is against your best interest. I will use any method of reaching you I have available, including sending you into a frozen panic, to stop you from making a bad trade. I stand for caution, the preservation of capital, and taking things slow and easy rather than taking wild and impulse leaps. While I prefer that you use your logical, rational voice to stay disciplined, I know sometimes I must step in to save us, especially from the savage advances made by your greedy voice.

Greed: Fear, you're a wimp! Get out of my way and let me push him into action or I'll bowl you over, you shivering bowl of jelly! You think you're keeping him from making a dumb trade. But all you do is scare him until he can't see straight. I'm his desire for higher returns, more possessions, more vacations—everything that is fun and adds to his life.

I am the engine that powers the locomotive of material bliss! When he follows my voice, I will help him feel good about himself and gain the envy of others through having so much to show off. I'm every bit as powerful as you are. Where would he be without my push?

You may despise me but you just watch and see how I can lure him into taking risks in pursuit of our desire to hit it big. You think you're a match for me? I'll leave my tire tracks on your face as I run over you, jumping into those juicy Internet stocks. Even his discriminating logic can't stop me from making myself felt. I can push his good judgment into taking a bigger risk. And when the risk works out, he loves me, so don't fool yourself.

Fear: There you go again, always trying to intimidate me, always acting like the big shot, throwing your weight around, as if you know what's right for him. Can't you see how many times he's lost money by acting on your voice, when he didn't hear or act on me?

Can't you see how much of who you are is just bravado, trying to live up to some image? You lead him to take chances that could cost him large amounts of money. Give me a break! And stop screaming at me, you loud-mouthed blow-hard.

Greed: That's awfully aggressive talk for someone who's shivering in his or her boots, always thinking of the worst that can happen, always afraid of catastrophe, and too scared to take a real risk and make bigger returns. Why can't you trust me a little more? Why don't you appreciate what I contribute?

Fear: OK, tell me what you contribute. I'll listen to you with an open mind. Please tell me how you're helping our goal of earning a good return for our investment capital without taking undo risks. Go ahead, tell me. But in return, I ask that you stop calling me names.

Greed: All right, I will. Don't you see that with everything you're whispering in his ear about all the bad stuff that can happen, he would take no risks if it weren't for me? Don't you remember what Gordon Gecko said, that I am good? Well, he was right! I represent desire in its most pure form, the desire for security and happiness through wealth accumulation. Is there anything wrong with that? Just because I may get overzealous and pushy at times is no reason to turn against me.

Fear: There is nothing wrong with you as desire. The problem is that you use heavy-handed means to get him to risk. You promise him sugar plums and all kinds of things that you can't deliver. You tempt him with all that is possible. You try and trick him into thinking that all he needs to do is have more money and then he'd be a happier human being. All I do is give him a scare so he doesn't make short-sighted decisions. But you are downright deceptive, tantalizing him with all the glitter of possessions.

Greed: What are you, a naive fool? Don't you think more money would make the guy happier? More money makes everyone happier! I am the force behind earning the money for his fancy European vacations, practicing and playing golf, buying nice clothes, having money to invest in the market, and everything else that brings a measure of joy to his life.

I'm what affords the simple material pleasures, from a coffee latte to a CD to a new piece of software. You think I'm all possession driven? Think again, baby. Without me, he wouldn't have the luxury of time to sit around in his garden and reflect on life or to meditate. Who do you think pushed him all those years to accomplish, get all that education, and make money?

Don't you get it? Without me, there's none of that stuff—no philharmonic concerts he likes so much, no books he loves to read, and none of the money to remodel the house. Without me, life is a drag. Without the money that comes from my motivation, who wants to live? Who wants a crappy existence, worrying about the basic necessities of life? I represent abundance, not just scraping by in life.

Sure, sometimes I promise him things I can't deliver. Don't all the other parts of him do the same? We all promise more than we can deliver. And, yes, I admit it—sometimes I push him to desire things he doesn't really need. I mean, this is America, land of conspicuous consumption, right?

You want him to sit there feeling fear when he is trading? You want to undermine his strength and courage?

Fear: Please don't misunderstand. He is not being undermined just because I make sure he feels my presence. I would be willing to make room for you if you will respect the part that I play instead of always calling me names and never giving me my due.

You're pretty full of yourself, aren't you? I mean, taking credit for his motivation to achieve, establish a profession, do well, and build a solid life—all because of you, huh? Get real! I don't believe that for a minute. There are so many other motivators beyond you that you can't acknowledge as playing their part. Like every other voice, you overemphasize your own importance.

Greed: OK, I'll stop calling you names. I have resisted seeing how much you and I are similar in certain ways. I can't seem to get past the difference in our style. All you do is make him fearful of loss while all I want to do is pump him up, make him feel good. We are both afraid of being dismissed, of not being taken seriously. But we really do seem to need each other for our mutual survival. I guess if you weren't around I might push him too far at times, then he'd hate me and maybe permanently stop listening to me. I couldn't live with that.

Fear: Yes, did you see how he was flipping back and forth between us this morning, when the NASDAQ was down 85 points? After last week's miserable down market, today the techs continued to plummet.

He heard you say it might be getting close to the time to strike, that while the blood is not yet covering the street, it's looking pretty brutal. Then I came in and reminded him to hold off, that it's still too early to do any bottom fishing. Still too much chance of further decline. In fact, I've been whispering in his ear for some time now to take some money off the table as the year winds down. I think he's listening, with all this Y2K uncertainty and all.

Greed: Yes, but how do you expect me to do my thing if you keep trying to pull back on the reins? At least he's got his eye on some of those Internet "backbone" IPOs that are hot. That's enough action for now. If he gets in at the offering price, it's a sure bet to make some money with zero risk. Double his money in an hour or so—that's my kind of action!

Fear: You're too much. Always looking for the quick killing, aren't you? But I agree with you that getting in on the offering price is about as safe as it can get. Nothing for me to be concerned about. I'll sit back and be quiet on that one. In fact, I might even enjoy the short ride. Just don't tell him to hold that past the first day, since they tend to dip after the initial surge.

Greed: I will try and hold back from pushing myself on him if you will also ease up and let his rational, discriminating part run more of the show. You know he can make better decisions about buying and selling when neither one of us gets in the way. I will contribute just enough of a push forward so that he doesn't lose interest in some of the glitter of the world. And maybe help him take a reasonable risk now and then, like he is with the IPOs.

Fear: Yes, and I will try and alert him using only the amount of me that is needed to make him pull back and reconsider. Sometimes I just get carried away and try and pull the emotional bottom out from under him. But, for the most part, he is quite disciplined. I'm willing to have more respect for you if you will give me the same. Let's try to remember that we're in this together, both trying to help him keep it together to make the best decisions possible.

Greed: I just thought of the perfect way to express this. You know how when the Dow is hovering around the unchanged mark, they say that it is "hugging the flatline"? Well, we want him to be "hugging the *emotional* flatline," never getting too far away from solid, clear thinking, never indulging in either one of us to the point of no return. Always coming back to the flatline. How's that sound to you?

Fear: Yes, I like that a lot. You're a pretty clever guy, Greed. We'll help him "hug the emotional flatline." Then his rational part can predominate. Maybe we can become whispers to him rather than irritating or redundant voices always battling to be heard.

Greed: Whispers? You mean like a whisper number at earnings time?

Fear: You know exactly what I mean. Now let's just try to cooperate.

Applying the Voice Dialogue Technique

As the previous example illustrated, when we can get both inner voices of fear and greed to really hear each other, it then becomes possible for them to stop fighting and work for the common cause. Each is then willing to quiet down a bit, and let another part, the voice of reason, be heard more clearly.

When you try this, it may take a while to really hear each voice as it comes up. But it is well worth the effort to not only know that you are feeling a specific emotion, but to also *hear the associated thoughts* that go with it. This is especially useful during trading, as fearful thoughts may then come through loud and clear. Then you can determine whether you ought to pay attention to what fear or greed is signaling. Here are the directions for you to work with this balancing tool:

1. Close your eyes. Get in touch with your own fear. If you have any trouble identifying this fearful part of yourself, remember the last time you felt fear while making a trade or watching the market. If you need to go back to the last real shot of anxiety you felt, do so, feeling the fear that was just behind the anxiety. Be very clear on what you were afraid of.
2. Now feel the fear again related to whatever you recall. Stay with it long enough to begin feeling it *now*.
3. While you're still feeling the fear, give this fear a voice. Begin to speak out loud, keeping your eyes closed so you can stay with the feeling. Begin with, "I'm the fearful part of you . . ." and continue by describing yourself as this part.
4. Say out loud what your function is, what role you serve to the larger complex of parts that make up the whole self: "What I do for you is . . ." "If it weren't for me, you'd . . ."
5. Be sure to include how you want to be appreciated for your contribution to the whole self. "I want you to appreciate me for . . ."

6. Now say out loud why you sometimes push too hard to be heard: "Sometimes I'm afraid that . . ." It is important for each part to understand the threat it feels to its survival. It is at this point you want to voice this fear directly.

7. Let each part express its mistrust of the other part. "The reason I can't trust you is . . ." Parts often arise out of the need to compensate for certain interests the person has that are not being represented. When they are created, they may initially be mistrustful of other parts. They do not like to give up their suspiciousness unless they can be shown that it is safe and that whatever need they represent will be heard and considered.

8. Continue the dialogue, each part doing its best to really hear the other side, until each part feels satisfied that it can compromise and not be so pushy in being heard.

9. When both parts have compromised and been able to give something up, let them make an agreement to work cooperatively for the good of the whole self.

Do not hurry this dialogue and do not quit when it becomes tough to come up with words for a part. Learning to hear your inner voices is a very potent tool in knowing your own mind more intimately. In the course of practicing psychotherapy, some of the most significant changes people have made were the result of the insights gained through outwardly dialoguing with inner voices. If we want to balance fear and greed, having a grasp of these voices and knowing how to temper them cannot be overestimated.

Working with Self-Talk

Self-talk is related to inner dialogue but distinct from it. The inner voices are parts of ourselves, representing different needs clamoring for attention and battling with each other for power. These voices are what we hear inside when we separate out the chatter and confusion. They are not usually brought out and verbalized. Because they inhabit the mental realm, they are often slippery, vague, and not easy to hear clearly without some practice.

In contrast, self-talk is more conscious, purposeful, and often is actually spoken out loud, sometimes popping out without much forethought. When people berate themselves for hitting a slice off the tee while playing golf, spilling juice on the carpet, getting a speeding ticket, or being late for an important appointment, self-talk is what comes out of their mouths as a self-condemning reaction.

This self-talk is usually coming from two basic parts of us: A critical parent voice (the part of us that has internalized our parents) or an adult, rational ego voice. When it comes from the adult rational ego, it is usually heard in the form of guidance, support, instruction, or for self-orienting, self-affirmation, and self-stabilizing.

Self-talk is useful to keep us on a specific, disciplined path that we might be wavering from. For example, we may have set a certain limit at which to sell a stock. But if we have not put in a limit order to sell ahead of time, when the stock price reaches our limit, we need the discipline to go ahead and follow our plan.

Now, as the stock hits the limit, it is easy to second guess and say inside, "Ah, maybe you should hold on a while and see what happens. Maybe we could squeeze a little more out of this." If we hear this internally, we can say *out loud*, "No, go ahead and follow your plan. Sell the stock and move on." This can be a useful kick to go ahead and take action.

Examples of self-talk that may temper or neutralize greed and fear, all of which should be said out loud right as the event is occurring, include the following:

1. "Stop watching the quotes and go ahead and execute the trade."
2. "Take a five-minute break; you're starting to get anxious."
3. "Turn off the sound to CNBC; they're contributing to the frenzy."
4. "Stay where you are—no need to chase that stock. Wait until it comes back to you. No need to get desperate."
5. "Stand up and stretch; you need some air."
6. "Stay with your plan; don't get scared (or greedy) now."

Begin to notice what you are saying to yourself when you talk out loud, both out in the world at large and while trading. Some people tend to speak out loud to themselves often during the day, while others tend to hear the same kind of statements in their heads but don't say them out loud. Sometimes self-talk comes out as a barely audible mumble. In whatever form it tends to surface for you, pay close attention to it and don't shy away from putting it out clearly, especially when alone during trading.

The benefits of saying the statements out loud are that: (1) it orients and stabilizes us in the moment when we may be unsure or confused; (2) it emphasizes more clearly the content of the message; (3) it acts as a supportive push to reinforce an action you wish to take; and (4) it demarks a shift from one activity to another, for example, "OK, its time to turn off the computer and get ready to go to the office."

You will also notice people talking to themselves during different activities. It is common for golfers hitting balls on the practice range, for example, to make comments to themselves after hitting shots, as a way to reinforce a good shot, or to think about something in their swing they want to pay attention to.

This kind of guiding self-talk is useful as a shaping device, as we monitor our behavior and make changes that are supported by it. Many athletes, musicians, and others doing physical tasks find it helpful to shape their behavior through self-talk. Especially during practice sessions, when one is working to improve performance, self-talk may be potent in facilitating the learning of new tasks that require repetition.

Watch out especially for self-talk that is coming from the "critical parent" part of yourself. This tends to come out negative, punitive, and self-critical and sounds like what has been told to you as a child. Examples would be:

"I'm a lousy trader, unable to execute fast enough."
"My decisions as to when to enter a position always seem to be wrong."
"I can't seem to get the knack of moving fast enough to keep up with all the data coming at me."
"I don't know enough about any companies to take chances with individual stocks."
"The analysts I hear on TV know much more than I do. Yet they all disagree. How can I trust anyone's opinion?"
"I can't seem to get the money I'm risking out of my mind."
"I'm not good at knowing when to sell."

Negative self-talk is usually not very useful, unless it can be done in a way that is forgiving and also tells us what to do to correct the mistake: "Come on, you're pulling your head up, keep your eye on the ball!" Since one of the most powerful and torturing inner voices we hear is the critical parent, this voice will only be reinforced if it is the one that you put into words. So, it is best to use self-talk that is verbalized for orienting, emphasizing, supporting, and demarking shifts.

EMOTIONAL DISCIPLINE
AND REACTIVE FLEXIBILITY

If our aim is to "hug the emotional flatline," the more mental control we exercise in dealing with changing conditions, the less greed and fear will enter into our decision making. When investment teachers talk about having a plan and following it, their intention is partly to eliminate strong emotion from trading by automatically following the steps that have been taught to deal with a particular situation.

Their intent is to give students a recipe or formula that can be applied uniformly under different market conditions. In this way, the numbers will decide, and emotion will be taken out of the equation. While this is not a bad idea in theory, the problem is that each new market condition is slightly different. And this means no one plan is necessarily going to fit best for what is right in front of us *now*, which is not going to be exactly the same as the last time, even if the conditions look similar.

While it is desirable to control strong emotion, some feelings associated with our thinking process can be useful in helping make trading decisions. For many, intuition based on previous experience is also valued as part of the process. This is where the creativity of the trader is required, knowing how to take the action that the moment calls for, without being overly rigid in our thinking or overly emotional.

The goal is not to turn into mechanical robots, unable to assess each new situation, where we are afraid to take reasonable risks when called for, even if the charts don't support us. The idea is to control fear and greed so they don't *dictate* the decision as they are wont to do.

We said that market psychology is based on belief and perception. Belief (what we think is true) and perception (how something appears to us) are influenced by changing emotions, which are always exaggerated in the short-run, both positively and negatively.

When we ask why belief and perception are influenced by emotion in the stock market, the answer has to do with the speediness of the market and the need to react very quickly to news. Because of this, traders don't have the luxury to sit leisurely and consider all trading decisions carefully before taking a position. What they think is true and how the market looks to them are often largely colored by passing emotions, as they react to the changing conditions—not by carefully considered rational thought.

So, the simple equation appears to be: *the shorter the gap between perception of a change and the belief that we must immediately react, the more likely we are to react from emotion.*

Conversely, the *longer the gap between perception of a change and the belief we must react, the more rational thought may enter and shape the decision, and the less reliant we will be on emotion.*

This is why the whole nature of the speedy market begs for us to react more from emotion than clear, rational thought. And it is why those who can "think on their feet" are apt to get less caught in the emotion of the moment and have a larger amount of clear thinking enter the decision.

What about the longer-term investors? If we are not in a hurry and don't care that much about whether we enter at one price or another, and don't care to react quickly to take advantage of news, can't we take all the time we need to weigh our decision? Yes, of course. But even without the push of the speedy market, even after the cognitive processes have been exercised in analyzing a stock, we often still end up making an emotionally based decision!

For example, after doing research on the past performance of a stock, finding out the moving averages, highs and lows over the last year, and knowing what a good price would be, they will still pay more for the stock to have it now than waiting patiently for it to come down to a level that promises a better return.

Valuation, in other words, while considered, is then tossed out the window when the actual purchase is made. They haven't got the patience necessary to take their time before making the trade. The greed of wanting to get into the action now wins out over waiting for the right time to buy. But there is another crucial reason at work.

And here is where the flip side of the ease of online trading contributes to the problem. It used to be that we were forced to call brokers, discuss a stock with them, let them do some research, then call us back and tell us what they thought. If the broker liked it and we wanted to go ahead, they'd place an order. The process itself made for gaps of time to consider what we were doing. And we had nothing whatsoever to do with actually placing the trade.

Now, with a few clicks of the mouse, we've bought the stock. The process might be as swift as a scan of short- and long-term performance charts, an earnings report, maybe a comparison to other stocks in the sector, a look at the web site for information and the fundamentals, and perhaps a few online analyst reports and a scan of a couple bulletin boards to see what those in the stock are thinking. Very quickly we can know a lot about the stock. Expert and amateur opinions are widely available with just a click on a handful of bookmarks. There is no need to dig for information.

The point is, having this instant information at our fingertips encourages us to go ahead and jump in rather than to take some time and think about it. And because of this, many will find themselves in positions that two weeks later they will be wondering how they got into.

And this is actually a fair amount of research compared to those who buy stocks on a tip or a message board comment where they have absolutely no idea what the company actually does but are still willing to jump in. They will put more consideration into the color of their new car than what risks they are taking in committing large sums of investment capital.

Since there is no logical explanation for this lack of consideration before making an investment, we need to call on a psychological one.

And that would be the uncomfortable feelings of being unsure of ourselves if we spend too much time investigating a stock. Whereas we would think that we would feel more comfortable with more information, for some this just isn't true. They actually get more anxious with more information because the information only serves to confuse them and create uncertainty.

So, like other decisions in life that make us uncomfortable, it is easier to simply take a leap rather than tolerate the discomfort of not knowing. If you think about this explanation, you may remember an instance in your own life where it was true. It is easier to jump into something with limited information than tolerate the anxiety of having to slowly learn something new and then make a decision, even though we may be unsure about the correctness of that decision.

The other part of this phenomenon is that it's just as easy to change our minds and get out if it doesn't pan out, and it doesn't cost much to do it. This "easy in—easy out" mentality is the delight of online discount brokerages. The whole emphasis on becoming more disciplined traders is simply to counter the ease with which we may get carried into the tide of emotions on the one hand, and inconsistent, haphazard decision making on the other.

In trying to be mentally disciplined, some investors like to rely strictly on various technical indicators, letting the numbers tell them when to enter and exit positions, rather than making subjective decisions. They simply follow what their charts tell them. Others read the charts to help them assess a position, and then call on their feelings to augment the decision process. This is where knowing your personality type is useful, as some types would not be comfortable without letting some feeling be part of the process.

Perhaps the best example of trading without emotion is not done by people at all, but by the computers that are used for trading by institutions. This programmed trading, which is a strong influence on the market because of the large share size of the trades, is all done by technical indicators, so that emotion may be kept completely out of the equation.

The closest individual online traders can get to this type of programmed trading is by using various charts and technical indicators to help in deciding buy and sell points and then locking in what the charts tell them by setting limits on their trades. But, as we said, this method is not for everyone, since not all investors have the personality to dedicate themselves to charts.

In addition, technical indicators, no matter how precise, tend to create a false sense of security that the formulas the indicators are based on will always be correct in predicting moves in a stock or the market as a whole. The reality is that *everyone makes the wrong bet more than half of the time, no matter what they rely on to help them beat the market.*

Popular opinion, for example, is that specialists on the New York Stock Exchange and institutional money managers make between 70 and 350 percent gains per year. Market makers on the NASDAQ make between 60 and 150 percent gains per year. And yet 65 percent of all trades even for these most experienced professionals are losers!

Now, just to keep a balanced perspective on the role of rational decision making through strong reliance on technical and fundamental indicators, here is what James Cramer has to say on the nature of trading, from his column at "The Street.Com" on September 30, 1999:

> It wasn't me that turned it into a casino. It was just me willing to admit what market professionals won't do because it savages the veneer they have cultivated all of their lives. Maybe it's because I used to play the horses. Maybe it is because I used to bet large on Sundays. . . . I can smell betting when I see it, and when we are out there taking Amazon up six points, we are gambling and we should just own up to that. We are assessing the odds and making a wager. I can't stand the sanctimonious people out there who would call this something else in a vain attempt to dignify what they do for a living. The worst ones are the ones who think there is a science behind it.

> A Nobel-awarding science. They are totally bogus. It is about an edge. It is about being early, or ahead of the crowd. It is about perception and psychology and capitulation and hubris. It ain't about P/Es and price-to-book anymore. Maybe it never really was.

Now Cramer is referring to frequent (but not necessarily day) trading when he makes these comments. For longer-term investors, the time horizon tends to smooth out some of the unpredictability and hour-to-hour gambling that occurs in the market. But our attempt as investors to balance greed and fear must still take this gambling aspect of the market into account.

In a market that may move unpredictably through wild swings based on greed and fear, to eliminate all emotion would mean to lose touch with the basic forces that are creating this movement. Again, the idea is not to eliminate all emotion but just not to let it dictate any momentary decision. Perhaps the best way to say it is: We use emotion as one input in our decision-making process, rather than let emotion use us.

To eliminate emotion altogether would be like saying that because emotions are sometimes painful and cause us to make decisions we later regret, we should give up on ever feeling emotion in our lives. We couldn't do it even if we wanted to. It doesn't make sense in our lives as a whole and it doesn't make sense with regard to the stock market.

It's just not as simple as surgically cutting out a fundamental human orienting system, not to mention the very core of human relations. Intuition and "gut feeling" should never be entirely eliminated from the picture. They will have a place, alongside our best critical and analytic judgment, using whatever fundamental and technical indicators we have found useful in our decision making.

One way to include emotion and strong hunches in this process guards against making any decision based too heavily upon them. It is especially appropriate for longer-term investors who do not make a lot of trades. Here is the mental discipline in the form of a rule: *Never make a decision in the moment after a strong feeling or flash of intuition strikes.*

Hugging the emotional flatline means showing the discipline to acknowledge the emotion or flash of intuition, letting it stick around for consideration, but not immediately jumping into action based upon it. This is especially important when it is so easy online to click a few buttons and own a stock. Momentary impulse can so easily be followed that we need to have a few simple ways to guard against both the strength of the impulse and the ease with which it can be put into action.

LIMIT SETTING AND RISK MANAGEMENT

Here are just a handful of tactics for balancing fear and greed that may be exercised by the disciplined online investor. First think about them and consider how they may fit with your personality. Then try them and see what you have the tolerance to stay with. If nothing else, some of them will clearly let you know your level of mental discipline and willingness to follow through with a plan. Many more considerations may be found in any good book that focuses on money management and trading tactics.

1. *Know what you can afford to lose.* Before investing anything, calculate what amount you can afford to lose if your stock goes down the drain. If it is 20 percent of your planned investment in this position, enter a stop loss at that figure. Although there are those who argue against the use of stop-losses, especially with volatile stocks, if capital preservation is of highest priority, they must be viewed as a useful tool. What they do psychologically is assure you that you will lose no more in your position than what you have determined you can handle. This helps deal with the fear of catastrophic loss.

2. *Know your price target.* Know what percentage gain you want when you enter a position. Write down this number and vow to stick to it, even when you begin to think it may be exceeded. The dictum of "letting profits run" is fine if you don't mind the added risk. But if you want to limit the likelihood of losing your profit, know your number and put in a limit order to sell at that price, at the same time you make the purchase.

Even if you think it will take three months for your stock to reach your number, still put the limit order in to sell at that price right after you make the trade. You can always change your mind. This will require agonizing discipline for some but it takes all second-guessing out of the equation. Think like a disciplined day trader, even if you're a long-term investor. Use stop losses liberally to protect downside loss. And use limit orders to sell to protect profits.

3. *Sell partial positions.* This tactic is common with professional traders and experienced investors. If you think there is further upside potential and have bought enough shares to do so, consider

selling a part of your position when it reaches your target and holding part of it for further gains. You may, for example, sell one-half of your position at your target and hold the other half, setting a new target price for those shares. Again, put in a limit order to sell the remaining shares at that new target. This risk management tool satisfies the greedy side to have something of your profit in your hands, limits all-or-nothing liability if the stock moves down, and keeps you in the game for further upside potential.

4. *Make your efforts tangible—take profits periodically.* Shorter-term traders don't have to be told but intermediate- and longer-term investors do.

Cash in a portion of your profits periodically. Resist the old line hold-forever mentality that fosters no enjoyment by ever taking any profit.

Even if your investments are for a retirement account and you can't get your hands on the money, sell when you've hit your target price and enjoy the feeling of your successful efforts. Retirement accounts are the best for taking profits because you don't have to pay any capital gains taxes when you sell.

The market is too volatile to put your money in and fall asleep for 10 years. If you're going to get actively involved in online investing, make it acceptable to take profits without apology. And don't let having to pay taxes (if a nonretirement account) stop you from raking some of it in. This appeases your greedy part and also increases confidence in your trading ability.

5. *Make sure to have cash for a crash.* The fearful side says never be fully invested, always maintain a healthy cash position. No matter what the market does, the cash sits and earns a little interest. The fearful side requires this security and wants your cash position to be even higher than the 5 to 10 percent often recommended in asset allocation models.

For intermediate- and long-term investors, having a healthy cash position is the equivalent of the day trader going home "flat," with no positions held overnight. The psychological security of a larger cash position or a chunk in bonds tends to be underestimated, especially when the equity market is hot. The greedy side wants all of our money working in stocks all of the time. But the fearful side needs to assert and make sure it is covered with adequate risk management.

The added benefit here is that the greedy side is just waiting to put that cash to work when the market takes a dive and everything is going at a big discount. While you will still need to find the courage to commit this cash, or at least a portion of it, when the market takes its dips and dives, at least it will be sitting there, ready for you to invest.

6. *Commit to watching your investments closely.* This one is to neutralize the common fear we feel when we don't have adequate information. If you are going to invest online, make it your responsibility to check your portfolio regularly. We are no longer living in a time when we can simply buy individual stocks or mutual funds and not pay attention to their performance. If you are going to be your own broker, then you have to act like one and commit to following your stocks as a part of good investment management. There are many good portfolio trackers at various stock sites that make this easy to do.

Even if you plan to hold your stocks long term, stay on top of the news related to your individual positions. Read online and off-line articles to stay informed. Never has it been easier to access all the information you could possibly want. Not only will you lose some of the fear associated with the mystery of how the financial markets work, you will also feel more confident to make adjustments in your holdings to keep up with changing conditions.

7. *Be aware and take advantage of the competition between discount brokerages.* This one is to appease the greedy part's need to get everything possible from a discount brokerage if they are going to hold your money. Don't get married to any one brokerage. Stay flexible and ready to move from one brokerage to another.

Consider opening accounts with more than one brokerage, even if you don't want to fund more than one of them. Having an account can qualify you for a number of online privileges that may supplement any other accounts with other brokerage firms you are using.

This is not like the old days where people found one broker, formed a personal relationship, and stayed with him or her forever. With online trading, you don't need the personal relationship but you do need service when you want to reach them.

As mentioned earlier, the best site I have found for analyzing and rating the whole gamut of discount brokerages, whether you are an active trader or long-term investor, is at *www.sonic.net/donaldj*. It is updated regularly as new information comes in from customers regarding problems at the various brokerages.

Things are changing very rapidly. In August of 1999, there were two discount brokerages offering after-hours trading. Two months later there were at least a half dozen. Now, as you read this, it is the norm for any competitive online brokerage to be connected to an after-hours trading partner. You can be sure that the game of enticing us with added benefits is only going to get juicier as we go.

Stay aware of what various brokerages are offering their online customers. If you are unhappy with the service you are getting, don't hesitate to jump ship. Don't get stuck with one just because of the hassle of paperwork for a trust or retirement account. The advantages may far outweigh the hassle in filling out some forms and transferring funds.

Use the message boards on stock sites to find out what experiences others are having. Others are very helpful in saving you the wear and tear of repeating their bad experiences. Fear is reduced when we feel we are getting the best treatment and services we can find.

One online brokerage (A. B. Watley) is offering free Level II quotes without a minimum number of trades and without having to maintain a minimum balance. The only requirement is that you open the account with $10,000. What Watley is offering is the direction other discounters will be moving in.

A number of brokerages are offering opportunities to get in on IPOs. While a few, like Wit Capital, feature IPO participation as a drawing card for new accounts, the reality is that being allowed to file a conditional offer along with thousands of others does not mean actually being allocated the shares. It is easy to get excited, emotionally caught up in the anticipation, only to be let down when you get the "Dear John" e-mail informing you the offering is oversubscribed. But at least the odds of being a part of IPOs are higher than they used to be. In summary, let your greedy part rejoice at finding the very best trading arrangement possible.

NEUTRALIZING FEAR AND GREED

When we feel fear and pull back or think greedy thoughts leading us to taking unreasonable risks while trading, there are ways we can neutralize both feelings and thoughts so they are unable to get the best of us.

Invoking a Trigger

One psychological tool is to use a trigger to set off a positive behavior that counters the negative emotion. The trigger is a sense-related behavior that is associated with something positive and neutralizing of whatever emotion we want to pull away from. When we use a trigger, we are simply using an effective gimmick to pull us out of one state and help us enter another.

So, if we are feeling fear, we create a trigger that will remind us of a neutralizing thought that pulls us out of the fear. The trigger may be to look at something in the room, hear a sound, or touch something. For example, I have windows that look out to a lush green garden and trees in my backyard. When I turn to the left, away from my monitor, and look out to the garden, I associate it with peace and tranquillity. Trades will come and go, but the garden will still be sitting there unfazed by monetary losses related to the stock market. The garden helps emotionally ground me, making me less susceptible to the tides of emotion.

The triggers, then, are the visual stimulation of looking at the garden and slightly shifting my chair to the left to be able to see it. Both visual and kinesthetic triggers (the physical movement of my body to the left) take me away from any fear to something calm, stable, and balancing that gives me a moment to remember that there is more happening than just stocks going up and down.

While it is not a substitute for periodically getting up and going out into the garden to be completely away from CNBC and the streaming quotes, it gives me a moment of visual and mental refreshment and perspective that lessens the intensity and duration of any emotion or fantasy which may arise.

While it is easier to make the mental shift with an actual view to turn to, it is not required. You can use a trigger to associate to a positive thought or to access an inner image that will serve the same purpose. For example, the trigger can be as simple as touching your left thumb to your left forefinger, signaling the inner search for the pacifying image that immediately neutralizes the fearful or greedy thought.

Choose a trigger that is readily available and associate it with a neutralizing image that will work for you. When you experiment with this for a while, you should notice that the association between your trigger and the positive thought or image becomes stronger. Try it and see.

The reason the trigger works is that you are building a body-mind connection between your trigger and the positive thought or image. While it is certainly possible to simply shift from negative to positive without a trigger, it serves the function of making the shift occur more quickly and with more emphasis. And anything we can use to make the process easier when caught in the undertow while watching the market is worth using.

Stabilizing with an Anchor

A second tool we can use for neutralizing emotion also relies on the association between body senses and the mind. It is related to using a trigger. But instead of the aim being to do something that helps make the shift, this one aims at stabilizing the shift. This is called *anchoring*. Once we have made a shift, we can hold on to the neutralizing thought or feeling by again performing a simple connection with the visual or kinesthetic (touch) senses.

For example, let's say we were feeling a little anxious after watching Citigroup go down. We employ the trigger behavior, let's say to lightly pull on the left earlobe, and this helps take us to neutralizing thoughts, such as "Don't get excited. It's only short term, based on the whole financial sector dropping today. You know how the financial sector moves in relation to changes in bond prices. The fundamentals of the company haven't changed. First piece of good news and it's back up there again." This can then be reinforced by an anchoring behavior, such as looking at a smiling Buddha statue on the bookshelf.

What this does is begin to build a mental and neurological association between the positive, neutralizing thoughts and the anchor of a pleasant, smiling Buddha statue. And over time, it is possible that just glancing at the statue will further reinforce the positive feeling that goes with neutralizing the negative thoughts.

And here's the good part: Once a firm mental association is made with the anchoring object, it can have its positive effect without even having to consciously think about it. In other words, the anchor becomes unconsciously reinforcing simply out of habit. Since bad habits work this way, it makes sense that good ones will too.

One of the reasons I think it is to our advantage to have a relatively clean and organized office setting for our trading is related to the use of triggers and anchors. Since we can use various objects in our setting to trigger and anchor positive shifts of thought and associated feelings, it is a good idea to have things in a set place where every time we look there, our eyes will find the same object, not have to search around for it.

The more orderly and consistent trigger and anchoring objects are in the office, the more automatic and unconscious these mental connections may be made. Mental associations are being made all the time with events and associated objects or movements of the body. All we are trying to do is more consciously use these associations to our own benefit. Then, when set in place, they can operate largely on their own.

Here's a simple example of how professional golfers use a trigger to help them enter into a set sequence they want to go through as they step up to hit the ball. This is called a "preshot routine" and is a common sequence that good players go through before every shot. One pro on the tour decides on a club, pulls it out of his bag, and then stands behind the ball to line up the shot. He visualizes the path he wants the ball to fly. Then, just before stepping toward the ball, he hitches up his pants.

Now, this hitching up of his pants, which appears to the outsider as just a nervous habit under pressure, is something more. It is a trigger behavior that launches the approach to the ball and may have a positive thought associated with it, such as "Just put a nice, smooth swing on it."

Using the same example of a professional golfer, an anchoring behavior would be holding his position on the follow-through of the swing, which builds in a mental/neurological connection between a good swing and a good shot. Holding the position allows for this connection to be remembered in the body.

Working with a Journal

This technique is more cognitively oriented than the last two. It is to keep an ongoing journal of your trades. But the focus is not on buy and sell points; it is on your thoughts and feelings before, during, and after the trade.

This one requires some discipline to stay with and will be especially challenging for those active traders who don't want to be distracted between trades with having to monitor their own mental processes. But even active traders should try this, as it may help them discover common thought patterns hampering their trading of which they otherwise may not become aware.

Each time you trade, make a note of what you were feeling and thinking leading up to the trade. Were you feeling anything at all? Or were you just thinking? How did you know you wanted to make this trade? How fast after deciding to make it did you actually go into action? I want you to become very aware of exactly what you are thinking in the minutes before making a trade, and any feeling tone associated to your thoughts.

Did you notice any apprehension, anxiety, or fear? Make a note of it if you did. If not, notice if your thoughts changed as you actually made the trade. Did your heart rate change at all? Did you notice any sensations in your body as you made the trade? Any excitement?

Now, I understand that a certain amount of your attention is going to be focused on the mechanics of simply making the trade. But there is plenty of awareness that may still be focused on what is going through your mind and any bodily sensations.

Notice any reactions after you place your trade. What thoughts come up? Any feelings? Write down key words that are enough for you to remember when you come back and review your journal entries. Keep trades by date and write down the time the trade is made. Then leave spaces to fill in your internal process under the headings "before," "during," and "after."

If you can manage to stay with this exercise, you will most likely discover certain patterns begin to emerge. You may, for example, have a similar thought or feeling come up just before you place the trade or just after it is executed.

Should you use any triggers or anchors, make note of what they were and how they worked. For example, an entry might look like this:

> Was feeling some excitement but then had negative thought that I might be paying too much. Neutralized this thought by using trigger of shifting chair to left and looking out window to garden. Neutralizing thought kicked in: "Big deal, so if you pay a little too much what are you going to lose? If you think the stock is going up from here, that's all that matters." This allowed me to go ahead and make the trade feeling more positive. Noticed I felt good after trade made and was glad to own this stock after watching it for so long.

Review your entries every week or so. In keeping a journal of your trades and the mental processes that accompany them, you not only begin to see patterns of thought that are useful but also patterns that are interruptive. Journal keeping itself is an anchor in feeling more confident of your ability to know your own mind while trading. You end up feeling more able to control the trade rather than have the trade control you. And that's exactly what makes more disciplined online investors.

Visualize the Chart Before It Happens

The problem with charts, even real-time ones, is that they are being drawn after something has happened. The chart is always lagging what is happening right now, even though it tells us the trend of the last few minutes or more. Some good traders try to visualize the movement of the chart line before it transpires. The edge that they want is the confidence to follow the direction the stock is moving but be able to correctly predict what will happen before it occurs. While they never know for sure, some get quite skillful at predicting where it is going. They are not afraid to visualize the upward or downward move before it takes place.

One way to develop this is to look at a real chart and then close your eyes and imagine how the chart continues. The idea here is that you simply want to be able to draw it clearly in your mind's eye. Open your eyes, again look at the actual chart for a minute, then close your eyes and visualize it again, adding something to what you last saw.

Shuttle back and forth from the actual chart on the monitor to your inner imagined chart. In practicing this shuttling back and forth, you will enhance your ability to visualize clearly in the mind's eye, and also to visually add to the chart in the direction you would like to see the trend line move. Besides enhancing confidence in your predictive ability, doing this exercise helps you feel more as if you're leading the market rather than following it.

This is one form of what the "edge" is all about that the professional traders are always trying to achieve. Let's be clear: I'm not saying that you can *make* the chart move in the direction you want to see it, only that you can imagine it positive so that your confidence to make the trade is increased.

To be able to imagine something in the mind's eye, to see it clearly as a real possibility is the first step toward being able to make it a reality. Put negatively, if you can't imagine something as possible, you are not going to ever make it a reality.

MEDITATION: A METHOD FOR INCREASING PRESENT-CENTEREDNESS

Watching our own thoughts requires the ability to decipher them from the inner chatter that fills our minds. The nature of the mind is that it churns out thoughts on its own, most of which are totally out of conscious control.

Tuning in to the feeling tones associated with these thoughts also requires the ability to see how thoughts create feelings. And being able to stay focused on the monitor without undue distraction by fear or greed means knowing how to come back to the present, as we notice the mind drift away into thoughts and fantasies. All of these skills can be enhanced through learning a basic centering meditation.

So, to close this chapter, I would like to offer instructions for a beginning meditation that may help you be able to watch thought, see how feelings become associated with it, and spend more time in the present and less time in fantasy when you are watching the market.

For our purposes, let us think of meditation as simply the process of catching ourselves when the mind wanders away from the present, and gently and uncritically bringing it back to the present. Although this may sound easy to do, a cursory trial will prove that it is not easy at all.

A benefit for traders and investors of learning to meditate is that they will find their focus of attention can be sustained longer and in a more concentrated manner when they know how to stay present-centered. Since our life-sustaining breath is the most powerful anchor we have to work with, breath will be the object of our meditation.

Breath Focus and Counting Anchor: Instructions

Considerations before beginning: Make sure there is nothing you need to do which may distract you. You won't be able to concentrate if you think there is something else you should be doing. Make sure you are not being affected by alcohol and avoid caffeine at least two hours before doing the meditation.

Find a comfortable chair to sit in. Make sure your feet are flat on the floor. Place your hands comfortably at your sides, where they may rest on the arms of the chair or hang loosely. Let yourself sit relaxed but stay alert. Your back should be straight but don't strain to make it erect.

Take a deep breath. Notice the tendency to want to control your breathing. In meditation, you don't want to control your breathing; you want to let it go naturally, just as it wants. When we begin to focus on the breath, it is natural to want to try and control it, so you want to resist this temptation. Breath through your nose, letting the air come in naturally as your diaphragm expands. Then let the breath go out of your lungs slowly, letting all the air out. As you exhale slowly, mentally count 1.

Now, inhale again without forcing, just letting in as much air as you need. Then exhale again and count 2. Continue focusing on your breathing, letting the air come and go, without altering the natural rhythm or forcing it in any way. After each exhalation count the next number until you reach 10. Then begin again with 1 until you reach 10 again.

Don't be surprised or upset if you can't make it to 10 without being distracted. If you become distracted by a thought or a sensation, notice it, let it go, and return to your breathing, again beginning with 1 each time you lose your place. Simply notice whatever may grab your attention, and as soon as you catch your mind wandering, come back to your breathing and your counting.

Don't be judgmental if you lose your place, just keep returning to your breathing and your counting. It is perfectly normal for the mind to wander—that is simply the nature of the mind. Try to stay with this meditation exercise at least 10 to 15 minutes, staying as physically still as possible and resisting any temptation to move. Just notice the impulse to move and then come back to your breath.

After 10 to 15 minutes, when you feel ready, gradually open your eyes and sit quietly for a minute or so. Notice what you experience in your body and anything you may be feeling. The purpose of silently counting from 1 to 10 is to help keep your attention anchored in the present and with your breath. Do not count absentmindedly. Using the preceding instructions, let yourself take some time now to try this basic meditation.

As a way to modify this meditation when you are sitting at the monitor following the market, you can always use this mental counting as you take a breath. This will pull you immediately back into the present when you find your mind drifting away. When you get pretty good at staying focused on the breath and are able to count all the way to 10 a number of times without losing your place, then try the following exercise.

Going Beyond the Breath: Focus on Thoughts

After learning to let the breath come and go on its own, without needing to change it in any way, and learning to let various sensations come and go without focusing too intently on them, the next thing we notice as we continue meditation practice is the persistence of the internal chatter of the mind.

Some of this chatter is in the form of the parts of ourselves we worked with earlier in this chapter. And some of the chatter is just gibberish that does not come through in a clear voice. Now we want to begin to hear more clearly exactly what is going on inside that may be of use to us.

We hear this incessant chatter when we begin to quiet down the mind. That is why it is useful to first practice the counting meditation which keeps us focused on the breath. As we do this, the mind begins to quiet, and this allows distinct voices to come through more loud and clear.

It is this incessant chatter of the mind that is taking place continually during our normal waking lives that contributes to our lapses of concentration, confusion, and poor decision making. Fear thoughts and greed thoughts are part of what may filter through. This exercise aims at more clearly being able to identify exactly what voice is clamoring for attention.

Now, for this exercise, rather than bringing the mind back each time it is whisked away by a thought, we are simply going to follow it wherever it chooses to go. We want to begin to understand how our mental associations work, and how subtle feelings become associated with our thoughts.

With eyes closed, begin to simply observe the thoughts that arise. Without getting caught in whatever the content of your thoughts is, see if you can simply watch as one thought arises and how it leads to another. Following the chain of your thoughts may lead you into a fantasy that includes images. With the eyes closed, it is easier for images to accompany your thoughts. You may also notice that certain thoughts lead to subtle feelings. See what feelings, if any, may come up as you watch your own chain of thoughts.

Thought watching, besides being instructive in knowing something about how your mind operates, can be entertaining. You can get to the point where you view watching your own thoughts as every bit as enjoyable and entertaining as watching a television show or a movie. Because, as you get into the content of your thought chains, it is quite similar to a movie, with images, feelings, elaborate story lines, and even dramatic endings.

One important thing we realize from thought watching is this: Feelings do not just arise out of the mental cauldron all by themselves. If you pay close attention, you will notice that even subtle feeling states are preceded by a chain of thoughts. So, the equation is this: *Thought leads to subtle feeling and subtle feeling states lead to stronger emotions.*

When you notice fear or desire come up as end states, realize, then, that they are always going to be attached to some kind of fearful or desirous thought. See if you can identify the fearful thought that has led to the feeling state. And then do your best to neutralize the fearful thought. As soon as you can confront and neutralize the fearful thought, you will see that the feeling state is diminished. But you've got to be willing to do the mental investigation work of tracing back to the fearful thought.

The Next Step: The Ability to Witness

The next step in the process, after we have learned to keep the body still and are able to bring the attention back to the breath without getting lost for too long in thoughts, is the ability to witness our thoughts as they come up without having to get caught in them.

Instead of each thought dragging us into its whirlpool and then being sucked into all its associated thought swirls, the observing ego is able to witness our thoughts coming and going and still maintain the focus of attention on the breath.

It is this observing ego, or witness, that makes it possible at a concentrated level of attention to sit back and actually watch the origin of an association. We see how it develops into a full-blown thought, how it reaches its height and may have an associated feeling that goes with it, and then how it begins to diminish in intensity, slowly breaking up and then passing into oblivion. This takes a good deal of concentration and clarity to observe.

The witness is that part of us that is nonjudgmental, just watching whatever comes up in the form of mental and emotional contents. It doesn't care what voice may be strongest and has no interest in fighting or winning any battles. The witness is a natural part of our awareness. It is a stable, consistent part of our essence that helps provide a sense of continuity in our lives from day to day.

Witnessing is a state, and consciousness is the means toward witnessing. When we practice witnessing we are really talking about working with our own attention. In working with our own attention, increased ability at witnessing is a by-product.

We may nurture the witness by learning to disidentify with all of those identifications which help fortify our normal, everyday sense of who we are. It is as if we let go of what we identify with and begin to *identify with the identifier*. One way to strengthen the observing witness is to repeat the following statements to yourself slowly and with total concentration, letting what they really mean seep into your awareness just long enough to get a taste of the observing witness.

Say the following out loud and listen to yourself as you do:

1. I *have* thoughts but I am *more* than my thoughts. I can know and intuit my thoughts, and what can be known is not the true Knower. Thoughts may come and go but they do not affect my true I. I have thoughts but I am *not* my thoughts.

2. I have a body but I am *more* than my body.

3. My body may be tired or excited, sick or healthy, heavy or light, hot or cold, but that has nothing to do with my inward I. I have a body but I am *not* my body.

4. I have desires but I am more than my desires. I can know my desires and what can be known is not the true Knower.

5. Desires come and go, floating through my awareness like bubbles in the air, but they do not affect my inward I. I have desires but I am *not* my desires.

6. I have emotions but I am not my emotions. I can feel and sense my emotions, but what can be felt and sensed is not the true Feeler. Emotions pass through me, but they do not affect my inward I. I have emotions but I am *not* my emotions.

When you complete saying the foregoing statements aloud, begin again and this time say each statement silently. Try to feel the truth of your words. This exercise helps us experience how all our senses can be operating but we are not the "doer" of what is being done. The witness simply notices what is happening just as it is happening, without interfering, judging, or identifying with what is occurring. When developed so that we can trade from this observing witness, fear and greed can never get the upper hand.

6

Balancing Isolation and Information Overload

The setting providing the greatest degree of freedom for the disciplined online investor is the home office. It is here that attention need not be divided with any other activities, and unwanted distractions may be kept to a minimum. For active day traders or those considering active trading, the only other viable setting is a day trading room run by a retail firm. We will consider the pros and cons of each setting in this chapter.

Some occasional traders sneak in a trade on their computer when they have a spare minute while in their work setting. Others may make trades to be executed the next morning from a laptop at night while lying in bed. But our focus is not on these settings. Neither is the optimal environment for the kind of concentration that is required to do a good job of trading.

What does the ideal environment for the online trader look like? What are the psychological considerations in this setting that facilitate active or occasional trading?

In this chapter we will examine the nuts and bolts of trading at home, with particular emphasis given to how we may balance the isolating aspects of trading at home alone with the always looming threat of information overload.

Before we examine issues related to the trading setting, we need to begin by summarizing the different types of traders that have been previously mentioned. As discussed here, there is more than one way to define a day trader. It is not quite as simple as thinking of a day trader as just the hypermanic person sitting back making dozens of trades per day.

DEFINING TRADING APPROACHES

According to the way one teacher of traders defines the word, I would be considered a day trader. Oliver Velez is the founder of Pristine.com, an educational service for active self-directed traders. He thinks of a day trader as anyone who is "committed to his trades and applies focus and attention to the market each and every day" (Keynote address at International Day Trading Expo, Ontario, California, September 25, 1999).

The interesting distinction Velez makes in his definition is that you don't need to be acting every day on your trades to be considered a day trader. Those of us who are committed and watching the market daily would thus qualify, under his definition, as day traders. If we accept this more inclusive view of the day trader, obviously a much larger number of investors would fall into this category than when defined more narrowly.

I offer this alternative definition because it has some psychological validity. When you think about it, perhaps the commitment to, and amount of time and attention put in, watching the market is a better criterion for defining a trading type than the number of trades executed in a specific period of time.

One reason Velez defines day trading this way is that he teaches a method that is called *swing* trading, in which a stock may be held from two to five days. The trader may be watching closely while in a position over a period of days but not necessarily taking any action on it.

Velez focuses on this period of time because he sees it as a market niche that may be taken advantage of by the individual trader. Since large institutions can't move quickly enough in this short period, they do not, he believes, pose any competition. Likewise, it's too long a period for those who want to be in and out the same day, so they aren't going to be the competition either.

Those practicing this style of trading, while they certainly fall under the category of short-term traders, don't fit the more common narrow definition, in which one doesn't hold a position overnight. For review, here are the typical types of traders:

1. *Fraction traders.* Also known as scalpers or grinders, they make numerous trades a day, looking to make fractional

gains, usually 1/8 to 1/2 of a point, on 1000-share lots. They trade in a day trading firm or on their own, and often have hardware and software that gives them direct access to exchanges and electronic networks, which is much faster than trading through a browser and online broker. They hold stocks for less than five minutes and sometimes less than 30 seconds. At the end of the day, all positions are closed.

2. *Swing day traders.* These can be active traders but will hold stocks for longer periods than the five minutes a day trader would. They may hold a stock for three hours or longer. This type of trader is looking for more than just fractional gains. They are trying to capture intraday price swings caused by news events, stock splits, or other events that move the stock within the trading period. They will also settle all accounts by the end of the day. They may use a trading firm or browser-based online broker.

3. *Position traders.* Also known as swing traders (not swing day traders), this type tries to capitalize on a stock move over a period of a few days or longer. They may sometimes exit positions the same day they enter them. They will hold positions overnight, aiming to maximize profits from a swing in stock prices over a few days or longer.

4. *Online investors.* They make their own investment decisions without the assistance of a broker and save on commission cost. They typically buy stocks for investment purposes, intending to hold them for months or years. They have accounts with a browser-based online broker. They may also trade on a shorter-term basis, but not as often. The powerful bull market and the volatility in stock prices have turned some who initially traded only sparingly into more dedicated frequent traders. A growing segment of these investors are increasingly willing to take higher risks, trading over shorter periods, in hopes of significant gains.

The first three types use short-term trading strategies and are considered short-term traders. The main difference among them is how much risk they are willing to take in their money management. That is, ending each day flat, having closed out all positions, versus what is considered more risky, holding positions overnight. The thinking is that there are too many outside variables that may affect a stock overnight, so it is viewed as more risky to hold onto it.

Many longer-term investors simply do not make this kind of distinction, viewing much more risk in trading short term, whether or not the position is held overnight. They view any attempt to time the market as fraught with peril. They are concerned about the commissions raked up in trading frequently and the short-term capital gains taxes that must be paid that take a significant bite out of profits.

FOR ACTIVE TRADERS: HOME OR AWAY?

For those who are considering active trading, which we will define as a few trades per day to a few trades per week, combined with dedication to ongoing monitoring of the market, the two basic choices are to trade in a trading room at a professional retail firm or on one's own at home.

The Trading Room

The benefits of using a trading room include the following:

- The use of state-of-the-art hardware, software, and direct access connections for instantaneous execution and feedback.
- The emotional support of other traders.
- The availability of an expensive but hands-on training course using their sophisticated computer systems and software.
- The availability of experienced traders who help a novice learn the ropes when they have free time and give valuable feedback on mistakes made.
- A focused environment, free from the possible distractions in a home setting.
- Hardware, software, and connection provided, no need to weigh or decide on options.
- The possibility of social contact, information sharing, learning from others.
- More reliable computer systems, less chance of downtime.
- The distinct separation between work environment and home, making it easier to get away from work for those who find this desirable.

For those who want or need the structure of going to their "office" of the trading room each morning and who don't do well in getting down to business on time on their own, the trading room offers needed structure.

In addition, you are less likely to have technical problems using a trading firm's terminals. Even with a speedy cable modem in a home setting, for example, I have had it go out during trading sessions. Short of a major power failure, you will never have this kind of interruption in a trading room.

More common than modem failure is difficulty getting through fast enough to my online broker. But part of that difficulty is not being set up with a firm that is tailored for the fastest possible trading executions. Even with the fastest of the browser-based brokerages, using an online brokerage to execute trades is nowhere near as fast as the super-speedy direct executions you get using trading room systems.

Another benefit of the trading room is that the level of information available is going to be more than most traders will get using home software packages. For example, Level III information is included, showing the institutional traders and the prices they are paying to buy and sell to each other through Instinet and other electronic communication networks (ECNs). As well, you have three Level II screens running, allowing you to track three different stocks at the same time. At home, you are more likely to have only one Level II screen running, which for most, is adequate for the job.

In learning how to use the software and understand the various screens, the beginner is allowed to do simulated trading until he or she is comfortable enough to begin trading live with money on the line. However, as I argue here, once the novice trader is ready to trade live with money on the line, there is pressure by some firms to trade in larger share lots, which is too risky because of the amounts of capital that must be wagered.

Because you are going to have to pay $1000 to $2000 or more if you want to take the training course offered, it is not in the interest of those who manage the trading room to see new students quickly lose all of their capital and go away feeling angry, frustrated, and ripped off.

They are making money on your commissions, not on the money you lose. So it is in their interest to keep you at the computer making trades for as long as possible. Managers are quite patient in allowing new students the time to get used to the intimidation of the scene, the technical aspects of operating the hardware and software, and the anxiety of putting their money on the line.

When I was spending time in the trading room, I found the managers to be cordial and open to my questions regarding the meaning of the data bombarding me and various strategies of trading. I did not feel pressured to hurry to set up an account or deposit funds.

In fact, I was permitted to use a computer with all the usual software to simulate trading for days at a time without anyone ever asking me to open an account. This might not have been available to me had someone needed my seat for live trading. Fortunately, every time I visited, there was always at least one empty seat. They were aware that I had not gone through their training program and did not pressure me to do so.

There were other new traders also there to learn who, after a couple of visits, would be called into a manager's office and asked to make a deposit if they wished to stay. It was not altogether clear why they were given less latitude than I.

For those who don't like to spend many hours alone, the trading room offers the opportunity to chat with other traders when they are taking short breaks or between trades and looking for distractions. In addition, at the trading room I visited, an effort was made to encourage after-hours camaraderie by going out for drinks together at the end of the week. Some will find this option of having other traders with whom to talk shop and socialize appealing.

In some trading rooms, one or two of the more experienced traders will be hooked up to a microphone, calling out their trades as they are getting in and out of positions. No one is ever directly pressured to join in. But there is some indirect pressure by suggestion for others to join these leaders, making it a group bet rather than that of just one individual.

This can be viewed in two ways—either as a supportive group effort that pumps up the individual trader's confidence that he or she is making the right move—or as a not so subtle pressure to jump in and follow the herd. While the experienced and self-sufficient trader is less likely to be influenced by the "group think" mentality, the novice is more susceptible to it.

This aspect of the trading room seemed only to further jack up the anxiety level in what was already a stressful scene. Additionally, it may also foster competitiveness among the traders.

If you want to trade with others around you, using state-of-the-art systems and software and direct connections that are super-speedy, the trading room may be your best bet. But you had better be what psychologists call *field independent*, that is, able to be around dozens of other traders without feeling the need to join in and follow the herd. It is useful to have good assertive skills and the ability to focus your attention independently of others. Otherwise, it is likely you will be overly influenced by what others are saying and doing around you.

The scene can be especially intimidating for beginners, as you notice the multiple monitors and overwhelming amounts of data coming at you. For those who prefer a calmer, quieter, and more controlled environment in which to do their trading, the trading room scene will not be for you.

Further Considerations

There are a couple of other issues worthy of mention. One is the implication in the room I visited that there is just one way to trade correctly—in 1000-share lots. Even beginners were encouraged to trade this amount, which often requires putting between $30,000 to $50,000 or more on the line just to make a fractional gain. This is not the way to start someone off. It is both psychologically and financially more responsible and sensible for beginners coping with the anxiety of trading to start with much smaller share lots.

Why not begin with 100 shares and get comfortable entering and exiting trades, without adding the extra anxiety of having to put so much money on the line? You don't take someone just learning how to swim and throw him or her into the deep end of the pool before he or she has even gotten used to the water.

The rationale for encouraging traders to trade in 1000-share lots is that with anything less, no worthwhile amount of money can be made on fractional gains. Yes, you will be paying too much in commissions to make any money on trading 100 shares and gaining only a quarter point.

So, the answer might be not to make dozens of trades as one is learning, only a few. Slowly, as one gains skill and comfort, larger share lots could be wagered. Any other way is far too risky when so much money is on the line and disrespects the psychological need to ease into trading.

It is insufficient to try and approximate the anxiety of having real money on the line by what is called "paper" trading. While doing simulated trading with no money on the line is helpful in learning how to handle pressing the right keys and getting comfortable with the software, it will not help much in dealing with the added anxiety that goes with real wagering.

So, the next best thing would be to trade in small share lots with limited amounts of capital being risked. Even if no money is made for a while on these learning trades, the small price paid in commissions is far preferable to risking significant losses by putting much more money into a trade. This approach would be consistent with research on how we best learn new tasks. Behavioral psychologists call it *successive approximation*. This means you want to take small steps in the direction of your goal and be rewarded for each one, which then reinforces moving further in the desired direction.

The trader has got to get the feel for when to trade and when to stay out of the action. Experienced day traders know that their odds improve when they are trading in a strong market, a strong sector, and a strong stock all at the same time. When all three line up, scalping for fractional gains becomes somewhat less risky. Then traders keep buying at the bid and selling at the asking price all day long, chipping away a profit and trying to lessen their risk.

Another consideration is the *demand* characteristics that we mentioned in Chapter 3. One is the tendency to make too many trades because that is the way the game is played in a trading room. Those who are more sparing in their trading stand to hold more of their gains by not mounting up commission costs. Again, this requires going against the grain of how you will be taught in this scene.

There are some atypical traders who come in to make a few trades and then leave, not forcing themselves to stay for the entire market session. This may be a smart way to take advantage of the hardware and software without risking getting too sucked into the demands of the scene. It can be compared to winning in Las Vegas and getting out of the casino before all gains are given back. Mental discipline is required for both.

A second demand characteristic is the feeling you can't leave your seat for very long without missing something. As previously mentioned, no one walks out of the trading room for a break, which is a mistake.

A third characteristic is less of a demand and more of a choice: the scene is riddled with anxiety. How much of this will affect you just by being in the setting with others who are anxious? How sensitive to it are you? Do you thrive in this type of setting? Or is it too uncomfortable? How much distracting noise can you handle? How do you feel about others walking up to you to ask questions or chat about the market? Do you welcome it or prefer not to be bothered? How much will the competitiveness of the scene affect you? Will it tend to make you take chances that you would not otherwise take if others weren't there letting you know how they are doing? And how do you feel about others looking over your shoulder, checking your trades?

To summarize, by far the biggest advantage of a trading room is the speedy direct connections to the electronic networks for instantaneous execution of trades, as well as the amount of data offered through the software. You also have access to support from experienced traders and a structured environment to do your trading.

Trading Room Update

The experiences in and reactions to the trading room were during numerous visits in 1997 when it was operated by Block Trading. Since then, Block has gone out of business and Momentum Securities has taken over the offices.

I went back to the same trading room in November 1999 to find some things had changed. I had been invited to a complimentary four-hour class on using Level II. In the service of painting a fair and current picture, and because I think the changes at this facility may be indicative of the direction the day trading industry is moving, I want to mention what I found in returning to the scene.

To begin with, the trading room had been reconfigured to accommodate many more trading stations than it had previously. This made it appear more congested, with less space between each trader, a tighter fit between chairs and monitors. What before had been designed to accommodate maybe 50 to 60 stations was now handling over 100 in the same space. Clearly, the interest in day trading had increased to warrant squeezing every bit of space out of the rather large room.

Secondly, an area had been separated out from the main room up on a platform in a corner. This was reserved for 20 or so hypertrading scalpers who were doing hundreds of trades per day.

Another small but perhaps telling sign of the altered thinking was that donuts were no longer available but bagels still were. Instead, there were five plastic containers each filled with a different kind of cold cereal.

There was now an adjoining room that was used for the Online Trading Academy, which taught the classes that traders were now required to take before they would be granted a seat on the trading floor. The room has a number of platforms for simulated trading. The fee of $3000 for the class had remained the same as it had been for Block Trading. But the training was far more organized and structured, with a set daily curriculum and a regular staff of teachers. There was also an arrangement for the fee to be refunded in the way of a discount on commissions for the first 600 trades made once the student began actual trading.

The one-week "boot camp" was for six hours each day, covering the fundamentals of trading. Students were tested at the end of the week to see if they had learned the basic material. If they didn't pass the test, they could go back and repeat the one-week course free of charge.

A second-week advanced "immersion" course followed for those who wished to go further. This class was also for $3000. Both of these classes had to be completed satisfactorily before a trader could take a seat on the trading floor. Yes, $6000 is a steep investment to get a seat on the floor.

Another change that new technology made possible was the one-month-old introduction of a "virtual mentoring" service, which was a real-time voice chat over the Web to help traders on the floor and those trading from their homes to be guided through various trades and trading issues they wished to bring up. It was now possible to be connected to the trading room expertise and have immediate dialogue with the teachers and other traders using their proprietary software from your own home. This component included classes that were offered at the lunch hour for those who wished to participate.

The advances in the technology that made for voice chat and immediate audio and visual feedback were impressive. The fee for the full service offered, which was for graduates of the week-long "boot camp" only, was $1000. Lesser packages were open to anyone.

Finally, my concerns regarding beginners not trading in large share lots had been addressed. Beginners were not allowed to trade more than 100 shares for the first couple of weeks, and then could slowly increase the number of shares as they felt ready. It was good to find out that the new operation was understanding of the need for going slowly.

They also seemed more flexible in allowing traders to come in for a couple of hours in the morning and then go to other jobs. They were now talking about and teaching swing and position trading, not just scalping for fractions.

All in all, the changes in the philosophy and teaching methods seemed to be a reflection of a maturing industry two years later, trying to address some of the concerns and criticisms that had been aimed at it by the press and government agencies.

FOR TRADERS AND SERIOUS INVESTORS: THE HOME OFFICE

The home office setting provides the greatest degree of autonomy and freedom for the online investor. In this setting, you may configure your environment to suit your trading style and comfort. You are under no pressure or suggestion to make a certain number of trades or risk amounts of money you may not be comfortable with. You may learn and trade at your own pace, in your own way, and may divide your time between trading and other work interests, as you wish.

Advantages of the home office setting include the following:

- Convenience of coming and going as you please, taking breaks as desired, without the *demand* characteristics of the trading room.
- Comfort of your own personal space versus commuting to an office building.
- Familiarity with your personal computer system's hardware and freedom to choose software and connection as desired.
- Higher comfort level without intimidation factor of competitive trading room.
- Higher degree of focus of attention without distraction of others for those who prefer a quiet work setting and to work alone.
- The ability to watch TV, listen to music, or mildly distract yourself in any other way you see fit that is not possible in a trading room.
- Potential nourishment of home setting: do other tasks like gardening, reading, making lunch, etc., when you wish to take break from following the market.
- No monthly seat charge as with some trading rooms.
- Freedom to access "virtual mentoring" for follow-up education and guidance, lessening isolation (see the following) and providing support.

While the home setting for trading offers a great degree of personal freedom, there are some disadvantages as well. You must be able to handle the isolation factor of spending large amounts of time alone. This requires enjoying your own company and functioning well alone. It means as well handling all the thoughts and feelings which arise while watching the market. We will explore this issue more thoroughly.

You must make a number of decisions regarding hardware, software, and connections that are already taken care of in a trading room. It is wise to talk to others and see what their experiences have been in using the different online sites aimed toward the active trader. There are numerous trading sites offering software packages, some of them quite costly, depending on the number of trades you plan to make.

None of these decisions should be made without careful consideration, as expenses will mount up each time a decision ends up not working out. This is one area where feedback from others who are familiar with various alternatives can be of great help. This feedback ought to be both in personal discussions with traders and from trading site bulletin boards.

Especially for active traders, the type of Internet connection you have is important. It is here that those trading from home are usually at a disadvantage compared to those in trading rooms. As you get your trading feet wet, you begin to understand that the market is moving so fast that the person who has the fastest connection to execute trades is at a clear advantage.

This is not as significant an issue for the occasional trader who is a long-term investor, who can get by using a standard Internet connection through a local independent service provider. But even for the long-term investor, my strong bias (based on my personal experience) is that you settle for nothing less than a cable modem or DSL for your Internet connection. Anything less than this puts you at a disadvantage if speed of accessing your broker and execution of trades matters to you at all. But that's not the only reason I strongly suggest it.

Not only will you have your data come to you more uniformly and at the rate it should (meaning *real* real time), even more importantly, you will also find that using the Internet through a cable modem or digital subscriber line is 100 times faster than the typical telephone line modem connection.

In other words, it makes all the difference in the world as to the quality of your Internet experience, not just your online trading. Once you try a cable modem or DSL you will never again settle for anything slower. It's like the difference between driving on a congested two-lane highway versus whizzing along on a five-lane freeway.

While we're discussing the speed of connection, let's mention a related issue—what happens when you place an order to your brokerage house, as this is related to the type of software the home trader has to choose from.

How Orders Are Routed

It is useful for new and occasional investors to understand how the technology works when you enter an order using an online browser versus electronic direct access. It is logical to assume that an order you place is going directly into the system, heading toward a market maker or specialist. But this is not at all how it works.

Let's say, using a typical telephone or cable modem connection with a browser-based discount broker, you make a decision to buy 100 shares of Dell. You see a price you like, fill out the order form, and click to enter an order with your brokerage of choice. What happens to your order?

Your order is like an e-mail message, which is delivered to your broker. Brokers do one of two things when they receive it. They may work the order on their own trading desk, stepping between you and the larger market. In other words, they use their own supply of stock to fill your order. You are charged the normal commission per trade and your order is filled. This fill shows up on your screen as soon as it takes place.

The second thing they may do is sell your order to a wholesaler, or a "broker of brokers." This wholesaler pays your broker for this order being sent his or her way. Your broker gets this small fee in the form of the spread between whatever price you are paying and a slightly reduced price the wholesaler is paying.

This means that your broker is being paid twice: a small amount from the wholesaler and the commission amount you are paying. This spread that is paid by the wholesaler to your broker becomes significant when multiplied thousands of times from all the orders being sold to the wholesaler.

The point of this explanation of the routing of your order is to show that you don't really have direct access to trade with other traders when you go through a typical browser-based system. This is by far the most common system for online investors and is used by even some more active traders who are using Level I quotes rather than a more sophisticated software package.

The alternative system is called *electronic direct access*. This means your connection is not through a discount broker but directly with ECNs where there is no one stepping between you and the person who wants to sell you your 100 shares of Dell. It is both faster and cheaper per trade to trade this way but requires the direct access that comes only by paying for this privilege.

ECNs like Instinet, Island, and Archipelago are competing with the NASDAQ market makers and bringing buyers and sellers directly together rather than forcing you to go through a broker. You pay a fee to them based on the number of shares involved. But the more significant fee you pay is to have the direct connection to them. And it is this very fast connection and access to the ECNs that puts you in the position to choose where you want your order to go that trading firms have to offer.

It is possible to get direct access to the ECNs using home software packages, but you are going to pay a rather high monthly fee for this kind of speed and direct execution either through a required number of trades or a straight charge if you fall below the trade minimum.

Some day trading firms are now offering what is called "smart routing" software in an attempt to win some of the business of the online discount brokers and make negotiating the various ECNs easier for day traders ("Day-Trading Firms Create Smart Software to Seek Out Best Prices," *Los Angeles Times*, November 9, 1999, p. C1).

Companies such as TradeCast, CyBerCorp.com, and Tradescape.com have smart-order software that scans the NYSE, NASDAQ, and ECNs to evaluate where an order should be sent based on price and execution of the system at any moment. It will then automatically route the order to the one offering the best price.

This is a recent development that adds to the attractiveness of direct access trading. It ought to have some impact on the decision making of active investors when choosing whether to use the browser-based system or ECNs through direct access. The key for day trading firms in selling smart-order routing systems is in convincing investors that they will save more money by getting better executions than they will pay in additional charges for the system.

During quiet times of the market, the advantages of the smart routing may be negligible. But during the open and close of the market, when the volume is the heaviest and prices are most volatile, the software will be able to decide instantaneously which way to route the order. Like most of the other technology we have mentioned, this smart routing will be a common part of the online investor's tools within a few years.

Suffice it to say that the typical online investor will have more choices as these networks become more readily accessible. The fees for connecting to them will go down, just like everything else, as there are more traders aware of them and wanting to take advantage of them.

Connections will become more sophisticated as bandwidth broadens, so that within a reasonably short time, the technology of trading for the typical online investor will look quite different than it does today. It is only a matter of when, not if, just as our friendly discount brokers, to stay competitive, will have us all smiling as we enjoy trading without a commission, no matter how many shares we wish to buy or sell. Once again, welcome to the new millennium gold rush, where the individual online investor keeps getting better picks and fancier shovels.

Elements of the Home Office

Ideally, trading from home will be done from an office that is quiet, comfortable, and has the elements to facilitate concentration of attention on the task at hand, which is watching the market and executing trades. It will be large enough so you are not cramped and the space will be clean and organized to help you feel in control. The notion here is that if you are going to take trading seriously, you need to set up your office to reflect that intention.

Organizing your trading setting is a step toward disciplining your mind to create the frame to help you succeed. Online trading favors those who can take in a lot of information, pick from it what is useful in the moment, and block out data that is not immediately useful. To do this, you need to have your computer system, monitors, software, telephone, television, and anything else relevant to trading all set up to suit you and functioning properly, so that attention does not need to be diverted to these things.

It is useful to have a view out of at least one window from your office that is open, peaceful, and where plants, flowers, or trees may be easily seen, like a garden or backyard setting. This fosters turning away from the monitor often to refocus your eyes, looking out at least 100 feet or more. A garden setting is ideal, so that not only are you refocusing but you are calming yourself with the natural, living environment at the same time.

This helps balance the amount of time spent focusing on a computer screen in front of you and perhaps a TV screen to the side. Frequent looking away to a calm setting gives a visual and mental break from the intensity of the electronic information coming from the computer screen and the television.

Other elements of the home office include good lighting and room ventilation, easy access to past hard-copy trading records, a fax machine and copier, a separate telephone line so that calls may be made and received if your main line is being used for a modem connection, and an ergonomically correct chair to help you stay alert and comfortable when spending many hours at the computer.

For active traders, it is also good planning to have a back-up source of electricity should your power go out. Power outages mean you're out of the market if you're trading for fractions. Investors, of course, can still pick up the phone and call their discount broker to enter a trade.

In the same vein, brokerage web sites or quote sites are sometimes down or impossibly slow to get through to, no matter what form of browser-based connection you may have. Because of this, it is a good idea to have more than one source for quotes, and more than one brokerage account for trading. The occasional investor may perhaps view these precautions as overkill and unnecessary. But more active traders will climb the wall if they are unable to get through to make trades when the market is hot.

So, all of these things need to be considered, or they will only be thought about after you have learned from experience that, in the worlds of high technology and cyberspace, anything can go wrong at any time, and, sooner or later, will.

THE ISOLATION FACTOR

The mind does strange things when you are sitting alone at the computer for long stretches of time and watching the market go by. Many "home alone" traders and investors complain about feeling isolated, especially if they are dedicated to following the market on a daily basis. They feel cut off from other traders and want feedback on their own hunches and analysis of the market.

One effect of feeling isolated is doubting your own mind. Instead of the more common process of having ideas and testing them out against others, you find that your mind tends to question your own judgment when you have too long to think about the market and nobody readily available with whom to share your ideas.

Doubt thoughts may grow to the point that decisions already made are questioned and requestioned. Obsession may visit you often enough to become more than a passing acquaintance. These visitations may lead to prematurely undoing positions out of the fear that a mistake has been made. You may feel like you've been handed the city key and made a permanent resident of Regret City.

This is where having a set pattern or sequence to go through for each and every trade helps circumvent any impulsive decision making. If you have a plan that you are following before each trade, then it is a matter of having the discipline to follow your plan. This kind of discipline can be learned on your own but is often best picked up at courses or seminars on trading that emphasize trading only with a clear plan in mind.

So, one result of being isolated at home from other traders is the mental sloppiness which may so easily creep into one's thinking and behavior. When we talk about the disciplined online investor, perhaps in no other area is discipline so relevant as following a plan which will lessen doubt thoughts.

Specific personality types react differently to being alone. Some enjoy being alone and will not experience it as isolating. Other types will be more uncomfortable with themselves and be quick to reach out for contact with others when possible. Here is a summary look at how they react.

Personality Types and Isolation

The gambling-impulsive type likes the competitive factor that is found in the trading room. They thrive on the interaction with others. They are more likely to experience some loneliness and isolation trading at home. They are also more likely to take chances in their trading, not being careful to follow a trading plan for every trade. They may find it easy to overtrade when on their own. This would hold true as well for the longer-term investors who happen to be of this personality type but who are not interested in active trading.

The obsessive-disciplined type handles the isolation factor rather well, compared to the gambling type. They are able to use their obsessive nature to follow a trading plan methodically and like having total control over their personal environment.

This type actually prefers being alone to concentrate on their trading. Being alone is experienced more as a pleasant respite from the demands of others rather than isolating. When it comes to following the trading plan, nobody does it better than the obsessive.

Remember, though, it is the obsessive-disciplined who is also most likely to form online relationships in virtual trading rooms and bulletin board chat rooms, and even become quite dedicated to these sites. So, while they enjoy being physically alone, they often make persistent efforts to connect with others online.

It is more in the realm of doubt thoughts that the obsessive is likely to have problems. Because the obsessive mentally plays back decisions made, questioning his or her own thinking and judgments, it is not hard for this type to spend too much time in self-recrimination for trades that don't go as expected and end in losses. The obsessive far and away feels more guilt over losing trades than the other types.

It is difficult for obsessives to let go of their guilt, which they ruminate over in their minds in the form of self-recriminating statements. This may be punishing enough for some to want to stop trading altogether. Here is where the obsessive could do well to borrow some of the easy-come–easy-go attitude toward losses that the gambling-impulsive type is so comfortable with. But this is exactly what is so difficult for them to learn and why personality style is so important when deciding on a primary approach toward trading.

The doubter-timid trading style handles the isolation factor reasonably well, as they much prefer not to have to deal with the motives and personalities of many others trading around them. The doubters will of course do what they do best, which is to doubt what they hear on television from the pundits and to doubt some of their own thinking.

While they prefer to err on the side of caution, they end up watching a lot of the market go by rather than jumping in and taking a position. So, they are more the victims of isolation through standing on the sidelines than feeling isolated by trading at home alone.

The optimist-gullible trading personality feels the isolation of the home setting the most. Because they thrive on being sociable and like to take their cue from discussing strategies with others, they miss not having others to share in the trading experience. They are not fond of spending a lot of time alone.

Optimists would be first in line to join a local investment club to pool their knowledge and capital with others. Optimists readily admit that the club serves as much of a social need for them than as a serious investment club. One way you know this is true is to check the actual amount invested by each member to the group effort. It is often relatively quite small. In other words, these clubs satisfy social needs as much as investment needs.

Reducing the Isolation Factor

To cope with the isolation that accompanies trading from a home office, there are a number of avenues the investor has available to connect to others. These are through cyberspace as well as face-to-face contact. It is a good idea for the serious investor who spends a lot of time alone at the computer to take advantage of both of these ways of connecting to others.

What we want to do is try and balance the need for contact with others who are also trading and investing, on the one hand, with the danger of overdoing our hunger for gathering information about trading and the market. When contact is too focused on trading tactics, software, etc., it becomes one more way for us to end up overwhelmed with all the information coming our way. Later in this chapter, we will identify in more detail the ways we become overloaded with information.

So, it is useful for us to distinguish between the need for contact to gather information and compare experiences, on the one hand, and the social need to be with others, where money and the market are not primarily the focus, on the other.

Meeting with others needs to be for social contact more than for gathering stock tips or other information. While the exchange of market-related information may or may not be part of the interaction, the investor needs to keep in mind that it is the contact itself that is important, not so much the content of it.

This is why it is so crucial to have people in your life who can help turn you away from trading, the economy, or anything having to do with making money. Avoiding having anything to do with the market and making money is not as easy for some as it might first appear.

One of the occupational hazards for active traders and serious investors is the insidiously seductive nature of the market itself. The fascination that we may develop for it, especially when it is going our way, can make other things seem less interesting. So we may spend more and more time on the Internet with market and nonmarket-related surfing, and less time interacting with live people in the real world, who may not seem as interesting as the stimulation we receive on the Internet.

Add to the undertow of the market the lure of the Internet itself, and it is easy to see how some spend hours surfing from one stock-related site to another. Just as with any other topic on the Internet, the numerous associated links and magnitude of information they lead to can keep one busy researching and reading for weeks on end. We can stay continually involved, either watching, trading, researching, or chatting. And consider for a moment how this will be magnified when we can trade at any time of the day or night on any exchange in the world!

It is not hard to understand why so many online traders and serious investors claim they can't wait to get up in the morning and hear the opening bell. The always changing nature of the market tends to keep those involved in it on their toes. They cannot afford (literally) to become too complacent or to take anything for granted.

While passion to learn and develop one's skills is admirable and to be encouraged, we need to make sure the market does not suck us in to the point that we can't keep it in perspective with other activities in life. The point is: the more we get caught in the Web, the more isolated from others we may become.

The following types of interaction are available online to help diminish the sense of isolation when you are trading:

- *Trading chat rooms.* Some have a particular trading orientation and all cost a fee to join after initial free trial. May offer stock tips during the trading session and give ongoing guidance, leading traders in and out of trades in a supervised manner. May offer training and education in addition to chat room. Some offer data packages as well.

These will interest the active trader who wants close contact with others. In terms of style, these rooms look and feel like social chat rooms, with ongoing commentary being given in real time and where participants may have their questions immediately answered by those leading the room. In cyberspeak, these are what are known as *moderated* chat rooms, meaning they have a leader.

- *Message bulletin boards.* These may be found at many stock-related sites on the Web. Some of the more popular include *Yahoo!* (worst), *Raging Bull* (better), and *Silicon Investor* (best). *The Street.com* also has message boards on specific topics but they are in the process of building active subscriber participation. New bulletin boards are popping up at various sites all the time, as they are an easy way to bring people back to a site repeatedly.

These boards are unmoderated, free-wheeling forums where you will find everything from petty backbiting and "flame wars" between posters, to shameless stock touting, to detailed analyses on particular stocks that are knowledgeable, insightful, and useful. Unlike trading chat rooms, the subjects are far-reaching in content. A "thread" that is begun on one stock continues for years if there are enough interested posters to keep it going.

Sites that require membership fees, like *Silicon Investor*, tend to attract more serious investors than sites like *Yahoo!* where anyone can (and does) join in on any subject. Often, earnings reports and breaking news will be posted immediately on these threads. Isolation is diminished for those who become regular contributors, but you must be careful not to impulsively make trades based on tips.

■ *Interactive commentary and community sites.* Sites like *The Motley Fool* and *The Street.com* offer articles and daily columns written on a broad range of topics and encourage reader feedback. *The Street.com* presently has a free area and a subscriber area, and will be offering a cluster of investment-related sites by the time you read this, including *RealMoney.com, TheStreetPros.com, ipoPros.com,* and a community site called *TheStreetTalk.com. RealMoney.com* will be the subscription site, costing $200 per year, offering twice daily news and market analysis e-mailed midday and evening in addition to web site articles. Best for those with more than a passing interest in the market.

Briefing.com offers a live, ongoing commentary on the market, updated throughout each hour, that features short breaking news items, company and sector analysis, research, interviews, earnings calendars, and charts. This is a very useful site to help investors navigate through the daily market. It costs $70 per year and is well worth it.

■ *Investor coaching.* This is offered by a few sites on a one-to-one basis to help new traders and investors learn the basics of trading and to address some of the emotional issues that arise in trading. It allows for personal contact for those who are unable to get this kind of help in person, by telephone, or as follow-up to in-person contact. I recommend in-person contact with licensed professionals for the mental and emotional aspects of trading.

Be wary of those who do not have a doctoral degree in psychology and are not licensed to practice in their state. By calling themselves "coaches" they get around the legal prohibition against practicing psychology without a license. But anyone who is offering to coach you on your mental and emotional problems related to investing should be qualified to do so. Because of the growing number of active traders and the issues arising that relate to loss of capital, this is an area that is ripe for exploitation. Being an experienced trader does not qualify one to work with the emotional difficulties of other traders. Investor beware!

Off-Line Support and Education

In addition to what is available online, the investor may attend educational seminars, workshops and conferences to increase knowledge and trading skills. There are a wide variety of training workshops available, from the informational programs offered by brokerage houses to in-depth, intensive three-day workshops on trading techniques. In most areas, traders have formed support groups, where they can meet and discuss trading issues.

Local colleges now offer beginning courses for investors, covering such areas as money management, retirement planning, investing in mutual funds, and online investing. These courses may be another place to meet and gain the support of like-minded investors. And, of course, there are a growing number of books aimed for online traders and investors.

COPING WITH INFORMATION OVERLOAD

While the investor at home may feel isolated from other investors, there is no shortage of information flowing to him or her. While the Web has a tremendous amount of valuable information that may be accessed, one result of this abundance is the ease with which we end up feeling overwhelmed. This is certainly the case when it comes to sites related to the world of investing.

The number of sites for stock analysis, charting, quotes, commentary, portfolio tracking, company web sites, education, news, and chat is more than any investor can possibly manage to sort through. Even trying to get a grip on the thousands of web sites by going to a comprehensive site that helps organize the material is itself a daunting task. These comprehensive sites offer a broad cross section of various investment categories, approaches, and methods and often seem as confusing and overwhelming as doing a search of individual sites. We may even end up feeling stupid.

We think we ought to be able take in and comprehend more than we actually can. So most of us try and push ourselves, stuffing in more and more bits of information, both simultaneously and sequentially. And that's only what is bombarding us from the outside. While the outside is bad enough, it actually is relatively tame compared to what is happening on the inside, thanks to the chattering of the mind.

The plethora of sites related to investing is partly a result of the explosion in online trading and partly created by the structure for navigating the Internet itself. They call it a "web" for a good reason: Taking a step down the associated path of links to related sites and following up these links to still more links can take us on a fascinating journey that may last for months. Or it may lead us on a wild goose chase that wastes a lot of time. Before we know it, we've become ensnared in the web. Curiosity is a marvelous thing. But it may lead to a lot of linkages that we can live without, linkages in a chain that binds.

Investors may come away from trying to explore these sites with a sense that there is simply too much information that they will not have and will never grasp. And they wonder how much of this information is important for them to know and how much of it is irrelevant to their needs. How much information is enough? Each investor has to decide for him- or herself.

One way to cope with overload is to choose a few web sites and explore them thoroughly. Listen to what others recommend for news, analysis, and commentary. Much of the material from one web site to another is similar or duplicated. You don't need to explore every web site to get an adequate grasp of what's happening. Start slowly and add more as you feel ready.

Most good discount brokerage sites will have a certain amount of news, research, and charting available, as well as a place to set up and manage your portfolio. They may also have links to other related sites that can be your jumping-off point to explore more, if you wish.

So, a robust discount brokerage site is the place to start for most online investors. While some skeleton sites might be good for very cheap trading, they usually don't offer much research, charting, or retirement planning tools.

In addition to a brokerage site, having one or more additional sites devoted to world, state, and local news as well as market-related news is useful. For example, the Associated Press wire and CNN are good for this, as is the Yahoo! finance section.

The Yahoo! site allows you to customize a page to receive a few top stories in whatever sectors or areas of interest you wish. Because they are getting the news hot off the press from Reuters, and the style of the page is easy on the eyes, I find Yahoo! to be a good place to begin in the morning for general, business, and market news, including foreign markets.

Most of the quote packages you may subscribe to that offer Level I or Level II quotes have some kind of news component. The question is how fast will the news come to you if your intention is to get a jump on the market? And here is where we run into a problem.

This is an area in which it appears the individual investor is still not going to get the breaking news quite as fast as institutions are. The irony is that with dozens of web sites devoted to nothing but business and market news, you are still going to experience some lag between the event, the initial release of the news, and when you first read about it on these sites.

As mentioned earlier, institutions pay $1500 per month for a direct news feed. If I get the news even three minutes after they do, they will capitalize on it and I will be left in the dust. By the time CNBC tells me and everyone else about the story, it's too late—those who got it three minutes earlier have already made their move.

Sometimes, with a big event, everyone is getting the news at exactly the same time as it is breaking, like when the Federal Reserve releases their decision on what to do with interest rates. These releases are purposely planned so that no one is able to get the jump on anyone else. It is company-related news that affects a stock that some get faster than others.

For most investors, learning of a news event three minutes later than the next person is inconsequential. But for traders, it's like having quotes delayed three minutes—it matters. I have tried getting alerts on my stocks from sites that offer them, but so far, I can't say that anything has adequately done the job. The alerts are nowhere near fast enough to be able to take advantage of the market. In fact, by the time I usually receive an alert, the news has already been flashed on CNBC. As usual, in the speedy electronic world, the person with the most sophisticated and costly toys wins.

Sources of Overload

Besides the stock-related web sites and the intimidating task of searching the Web itself, other sources contributing to information overload include TVs, car radios, cell phones, newspapers, magazines, pagers, gossip, and the ongoing chatter bubbling up inside our own minds.

Would you ever think of your own mind as contributing to the problem? Maybe not when you think of information overload as only arising from outside of you in the world.

But the psychological reality is, what is going on inside in the form of doubting, rumination, planning, rehearsing, fantasizing, and second-guessing is actually far more captivating and potentially overwhelming than anything coming from the onslaught outside.

And we have not even begun to talk about how the unconscious mind affects our decision making and contributes to the conflict. One of the reasons we need to understand how our personality affects our trading is because if we don't, certain decisions are going to be made from the unconscious mind whether we like it or not. Another way to state the issue is to say that the whole reason we are so interested in mental and emotional discipline when we are trading is because unconscious motivation that, by definition, *we are not even aware of*, can be strong enough to counter rational thought and the best laid plans of the disciplined mind.

Returning to the conscious level, the mind has its own mechanism for selectively attending to only the number of bits of information it can take in and process from the outside world at one time. When it reaches the point of having more than it can handle, it simply blocks out whatever else is bombarding it. But this is in no way a rigid process and some people can take in and remember much more data at one time than can others.

For example, on CNBC recently, they were doing segments of the show from the Bay Area and Silicon Valley. They had a memory expert, David Markoff, look at 50 digits for 15 minutes and then say them out loud. He was able to remember all 50 of them in the exact sequence. If nothing else, this feat demonstrates that memory is elastic, that it can be expanded to include a greater number of bits of data than we usually believe.

Signs and Symptoms of Information Overload

Some of the indications of information overload include the following:

- Feelings of confusion in comprehending and processing information.
- Forgetting what is read or heard shortly after taking in information.
- Feeling anxious or tense as information is being presented.
- Feelings of mental and physical exhaustion and complaints of weakness.
- Losing interest in topics you usually follow and in hobbies.
- Noticing ringing in the ears or blurred vision when listening or reading.
- Feeling confused or unclear when discussing information with others.
- Dreams of being overwhelmed, confused, unable to figure out a situation or solve a problem.
- Sleeping for longer periods than usual, wanting to take naps while working or following the market, trouble staying awake.
- Procrastinating with work tasks.
- Increasing fantasies of escape or going on vacation.
- Changes in diet, especially eating more than usual.
- Reacting more emotionally to minor slights or disappointments or more sensitively than usual to nonpersonal events in the world.
- Developing new nervous problems/habits: skin irritation, stomach problems,scalp problems, back tightness, stiff neck, etc.

MANAGING THE OUTER NOISE

If you identify a number of these signs and symptoms as being true for you, here are some ways to manage the outer noise. Even if you don't identify with any of them, the following steps may be taken preventatively to help keep you from ending up with symptoms:

1. *Begin paying attention.* How much stimulation can you handle comfortably? Walk away from the TV or computer, phone or book when you notice that you can no longer adequately concentrate.

2. *Take your level of interest seriously.* Monitor it regularly. When it drops, ask why and experiment to find out what will help you regain it. Avoid those tasks and activities that you have no interest in if

at all possible. Pushing yourself to learn or do something uninterest-ing only drains mental and physical energy. And when you must learn or do something uninteresting to you, don't waste emotion complaining about it.

3. *Make sure you are getting enough sleep.* Walking through the world sleep-deprived makes everyday noise seem more excruciat-ing. It will also contribute to short-sighted decisions when we are trading.

4. *Limit the amount of gratuitous stimulation-bombardment that you subject yourself to.* Watching violent shows on TV; overdosing on negative and violent news; spending too much time around highly anxious, depressed, and negative people; and indulging in violent adventure films with special effects will all take their toll over time. Limit the amount of time you spend in loud restaurants, theaters, or concert arenas. Limit the amount of time spent listening to talk radio or senseless television shows.

5. *Listen to soothing music.* Do other activities that you know will calm your body and quiet your mind, such as slow walks in a natural setting, taking a bubble bath, lovingly preparing a meal, or giving and receiving a message with a loved one.

6. *Learn to meditate.* Become more aware of your inner world and quiet the body as a preventative against stress and burnout. We offered a beginning meditation in the last chapter.

7. *Establish a meaningful, consistent, and satisfying sexual relation-ship.* This will be nourishing, supportive and promote a deepening emotional connection. It will also help in relieving physical stress. Consciously learn to extend the pleasant *halo effect* (the time you feel more relaxed and open) after sex for longer periods of time.

8. *Establish a regular exercise routine.* This will help cope with stress, fight off low energy, depressive tendencies, and tone the body and strengthen the heart. This is especially important if you are spending a number of hours daily in front of the monitor trading.

9. *Make friends and acquaintances.* This will promote mutual sharing of activities, ideas, experiences, and problem solving. Oth-ers help us understand that we are not alone and may provide needed support when we are under stress. Try to share interests with others that have nothing to do with trading, investing, or the business and financial world.

10. *Take complete breaks from trading, watching the market, and from even turning on the computer.* See what it's like to be disconnected from the Web for at least a full day. Don't call for automated phone quotes or watch television business programs. Give yourself a one-day withdrawal from the market. Not only does this give you a necessary break from the action, it also shows you that you can live without constant attention to the market and your portfolio without anything terrible happening.

11. *Take periodic vacations.* Go to a different environment than you are used to. Go to the mountains, desert, seashore, or to another state or country. This is necessary to clear your mind of habitual problems and routines that are easy for us all to get stuck in. See if you can resist the temptation to turn on CNN if you travel to another country.

12. *Seek professional help.* Take advantage of psychological counseling or psychotherapy when needed. Do not wait until you are miserably depressed or climbing the walls with anxiety before reaching out. If things get bad enough, medication from an M.D. is always available and a psychologist can help determine if you need it.

Remember that psychologists are too good at what they have to offer to be limited to helping disturbed people. They can help you overcome obstacles that block you from higher-level work performance and more intimate love relationships. They can assist you in coping with the pain of loss and adjust to the developmental stages and changes that are part of life. Don't be afraid to seek help when you need it.

MANAGING THE INNER NOISE

While the outer noise that overloads us may be largely managed by manipulating the physical environment and altering relationships with others, controlling our own minds is not as easy. It is, in fact, *the most difficult thing that anyone can do.* If you don't believe this, try it for yourself and see what you discover. In addition to what was presented in the last chapter, here are more ways to work with your thoughts and feelings.

1. *Shuttle between inner and outer.* Pay attention to your own mental and emotional state while trading and watching the market. Develop a habit of shuttling back and forth between the data on the screen and the "data" inside your mind. Notice what inner dialogue comes up as you react to watching changes on the monitor or news events on television.

Spend at least one part of time focusing on your thoughts and emotional reactions for every three parts of outward focus on data and information. So, if you are watching the monitor for an hour straight, at least 15 minutes of that time should go to quickly accessing your inner world, observing your reactions. If you think this is a lot of time to give to your inner world, then you are underestimating the power this inner world has on your trading decisions.

2. *Identify and combat all negative thoughts.* Begin to notice which negative thoughts tend to arise the most. See if you can trace where they may be coming from and why they come up repeatedly. Are they triggered by certain events? If so, try to identify exactly what events trigger your negative thoughts. Then see if you can imagine another way to interpret the events so that the associated negative thoughts can be made neutral or turned positive.

For example, if the S&P futures are way down before the market opens, and this is the trigger for your negative thoughts about how badly the market will be that day, come up with an alternative scenario for the market that allows for neutral or positive thoughts. You can do this by remembering that often the market opens with the futures down and then recovers in the first hour or later in the session. Simply remembering your own previous experience is often enough to neutralize negative thinking.

3. *Mediate all-or-nothing thinking.* Make sure you are not thinking in extremes. Always try and find some gradations, or steps in between the end points of one extreme or the other.

For example, instead of telling yourself you must either make $500 in a day or you've failed, see the increments from 0 to 500 and assess what is a realistic amount to try and make. Then evaluate based on your actual average what makes sense to set your goal at. All-or-nothing thinking is not using what I have called the *discriminating mind* to see the components that fill in the spaces or gaps from one end to the other. When you can't see the gradations yourself, ask someone you trust to help you fill in the mental gaps. The more attached we are to one position, the harder it is to see various alternatives and to seriously entertain them.

4. *Refuse to allow strong emotion to dictate your course of action.* Whether you feel exhilaration or fear, do not allow yourself to make any trade until it has been processed through your critical mind. Get up and walk away from the computer if you are feeling you must make a trade based on strong emotion. Learn that you can tolerate whatever emotion you are feeling but do not have to take any action because of it.

5. *Persistently but gently bring the mind back to the task at hand.* It is normal for the mind to wander even with the compelling data flashing before you on the monitor. Over the course of hours at the screen, your mind will come and go from the task of paying attention over and over again. You want to bring it back each and every time to the monitor, getting to the point that all extraneous distraction can be eliminated for increasing periods when you are making a trade.

When you have made your trade and no longer need to attend, you can let yourself be distracted. In the same way we want to learn to shuttle between the inner and the outer, we also want to shuttle between intense concentration when needed and distracting ourselves when rigorous attention is not needed.

6. *Have a plan.* Start the trading day with a plan. And do your best to stick with it. Have a list of stocks that you are watching closely. Have an idea how many trades you are going to make if the conditions are favorable. Have a limit on the number of trades and the amounts of capital you are willing to risk in any one trade and for the day as a whole.

Know how much you can lose in a week, a month, three months and still have adequate capital to continue trading. Don't just guess at these amounts. Set realistic and conservative limits so that the chances of being overwhelmed by fear during trading is diminished.

If you resist doing any of these behaviors, ask yourself *why* you are unwilling to discipline yourself by setting limits. If you are going to be a disciplined online investor, you've got to be willing to set limits on your trading behavior. It is just too easy to make impulsive trades no matter how much we tell ourselves we won't indulge.

7. *Know your limits.* When you begin to feel that you are no longer concentrating well, that you're becoming easily distracted, give yourself permission to stop for the day. Resist the compulsion to sit at the computer and trade when your mind is not with it. You will only make bad trades if you fight your desire to get away from it. Turn off the computer and let the market do its dance for the day without you. Remember that there will always be another day and another trade.

7

The Paradox of
Self-Control

Some psychologists assert that one of our most powerful fears is losing control and that one of the strongest human motivations and most basic needs is to have control over our lives. Much of our thinking and behavior, they believe, is an expression of our need to gain and maintain a sense of control. We strive to feel a sense of control over our own minds, our behavior in the world, our ability to shape our environment to satisfy our needs, and to some degree, over our relations with others.

In support of this, feeling out of control of thoughts, emotions, and/or behavior is common to the complaints presented when people seek psychotherapy. And when the issues do not center on feeling internally out of control, they are often around control issues with significant others, either as the controller or the one being controlled.

If we define having a sense of control as "causing to influence something in the desired direction or believing one can if desired," then it isn't an exaggeration to say that at least a subtle (and often larger) aspect of control enters all human relationships.

Sometimes our efforts at control are very conscious and intentional. And other times they are only barely in our awareness or not conscious at all. Whether it be in the form of friends, lovers, colleagues, boss and employee, psychotherapist and patient, parent and child, acquaintances, or even daily casual encounters with strangers, we are usually trying to influence someone in some way.

That is, after all, what meeting our needs through interactions with others is all about.

When we talk about being disciplined online investors, perhaps the most transparent way we mean this is to have self-control. We have mentioned in previous chapters how hard it is to control our inner world, and we have offered a number of tools to try and gain mental and emotional balance while trading. We have also identified various personality types and their respective approaches to trading. We suggested that some trading types favor feeling more in control and, therefore, are less risk-taking than other types.

Because self-control is so important to the process of being a good trader and investor, in this chapter we will focus on the two basic modes of control, and strategies for employing them during and after trading.One of the reasons this topic warrants attention is that it is readily apparent that there is so much having to do with online trading in the financial markets that is out of our personal control.

Here is a sampling of the variables that as online traders we may experience as—or in fact are—beyond our personal control. Some of these are short-term conditions which may eventually come under control with further knowledge and experience. Others will never be in our power to accurately predict or to influence and may come suddenly and without warning:

■ *Feeling out of control of technical aspects of hardware and software.* Examples: How to find the right keys under pressure? How to make sense of all the real-time data filling the monitor? How to keep up on all the news of the markets when things are changing so rapidly? How to determine what news and data really matters and what isn't crucial? How to gain enough knowledge to make the data most useful for trading? How to make all the hardware function smoothly? How to know which trading software is right—not too sophisticated, not too simple? How to deal with technical glitches and system crashes in the middle of trades? How not to get caught up in obsessive "tweaking" of software, monitors, hardware? How not to blame hardware and software for poor trades?

■ *Physical and mental fluctuations while trading.* Fluctuations such as sleepiness, pain, distraction by outside noise, commotion, and interruptions. How to deal with periods of preoccupation with other life issues? How to cope with mental laziness? How to keep from making poor trading decisions when swept up in various passing moods, lapses of concentration, or fuzzy thinking? How to keep from letting too much anxiety, caffeine, sugary foods, or other substances give us an "itchy trigger finger" when trading?

■ *News events that come out of nowhere*. Events to jar a stock, like the resignation or death of a key officer; financial improprieties in record keeping; production problems; rumors of a buyout or merger; legal problems that become public; analyst upgrades or downgrades; insider buying or selling; and various other company intangibles, such as false or true rumors, that may move the stock.

■ *Perceptual discrepancies between company value and stock price*. You cannot control the perception Wall Street may have of a company and whether or not analysts choose to cover it, "pound the table" for it, or whether institutions are willing to get behind it. Some fundamentally good companies wither until they receive analyst and institutional support.

As individual online traders and investors, we have no control (and often no knowledge until after the fact) of all the behind-the-scenes gyrations being exercised by governmental agencies, company insiders, analysts, brokerages, arbitrageurs, venture capitalists, institutions, and any other significant Wall Street influence that helps move the markets. Despite real-time news, we are the very smallest piece in a very large puzzle and still the last to know the latest news of their machinations.

■ *Earnings reports*. Reports that meet analysts' consensus estimates but fall a penny or more short of the "whisper" number; reports that meet the consensus and then hit the whisper number but are followed by a less than stellar conference call; next quarter projections not meeting or exceeding present quarter; analyst interpretation of report and call and any upgrades or downgrades based upon them; any comments made by the "axe."

The axe is the most important analyst, by virtue of strong interest in the stock through either participating in underwriting or his or her research department following the sector and the company closely. The axe has gained influence through tenure, previous correct predictions, timely and influential connections to company management, and gaining the confidence of institutional money managers. When the axe speaks, everyone listens.

■ *Natural catastrophes*. Catastrophes like an earthquake in Taiwan that threatens to slow down around-the-clock production in a slightly damaged plant half-way around the world but immediately brings down the stock price of Dell Computer.

- *Economic statistics and reports.* Reports of the most bland and esoteric kind that in the broader scheme of things are relatively unimportant but can shake a jittery market. These short-term reports sometimes have an inordinate impact on the market when traders are looking for the least signs of a changing economic climate such as whether the economy is heating up, etc.

- *Any direct or indirect, live or delayed utterances of the all-knowing and all-powerful Oz.* Fed Chairman Alan Greenspan, arguably the single most powerful mover of financial markets in the free world. To a lesser degree, comments and proclamations made by other "Fed-heads" (members of the Federal Reserve Board).

- *Seasonal patterns of buying and selling within a sector or whole market.* For example, retail during the holiday season; strong technology sector in the fall; tax-loss selling toward the end of the year; "January effect," superstitious beliefs about anniversaries of past market crashes, etc.

- *Unpredictable , arbitrary, and gratuitous mentions.* Comments by CNBC commentators or guests that can immediately influence buying or selling by both traders and investors, rumors, touts by guests, innuendo by analysts, general emotional demeanor about market when things are good or bad and how this demeanor is projected to listening audience.

- *Trying to predict trend direction.* A stock in a fast market, where prices are moving so fast that you won't be guaranteed anything by anyone at any price. In the world of stocks, nothing is more chaotic and out of our control than a fast market, motivated by panic buying or selling.

- *International economic, business, and political news events.* Such events may not be immediately relevant to the U.S. market but are acted upon first by traders in a knee-jerk fashion who ask questions later.

Because of all of these concerns, we need to be able to clearly recognize what we can and can't control, and how to deal with all these variables that are truly out of our control. To do this, we must have a view of control, and specifically a *yielding* mode of control, that is positive and actually helps us feel *more* in control.

Even if it is not our more common mode of actively working to effect change and to feel more in control, we must begin to understand the paradoxical nature of the positive yielding form of control. We must see that the acceptance of that which is out of our control may be done in a way that actually makes us feel more in control.

MODES OF CONTROL: ASSERTIVE AND YIELDING

Research and the clinical experience of psychologists suggest there are two basic modes that people use to gain and maintain a sense of control. The first is an active, assertive, mastery mode and the second is a yielding, accepting mode (Shapiro and Astin, 1998).

It is common to think of control as only the first type—active effort to gain mastery of ourselves, others. and the environment. We want to actively do something to influence the situation. Or we want to see others do what we want them to do. We think of this active form of control as being strong, assertive, and engaged in problem solving. And it is.

We tend to contrast this active mode with a passive, negative, and resigned "giving up" mode when we feel that we have too little control and are unable to do anything to gain more control. Yielding, because we fight against it, ends up feeling like a total *lack* of control. This is due to not having developed a way to reframe it in addition to our own Western cultural belief about the meaning of control.

Eastern psychologies and philosophies focus far more favorably on gaining a sense of control through the yielding mode, rather than the Western assertive mode. The interplay of asserting and giving in, active effort and effortless withdrawal, are viewed as complementary and both necessary parts of a whole. When one won't get the job done, oftentimes the other will. And this is especially true when it comes to gaining a sense of self-control while trading and investing in the financial markets.

In addition to our negative bias against the yielding mode, we go on to believe that disciplined investors want to have as much active control as possible, doing everything in their means to make things go the way they want them to go. We take "discipline" to mean active, assertive control, either by active doing or by active *not doing*. Both have the quality of effort attached to them.

What I mean by active not doing is that we include in this active control mode the ability to refrain from taking action, such as not impulsively jumping in to buy a stock that we don't know anything about. But even this holding back we view as an active, assertive self-restraint of our own part through "will power," or "self-discipline." My point is, it is still an active, attempt to control ourselves. And all active attempts are fine when appropriate but miss the mark when they're not.

We can as traders schedule our time precisely around preparing for the market, follow our schedule of news gathering to be ready for the open, stay focused on the screen, and develop a trading plan and follow through with it. We can diligently prepare and use our time wisely, doing only what we have planned to do in our trading, following all our limits and stop losses. This gives us a sense of control of our trading behavior, at least to some degree. We can actively and purposely pursue trading goals with enthusiasm, energy, and courage to face the unknown. Isn't this a reasonable facsimile of what the investment world refers to as "discipline and self-control"? Becoming master of our own investment destiny, right? And it is certainly valuable for those areas where this kind of self-control can help us meet our goals.

But all of this is just half of the control picture. And from an Eastern perspective, it isn't even the most interesting half. The more psychologically sophisticated online investor will begin to see that he or she must, in addition to the active mode, be able to feel in control through a deep acceptance of that which can't be controlled.

Again, I don't mean a fighting back of our impulses through a lot of effort. And I certainly don't mean the negative form of yielding, which is defeated resignation. I'm talking about actively and even enthusiastically giving in when it is clear that the assertive mode is inappropriate or ineffective. And then feeling the sense of control that goes with it.

While we may not be able to influence the events of the market the way we would like, we can influence our *attitude* toward them. And it is here that the positive yielding mode of control has much to offer the online trader and investor.

The limited way trading classes and books have approached this is by saying that we should have a "positive attitude" about trading. If we are positive, we are told, we will understand that things will not always go our way but we will not be too disappointed. Being positive will help us approach each new trading day with interest and even passion. So far, so good.

But we are talking about more in this concept of positive yielding than just establishing and maintaining a positive attitude. Sometimes being positive is being out of touch with the immediate reality on the monitor! We are talking about controlling our own inner state despite what may appear to be outward chaos. So, the stock takes a dive; we don't like what we see on the monitor—nothing to be positive about, right? But we don't let what we are feeling interfere with our good judgment as to what action we may choose to take.

So, to repeat, it is not that we block out or expunge subtle feelings or even full emotions. It is that we are able to control (or regulate) how strong our emotions become. Further, we want to be able to mandate that our clear thinking be always at least a little stronger than our emotion.

One experienced scalper and swing trader put it like this: "I watch a stock nose dive when I've got 1000 shares on the line and I can feel fear or anger inside. But if you look at me you'll see no indication of how I feel. I do what I need to make the position work. Later, after the close, I might go outside and let out a yelp."

As all online traders and investors know, maintaining emotional equilibrium is tough to do. The very nature of emotion is that it is more powerful than thinking. We are, in a sense, swimming against the current in trying to go against the primacy of emotion. We are trying to develop what over a decade ago I called the *discriminating mind*, the mind that can stay one jump ahead of whatever emotional wave may wash over us. But this is the goal and the challenge—not, for most, the common reality. And, make no mistake about it, it is indeed a challenge.

The better we get at being able to do this, the less fear and greed (as we discussed in Chapters 3, 4, and 5) are likely to overwhelm us. To be able to consciously choose to drop into the mode of positive yielding and experience it not as negative, passive helplessness but as a position of strength and appropriate action is an important tool to have to call upon.

A sound-bite way to say this: We are graciously giving *in* but not giving *up*. We feel just as strong as if we had exerted active control.

One difficulty with operating only from an active, assertive mode of control lies in the grandiose belief that we can master aspects of the market that are actually out of our control. This promotes further inaccurate beliefs and the employment of ego defense mechanisms that take us away from what is really true.

These defenses include blaming the market, the market makers, the government, brokerages, software, or other people and denying facts that are clearly presented to protect our false pride in our decisions. Of course, without self-insight, we don't know that this is what we are doing. We then add the need to believe that we can find an order to the chaotic market, where there is, in actuality, no inherent, absolute order to be found (Shapiro and Astin, 1998).

Discerning Positive from Negative Yielding

Our Western cultural bias toward active control has made it difficult for many to view anything positive about the yielding mode of control. The clear distinction has not been made between *negative* yielding (passivity or too little control) and *positive* yielding (acceptance).

Since, as we itemized, there are so many variables of the financial markets that we can't control, we need to understand the value of the positive yielding mode; how to enter it with strength and confidence when we choose to adopt it, rather than feel even more out of control by framing it in a negative and disempowering way.

We can think of the active mode as having both positive and negative sides and the yielding mode as having the same. The positive side of active control would be to exert our best efforts to change those things that can be changed. The negative side would be to try and overcontrol ourselves or others, or to try and control things that just can't be controlled.

The yielding mode's positive side is learning to let go and accept those things that clearly are out of our control. And the negative side of this mode would be passively yielding when it is more appropriate to take assertive action, and when we feel too little control of those things of which we can actually have greater control.

The goal is to be able to use the positive control strategy (assertive or yielding) that is best for the situation, based on our desires, goals, and what is possible for the situation. Ideally, we want to be flexible in our ability to use both assertive and yielding modes of control and be able to get a sense of control when we are using either strategy. In addition, we want to develop an awareness of when desire for control has become excessive or misplaced.

We declared in Chapter 5 that we want to escape either/or thinking for the more flexible style of both/and thinking, which allows us to see how things can appear to be opposite but are actually complementary. Being able to see that both the positive, assertive mode and the positive, yielding mode are indeed complementary is an example of exercising both/and thinking.

Control Modes and Domains

We have distinguished between assertive and yielding modes of control and further divided each mode into a positive and negative form. Before presenting tools for working with each mode, we need to briefly give some online trading-related examples of each form, just to make the concepts clear.

Positive Assertive Mode

In this mode, we take active steps to control ourselves or the situation. Examples of areas we may wish to take assertive, positive control include the following areas or domains:

- *Time management,* including how much time in reading and preparation before the market opens, how long we stay with the market before taking breaks, how much time spent researching stocks in evenings or on weekends, time spent managing accounts, time allotted for other nontrading-related activities.

- *Procedural management,* including the sequence of actions before, during, and after trades; noticing thoughts and emotions arising before and during trades; ability to stay focused when watching quotes; ability to respond quickly when needed for executing trades; keeping journal entries of all trades and associated reactions, reflecting on bad trades for clues as to what to change; noticing habitual nervous, superstitious, or compulsive behaviors related to trading; managing volume of trades; building in triggers and anchors; ways of relating to others in seeking out, sharing, or withholding market-related information; and habits for tracking investments, reviewing positions, and limit setting.

- *Mind management,* including gaining greater control of thoughts and emotions through various tools presented, such as meditation, deep breathing, movement, inner dialogue, self-talk observation, thought-following, and witnessing from the observing ego. Working with fluctuations in attention during trading with the goal of being as present-centered as possible for as long as possible, then disengaging as needed.

- *Impulse management,* including any dietary substances while trading that may affect thinking, nervous system, emotions, and mental clarity. Controlling intake of food, caffeine, nicotine, glucose, and any drugs; keeping the body healthy and strong to cope with trading-related stresses; understanding the stresses of trading and how they may increase impulsive and compulsive behavior; obsessive thinking.

- *Knowledge management*, including learning computer platform operations, software operations, learning through reading, discussion, conferences, and experience various trading techniques, patterns of the market, individual and mass psychology, business and economic concepts that increase understanding of the context of the market, market-speak, trader-speak, and any other information and knowledge related to the functioning of the market that may be useful to trading and investing.
- *Environmental management*, including making trading space pleasing and functional enough to encourage and facilitate a positive approach to trading; manipulation of noise, clutter, other people, outside distractions to create optimal trading space for focused attention to the task at hand.

Negative Assertive Mode

All the areas mentioned at the start of this chapter are examples of potential traps of the negative assertive mode. Trying to control areas that can't be controlled, where the effort to control will only result in frustration, anger, disappointment, and resentment. Not being able to "go with the flow" of the market and to let the market's direction dictate trading rather than impose a plan on the market; not being cognizant and respectful of what the market is saying.

Trying too hard, overtrading, becoming addicted to trading, not being able to see the bigger picture through overassertion, demandingness. Trying to control family and friends when feeling irritated about losses. Reacting to feeling powerless and out of control by trying to overcontrol.

Positive Yielding Mode

Accepting losses gracefully; accepting not getting an IPO allotment, not getting in at the start of a market run-up; not getting your price met; being able to derive strength and comfort from giving in either by choice or by default, knowing that you're not giving up; allowing others to have their way when it doesn't compromise your self-respect or integrity; accepting the haphazard, random-walk aspect of the market rather than letting it drive you crazy and fighting against it; letting the market come to you; being comfortable making few trades or no trades; understanding that sometimes doing nothing is the best strategy and the best way of feeling in control. Accepting loss as an inevitable part of trading, no matter how skillful or experienced you might be.

Negative Yielding Mode

Feeling that we are losing control we had or helpless to gain control at all. Resignation, anger, frustration, and rage as reactions to not being able to effect change in our lives; having to accept unpleasant conditions against our own will.

"Learned helplessness" or giving up any attempts to gain control after repeated attempts to change one's life do not work; not doing homework to improve trading knowledge and techniques after a number of losing trades; giving in to depression and helplessness when money has been lost; passively letting losses mount up without getting outside help out of embarrassment, shame, and false pride.

Giving in to pressure of others to buy a stock on a tip, holding a stock longer than one wishes, staying invested when one wants to be in cash, or any number of other situations in which we give in against our own best judgment because of peer pressure, need for acceptance and approval, or fear of making our judgment independent of others; passively following the herd; not making the effort necessary to gain the skills needed to be successful.

The optimist-gullible trading type, presented in Chapter 2, is the most likely type to get caught in the negative yielding mode, although by no means is it a trap exclusively reserved for them.

CONTROL PROCESS AND TECHNIQUES

Now that we have distinguished between assertive and yielding modes of control and given examples of both positive and negative forms of each, we want to offer some strategies and techniques for working with the positive mode of asserting and the positive mode of yielding.

Whether we employ the active mode of control or the yielding mode, our strategies for control are to change the environment, change our behavior, or change our consciousness. All three of these strategies may be appropriate for the investor who wants to make changes toward greater control.

The Five-Step Process

To gain greater control in either mode, we need to satisfy a five-step process that has been identified by a number of research and clinical psychologists (Shapiro and Astin, 1998). It is due to a breakdown somewhere in this process that we are unable to effect the changes that we say we want to make. We will list the steps incorporating each mode of control, realizing that what is imbalanced on one side of the equation will be imbalanced in the opposite direction on the other side. The five-step process is made up of the following:

1. We must start with the *desire* for greater control. At this point, we need to focus on our choices, goals, and options. From the assertive mode, when our motivation is too low, we need to find a way to increase it or we never make the effort. If we are trying to gain control from the yielding mode, we must admit that we are overcontroling or that our desire can be too high for control.

2. The second step is believing we have the *right* to change, to act assertively, and that we are responsible for exercising our right for greater control. The whole movement of assertiveness training for women began with helping them believe they had the right to be more assertive in their lives. Often people are not sure they have the right to change, especially when they feel unworthy of having what they want.

On the yielding side, we may need to challenge our excessive belief in our right to control. The person who manipulates others and is insensitive to their needs often has an excessive belief in the right to anything he or she wishes in controlling others.

3. The third step is our *belief in our ability* to make assertive changes. Do we believe we can control our inner world? Do we believe we can gain greater control in the outer world? "Learned helplessness" comes about because of the resignation that we don't believe we have the ability to gain greater control over the external world.

On the yielding side, we need to increase our belief that we can learn to let go and accept those things that are out of control; that we can let go of chronic resentment and passive-aggressive ways of showing others that we want to be in control. We must also challenge any overblown beliefs we have in our belief to actively control others and the environment.

4. The fourth step is having the *commitment and skill* to make the changes toward greater control. We may have the belief that we will do something but not necessarily have the commitment to follow through with it. Along with commitment, we must also know how to use the tools to gain greater control—we must have the skill to perform the task.

5. The last step is the *recognition of success* at gaining greater control and feeling the sense of competence and mastery that goes with this recognition. We must clearly register any changed thoughts, feelings, or behaviors so we may reinforce ourselves for our efforts, making it easier to take on new challenges in other areas we may wish to change.

In the positive yielding mode, recognition of success means realizing the actual sense of control that goes with true acceptance of that which we can't change. It is important to recognize that this acceptance is relaxed and with relief—and not a forced, effortful holding back out of frustration of not being able to employ the assertive mode of control. This forced holding back is what I earlier termed a *not-doing doing*.

Assessment and Goal Setting: Examples

Assuming we have the desire for greater control, believe we have the right to have control, and believe we have the ability to make the changes, what else do we need to know to gain control? We need to have the skills, or tools to put into practice that which will achieve our goal. To set our goal, we first need to know what we want to change, which control mode is appropriate, and how we will measure our goal.

What is it we wish to gain greater control of? Let's say we feel out of control in using trading software and hardware and want to feel more competent. Beginners will, without exception, feel overwhelmed and out of control when they first encounter Level II data. Between real-time tick charts, various interval S&P futures graphs, time and sales data rapidly scrolling down the screen, a real-time portfolio tracker, and two or more Level II boxes with various colors being "eaten up" so fast you can barely discern what's happening, the common initial reaction is to sit dumb-founded at what is flickering across the screen!

So how will we tackle this? We decide that there is just one way to go: the positive assertive mode. Specifically, we decide we will gain greater control by watching and learning the software in mock trading for five hours. If we can't do mock trading, we will sit through at least one or more complete market session watching the indices and gaining an understanding of what the numbers mean. We also determine that we will seek assistance in interpreting the data from someone who knows the software and can explain the intricacies of its use.

The goal of knowing the software will be met when we are able to use it in real-time trading without hitting any wrong keys, which is objective and measurable.

We also decide that a second condition of reaching the goal is a loss of feeling overwhelmed and a growing comfort and familiarity, such that the software begins to feel like an aid, rather than a burden. This is a subjective judgment but one which can be reasonably determined as to whether we have met it. This is an example of an area in which the assertive mode of taking control by doing is appropriate to meet the goal.

Here is a second positive, assertive mode example. Let's say Janice, 44, an active trader at home for about a year, comes in and tells me she has developed a case of "trader's block." Although normally not an issue, suddenly she finds that pulling the trigger to enter a trade becomes problematic, fraught with fear and anxiety. She knows what she wants to trade and the price she want to trade it at. But when she goes to enter the trade, she shies away and can't seem to muster the courage to execute. She feels out of control.

We decide that in order to figure out what the block is about we will review how she has been feeling about previous trades. After a cursory review of her journal of trades and how she was feeling when she made them, it becomes obvious she made some bad trades that she wasn't sure about. She got burned, losing more than she was comfortable with.

In talking to me, Janice further realized that she was hesitant to tell anyone about the losing trades, because the amounts she lost were more than she was used to, and— truth be told—more than she could afford. She waited two months after she had the idea to consult me before actually coming in. Janice knew she was losing more than she could afford because she had set a daily amount that she could lose and not jeopardize her capital for other trading days. So, she was feeling embarrassed and ashamed, shown by not wanting anyone, including me, to know how many losing days she had sustained. And she was scared because she had lost too much, not paying attention to her established limits.

In addition, Janice was now doubting her skills because she felt she had some knowledge of the stocks she was trading. She had done her homework. But the trades, as they are apt to do, went against her anyway and she was now feeling gun-shy. This resulted in feeling paralyzed to make any further trades.

This trader's block was actually an alert from Janice's voice of fear, telling her she was in danger of losing precious capital that could not be risked. Fear's way of stopping her for a while was to paralyze her from being able to pull the trigger to execute any further trades.

The steps taken to regain a feeling of control were to respect the trader's block rather than struggle against it. I suggested Janice go for a period of days without trading, just watching the market or staying away from it altogether. She chose a little of each. She would check in to see how the market was going but also would take long breaks away from it.

Secondly, I taught Janice a deep breathing method to help her deal with the fear response that was coming up and causing her block. I had her visualize the trading situation and being ready to execute the trade. I asked her to let the anxiety come up that had stopped her from pulling the trigger. At the same time, while feeling the anxiety, I instructed her in a deep breathing technique to help her feel in control and to gain control of her physical response as well as her thoughts. I helped her neutralize her fear thoughts by offering some things to remember to counter them with.

Next, I discussed with her the idea that for a while she would need to proceed very cautiously to regain her confidence in her trading ability.

I suggested she trade in small-share amounts only, slowly building back up her confidence by a number of good trades. She accepted this suggestion and was willing to comply with it.

Within two weeks, Janice was feeling more confident and her anxiety was under control. The breathing technique helped her face her fear. She used it whenever she began to get anxious, allowing her to go ahead and resume trading after one week. After one month of smaller trades, she had recovered the amount she had lost.

Janice made a pact with me not to try to hide her losses from me and to come back in periodically for consultation so that we could review how she was doing. In the meantime, I asked her to let me know if she had any further problems by way of e-mail. She did, in fact, e-mail me a couple of times just to let me know she was continuing to feel more in control. I tried to impress upon her how important it was not to let shame and embarrassment lead her to withdraw from facing the reality of out-of-control trading losses.

Control Techniques in the Midst of Battle

In previous chapters we have already discussed techniques for working with changes of consciousness, which is the realm of our thoughts and emotions. We have also offered tools for altering the trading environment in the form of how to set up a home office space and to use it for shaping and reinforcing trigger and anchoring behaviors.

We have implicitly assumed that utilizing these tools would lead to a higher sense of personal control. But we will now more directly frame the following techniques in the context of gaining personal control.

We will emphasize how we may work with the positive yielding mode, since most of the tools offered—with the exception of meditation—have been from the active, assertive mode. Meditation is a powerful method that strengthens the ability to accept internal and external events that are beyond our control. It is therefore a very appropriate tool in heightening our ability to enter the positive yielding mode more easily and, once there, to end up feeling a greater actual sense of control.

Diaphragmatic Breathing

This type of breathing is associated with relaxation. It is a useful technique for periods of feeling anxious or out of control of our thoughts. Obsessive thoughts about trades, losses, or any other situation where we feel out of control can often be neutralized with diaphragmatic breathing. It is especially useful during market anxiety when we do not have the time or quiet setting to practice meditation. It is an "in the heat of the battle" tool that can make a difference.

Here are the instructions: Placing your hand on your abdomen with fingers barely touching, let the air come in through your nose without any effort to force it. As the air comes, notice how your stomach inflates slightly and your fingers move apart a little. As you exhale through your nose, notice that your fingers come back together. Take a few minutes to practice letting the air come in and watching your stomach inflate. Each time you exhale, your stomach returns to its original position. Don't force your breathing in any way, just let it come and go on its own. If you can stay with this for a few minutes, it will have a calming effect.

This form of breathing is too good to be confined just to controlling emotional states and thoughts during trading. You can use it any time you begin to feel flustered as a chance to literally "catch your breath" and to get back a sense of control. I should mention that sustained meditation practice actually habituates us to this form of breathing as our common mode, so that any other form (thoracic or chest breathing) seems uncomfortable.

Mental Scan

Like the thought-watching meditation offered in Chapter 5, the mental scan helps us focus attention on what thoughts we are using to feel out of control. Using diaphragmatic breathing as an anchor, we close our eyes and pay attention to any thoughts or subtle feeling states that may arise. We don't try to push any unpleasant thoughts away or change any feelings. We simply pay attention to what is there.

Are you having a reaction to the market that is not quite clear? Try and stay with it long enough to identify it. If you notice an obsessive thought that is market related, ask yourself: What function is this repetitive thought serving by not going away? What might it be trying to tell you? Is it giving you a warning about some action you are thinking about taking? Is it related to a past action? Is it related to a feeling about a stock you are watching?

Sometimes our previous trades with a specific stock will come to mind to scare us as we are watching its movement or thinking about trading it. See if you can determine the message of any obsessive thought so that you can let go of it. Obsessive thoughts are your mind's way of telling you to pay attention! Something needs to be attended to before it will go away.

This mental scan is not only useful to help us disengage from the monitor but also helps us pinpoint what we may be telling ourselves to feel out of control. The breathing method will then help calm us from any obsessive thinking and help us notice how jumping into the future with our thoughts creates anxiety.

Any time we can come back into the present, we can feel more control, as we give up rumination for the bad trade 20 minutes ago or the anticipated bad trade 10 minutes from now. The mental scan technique can be seen as a "minimeditation" when there is insufficient time or inclination to give to a more extended meditation.

Yielding in the Midst of the Trading Battle

The yielding mode balances the assertive change tools by helping us feel satisfied and accepting of things as they are. Market news comes that happens to turn one of our stocks down. We can get upset, fight it, panic and sell the stock, or sit back and let the wave of emotion wash over us without the need to do anything.

We give in to the market movement that is beyond our control. Sometimes the news will help our stocks and sometimes it will bring them down. That's the nature of news moving the market. Can we accept it, give in to it, without feeling out of control? It is not our right to always have the market go our way. But this doesn't stop many from acting as if it is. We must bend, accommodate, and go with the flow of the market, whether we like it or not.

The stock market, like life itself, is obviously in flux and constantly changing. If we take the first hour or two of the market as the trend for the day, we will not be prepared to swiftly shift gears when the tide turns in the other direction, as it so often does. By yielding to these moves and trading with them, we find control by not fighting these waves of change.

Think about the strategies you use to cope with other areas of life over which you have no control. It might be waiting in line at the bank, waiting for a traffic signal, standing in line to buy a sandwich, or at a checkout counter at the market. Everyday, common experiences of not having the world move just at the pace we might want it to.

Each of these experiences may be viewed as an opportunity to let go of control, allowing things to be just the way they are. We can get upset, impatient, and aggravated. Or we can use the wait to slow down and pay attention to our inner world. We could even use the break as a chance to close our eyes and meditate, or scan our thoughts.

Personally, if I do not close my eyes when I have this kind of break, I am bending and stretching, using the break to get back in touch with my body. I don't think about this any longer. I just do it. It helps me slow down and be more accepting of the wait in front of me without feeling like I'm "wasting" my time.

What makes yielding in the heat of the trading battle tough to do is that we are primed to be in control. All our data, speedy computer, everything coming at us—we use it all so we can feel in control and trade confidently. It is a skill to be able to drop into the yielding mode when it becomes clear that no matter what technology we have at our disposal, we still are going to have numerous periods of feeling out of active, assertive control. It is at these times we have a choice to either fight the tide with annoyance and frustration for the trade not going our way or to accept it and move on.

Self-Statements That Facilitate Yielding

Here are some self-statements that can be used to make positive yielding easier:

- The market will not fall apart if I let go and stop trying to control it.
- Even while trading, I have a right to take breaks to let go and not fight the tape or myself.
- I can trade only so long before I need to take a break and clear my mind.
- When I yield I can feel strong and in control; I don't have to feel passive just because I yield.
- I can use the traffic signs that read "yield" to remind me that just as I can give way on the road and still feel in control, so can I yield when trading and feel in control.
- There are times when making no trades at all makes me feel totally in control.
- I will yield to other trader's panic, stepping out of the way, rather than getting caught up in an active attempt to change the market.
- I will not actively chase a stock in desperation, thinking I must be in on it today; I will remember there will always be another chance to get in and allow the stock to come back to my price. When I hold back like this I feel in control and am showing strong discipline.
- To balance the speedy pace and stress of trading, I will make a point of having balancing activities where I slow down and allow things to unfold without grasping. I will not let the pace of the market become the pace of my whole life.

Balancing the Active and Yielding Modes

The active and yielding modes are used as needed: the active to help us feel more control of those areas in which we can actively do something to enhance our sense of control, and the yielding in those areas in which there is nothing we can do except give in and accept *what is*. Sometimes we will use the modes together in gaining control, one before the other. Other times they may work to counterbalance each other.

Like the Chinese concept of yin and yang—each needing the other to complete the whole—active and yielding modes of control, each contains aspects of the other within it. For example, it takes a lot of effort and discipline to let go and be more accepting of what is. In the same way, it is during periods of quiet reflection that we often realize it is time to make assertive change.

The positive yielding mode makes it more likely that our assertive change strategies will not lead to negative assertive overcontrol. Also, skillfully using the positive assertive mode helps ensure that a positive yielding approach in gaining control does not result in passive resignation (Shapiro and Astin, 1998).

We can do everything possible to learn about trading, stocks, business, and economics issues that make us informed and skillful traders and investors. At the same time, we need to realize that with all our knowledge, we will miss certain news, certain moves in the market, and make some wrong trading decisions based on limited information.

We can second-guess ourselves every trading day when we look back and see what we could have done differently. But this kind of wishful thinking and ruminating on what could have been isn't going to be as effective as learning how to let go and move on to the next opportunity.

We need to stay flexible and ready to change direction, even as we pursue our trading goals with positive, assertive steps to gain more personal control. We need to work toward realizing these goals while staying open to changing them along the way or even giving them up altogether.

This is the exquisite and paradoxical dance of self-control. And those traders and investors who learn the psychological steps well will still be standing on the dance floor when the music of the gyrating market has been silenced for the day by the closing bell.

Trading Perfection or Trading Excellence?

The conscious or unconscious desire to be the perfect trader pervades the live trading floors and electronic networks of the financial marketplace. Institutional and independent money managers want to be the best, to have the top performing fund in their sector. And, of course, individual online investors want every trade to make a profit. The whole financial world speaks a market language of "winners" and "losers." Everyone wants to make a bet on the winning stocks—for the day, the month, the quarter, and the year.

The fear of making mistakes, losing money, and feeling incompetent as traders holds back many from taking the assertive steps necessary toward gaining greater knowledge and self-control in managing their money that we focused on in the last chapter. These fears stop significant numbers of those who already surf the Internet from learning how to extend their online experience to stock trading. Once they have become initiated into the world of online trading, these same fears hold them back from becoming more passionate and sophisticated investors.

As mentioned in the preface, one of the purposes of this book is to help online investors gain more of the psychological knowledge they need to successfully manage their own accounts. One piece of this knowledge is confronting this desire to be perfect. This desire is so deeply ingrained in our culture and our psyches that some psychologists believe it is even genetically programmed as one of the mental templates (or archetypes) with which we are born. Let's begin by giving a simple definition of a perfectionistic investor.

A perfectionistic investor is someone who thinks that anything short of perfection in his or her trading is unacceptable.

Of course, it is not so much that we say to ourselves, "I want to be the perfect investor." It is more that our thinking and behavior reveal this as an underlying desire. In addition, in our performance as investors, we blur the important distinction between perfection seeking and striving for excellence.

The desire to be perfect may lead to paralyzing fear in the form of trader's block. Or it may led to foolhardy risks in the attempt to prove to ourselves and others how skilled we are. In this chapter, we will define the perils of perfectionism as they relate to online trading and we will make it crystal clear to you how perfection seeking differs from pursuing trading excellence. I want the difference between perfection and excellence to be etched into your mind so that it can never be forgotten.

The personality styles and trading types we explored in Chapter 2 are all infused by the desire to be perfect investors. For example, the obsessive-disciplined, of all the types, is most likely to suffer from perfectionism, with fears of loss that hamper reasonable risk taking and the willingness to make mistakes. While they exhibit many of the positive, disciplined behaviors required for good trading, they also are susceptible to ritualistic habits and compulsive behaviors that lessen their effectiveness.

The timid-doubter is unsure, always wanting more data, never comfortable making trading decisions based on incomplete information, even when it may never be available. They are timid because they can't take decisive action. And they are doubters because they can't stand the thought of making a mistake. Perfect investors, they think, don't make mistakes.

The gambler-impulsive jumps in head first and always at the deep end of the trading pool. They are trying to prove to themselves and to others how good they are and to satisfy their narcissism to be the best by making the biggest splash and the most money. At least they're not afraid to get their feet wet.

The optimist-gullible type wants to believe that positive, wishful thinking will translate into being a great investor. When they realize they aren't going to be perfect, they try and find a money manager, a full-service broker, newsletter guru, or someone else they think might be. And the victim-blamers know they're not perfect traders but can't stand the thought that somewhere out there someone else might be.

Disciplined online investors have to walk a fine line. They have to stay balanced on what I have called the "razor's edge," between trying to excel without falling into the trap of perfectionism. Often, they are viewed as one and the same. So let's try and be very clear on the crucial ways they differ.

ARE YOU A PERFECTIONIST?

Here are some of the characteristics of perfectionistic thinking:

- The perfectionist is motivated not by the desire for improvement but by the fear of failure.
- The perfectionist tends to view the world in all-or-nothing terms.
- The perfectionist has a large number of severe self-commands.
- The perfectionist tends to focus on the negative in a situation and not on the positive.
- The perfectionist is quick to jump to conclusions based on inadequate information. This leads to interpreting situations in a negative way without taking the time to gather sufficient information to warrant the judgment.
- Perfectionists, although often as critical of others as they are of themselves, tend to blame themselves for what is not their doing. For example, they may blame themselves for entering a stock position that goes down soon after they buy due to a news event that could not be anticipated.
- Hard-core perfectionists have obsessive-compulsive tendencies. As we have discussed with the obsessive-disciplined trader type, these tendencies have both an upside and a downside when it comes to online investing.

STRIVING FOR EXCELLENCE

We can help clarify the distinction between perfectionism and seeking excellence by describing the healthy characteristics of the person striving for excellence. As you consider these, think how they may relate to your investing behavior as well as other areas of your life. The person striving for excellence is:

- Able to accept less than a perfect trading performance without feeling inadequate.
- Able to not only feel acceptance but, in addition, derive personal satisfaction and pride from a good enough performance.
- Motivated by the joy of achievement and the challenge of reaching an investing goal rather than driven by the fear of failure and disapproval from others.
- Able to appreciate and enjoy successive steps achieved toward the investing goals as significant in themselves rather than stay focused only on the end goal of a specific return.
- Able to remember and utilize previous accomplishments to build a reservoir of self-confidence and self-esteem as support when taking on new challenges.
- Able to not only accept but feel sympathetic joy for the accomplishments of others without feeling envious or diminished by the others' success. Sympathetic joy is the feeling of sharing the other's accomplishment based on the ability to identify with the other in a positive, caring way, beyond the cut-throat, trader-against-trader mentality.
- Able to transcend exclusively making their identity, self-esteem, and self-worth dependent on personal performance and accomplishments.
- Able to take on tasks, play sports, games, and amusements for their entertainment value, doing their best, but without turning them into a competition with others.
- Able to lose gracefully and be a good sport without needing a rematch or walking away feeling that their self-worth has been diminished.
- Able to overcome depression and feelings of anxiety, hostility, anger, and resentment when they don't come out ahead.
- Able to enjoy their accomplishments without having to boast or put others down.
- Able to demonstrate a sense of modesty and humility, a sense of perspective on their own accomplishments. For traders, this means realizing they can do well one day, one week, or one month but their fortune may change very fast,

so they should not get complacent nor become overconfident, leading to unreasonable risks.

THE HENDLIN PERFECTIONISM INVENTORY (HPI)

If you are not sure whether you are a perfectionist, or want to determine how perfectionistic you are compared to others, take the following inventory, which was originally created as a tool for my 1992 book on perfectionism, *When Good Enough Is Never Enough*.

Instructions: For each statement, fill in the blank with the number from the following scale that best describes how you feel. Don't go back and change any answers and try not to ponder your answers for more than 20 seconds.

0 = I disagree strongly.   3 = I agree somewhat.
1 = I disagree somewhat.   4 = I agree very much.
2 = I feel neutral about this.

---

1. I think of myself as a perfectionist.
2. I take pride in telling others that I'm a perfectionist.
3. I am easily annoyed when others don't measure up to my expectations.
4. If I can't do something well, there is no reason to try it at all.
5. I am hard on myself when I lose a game, contest, or competition.
6. I set very high goals for myself no matter what I'm doing.
7. I like my material possessions in order and get upset when they are disturbed.
8. I like my work place very neat and clean and find it hard to work if it is disturbed.
9. I have trouble accepting the fact that others don't expect as much from themselves as I expect from myself.
10. I get angry when people I care about don't perform up to my expectations.
11. I get impatient and annoyed when I have to waste time because of others' incompetence.
12. I find it hard to accept how people can do such sloppy work and get away with it.

13. I can't imagine ever thinking I am too thin.
14. I don't like to have to be a beginner at learning something new.
15. I like to teach others the very best way to do something.
16. Striving for perfection keeps me performing at my best.
17. It is hard for me not to zero in on the inadequacies of other people.
18. It disturbs me that the world isn't a more fair place than it is.
19. If I couldn't excel at and be acknowledged for at least one thing I do, I don't think I could live with myself.
20. I often think to myself how other people are "idiots" when they make mistakes or don't perform as I think they should.
21. I get paralyzed by procrastination when it comes to tackling new tasks.
22. I hate to admit feeling envy when I find out someone I feel competitive with has achieved something I haven't.
23. Once I make a mistake, I should never make it again.
24. When someone does something better than me, I tend to silently berate them and minimize their accomplishment.
25. When something about my character is criticized by someone, I feel attacked and tend to get defensive.
26. I feel shame when I don't measure up to the goals I have set for myself.
27. When my work is criticized, I feel injured and humiliated.
28. When others I know get awards and recognition, I feel left out.
29. I feel very frustrated when I can't express my good ideas perfectly.
30. I get a perverse feeling of satisfaction in watching those with whom I feel competitive lose or fail, especially if they are losing to me.
31. I prefer the perfect world of my inner thoughts and fantasies to the outer world of human error and folly.
32. Those who are close to me tell me I expect too much of myself.
33. An average performance is not good enough for me.
34. People in my life don't seem to appreciate my special skills and talents.

35. Compliments on my physical appearance are important to me.

36. When my life is not in perfect order, I get anxious and do whatever is necessary to get things back in place.

37. If I don't wear exactly the right clothes for an occasion, I feel embarrassed.

38. Making jokes about others' foibles makes me feel superior to them.

39. It is hard for me not to boast to others when I have done something well.

40. Most of the time I don't feel satisfied with how my body looks.

41. I sometimes imagine that when I die and go to heaven, everyone there will be perfect and all my needs will be perfectly satisfied.

42. My feelings of emptiness go away for a while when I stuff myself with food and/or mood-altering substances.

43. Getting attention in my family meant having to accomplish a lot.

44. I felt I had to earn my parents' love rather than be loved just for who I was.

45. Being hard on myself when I don't measure up will make me do better the next time.

46. Sometimes I wonder if someone like me belongs in this less-than-perfect world.

47. Sometimes I repeat something over and over until I get it just right.

48. At all times, I try as hard as I can to be morally and ethically correct.

49. I tend to judge my sexual performance and technique and wonder how I compare to other men or women my partner has been with.

50. Sometimes I wonder whether my spouse/boyfriend/girlfriend is the right partner for me and fantasize being with somebody more perfect.

51. I wonder how much others think about me and the private things they say about me behind my back.

52. I am proud of my overall body strength and muscle tone.

53. I can't stand doing anything partway—it's either all or nothing for me.

54. I like to fantasize how my life would be if I finally got the recognition and status from others that I justly deserve.

55. I don't like to be around people socially who aren't at the same level of accomplishment and social status as I am.

56. Sometimes I have dreams about others giving me recognition and treating me special.

57. I try to change my partner to make a good reflection upon me.

58. It really matters what others think about me.

59. The thought of giving up the standard of perfection that I have set for myself fills me with anxiety in that I wouldn't know what else to use to guide my behavior.

60. I feel driven to accomplish more and more in my life.

Scoring

Add up your score on all 60 items. Your score will fall somewhere between 0 (if you disagreed strongly with all 60 items) and 240 (if you agreed strongly with all 60 items). In taking an inventory of this type, there are various subjective factors involved (for example, truthfulness in answering the statements) and statistical factors that affect your score.

Because of this, your global, or "universe," score is probably in the range of 15 points above or below what you have calculated. You may want to consider this when drawing any conclusions as to where you fit. Calculate the following:

_____ Actual Score   _____ Low universe score

(subtract 15 points)

_____ High universe score

(add 15 points)

Interpretation of Scores

In using the interpretive guidelines presented here, please remember that (even taking into consideration your universe scores), any general statements made may not be accurate in your particular case. One inventory instrument alone is not in itself enough to draw any absolutely valid conclusions as to where you stand in relationship to perfectionism. The HPI has not been rigorously tested or validated with significantly large samples and is for experimental use only. Interpretations should only be used in a general way as an aid in gaining information on where you fit along the perfectionism scale.

If your total score for all 60 statements falls in the range of:

80 or less. Assuming you have answered the statements truthfully, you do not have a problem with perfectionism. While you appear to have escaped the push of our society to strive for excellence, you may be on the other end of the scale, possibly not expecting enough of yourself and not feeling sufficiently motivated. Depending on your chosen lifestyle and values, this may or may not pose a problem. Striving for excellence may not be of concern to you, nor may much of anything else!

81–120. Assuming you have answered the statements truthfully, you have a healthy degree of perfectionism. While you do not escape the values of our society, you do not overly pressure yourself to perform and may have learned to value yourself independently from your accomplishments. You can read this book for information and pleasure to learn what the hard-ball players are dealing with.

121–160. You have a mild (lower end) to moderate (upper end) degree of perfectionism. A score in the midrange of this category (140) means you had an average score for all items of 2.3, or only slightly stronger than neutral. This category indicates perfectionistic strivings that for the most part are in control, where you might have certain tendencies that are balanced by other nonperfectionistic attitudes and behaviors.

161–180. You have a moderate to high degree of perfectionism. A midrange score in this category (170) would mean an average of 2.8 for all items, clearly an indication that perfectionism is part of your thinking and behavior. You might be a high achiever who expects a lot of yourself. A moderate amount of your self-worth is determined by your accomplishments.

181–200. You have a high degree of perfectionism. You have gone beyond striving for excellence and definitely are ensnared in the trap of perfection. "Good enough" is never enough for you. You may have a driven need to succeed, and strong feelings about how you and others ought to be in this world. You are in touch with yourself enough to know that you are perfectionistic and very likely view perfection as your "standard of excellence." You may be anxious about giving up this guideline as you would not know what else to use in determining your self-worth.

201 and above. For most people, their worst nightmare. But for the hardcore perfectionist, just what you hoped for—on the HPI you have achieved the category of "perfect" perfectionism! Believe me, you don't want to hear any more of the interpretation for this category.

Not for Compulsives Only: Taking It a Step Further

Item and Cluster Analysis

The HPI can be broken down into seven clusters of statements, based on different aspects of perfectionism. Here are the seven clusters and their corresponding statement numbers:

- *Perfectionistic self-identification.* 1, 2, 16, 55, 59 (five items).
- *Narcissistic traits (superiority, grandiosity, envy, need for attention, etc.).* 14, 15, 17, 20, 22, 24, 25, 27, 28, 30, 34, 38, 39, 42, 51, 54, 56 (17 items).
- *Body image.* 13, 35, 40, 52 (four items).
- *Severe judgments of self and others.* 5, 11, 32, 45, 49, 50, 57, 60 (eight items).
- *Unrealistically high expectations of self and others.* 3, 6, 9, 10, 12, 18, 26, 33, 43, 44 (10 items).
- *All-or-nothing thinking.* 4, 19, 23, 29, 37, 53 (six items).
- *Obsessive-compulsive traits.* 7, 8, 21, 31, 36, 41, 46, 47, 48, 60 (10 items).

By examining your answers to specifics items within specific clusters, you can get a more exact idea of which aspects of perfectionism with which you tend to most strongly identify. Look especially at items you scored "4" in each cluster.

"NEVER ENOUGH" THINKING

Our list of perfectionistic traits in the beginning of this chapter dealt largely with how perfectionists think about themselves, the world, and others in a general way. The following list focuses on how the "never enough" mentality influences the way perfectionists think and behave around a specific issue of overwhelming importance to them: that of their own performance. As with the excellence list given earlier, when you read these, think how they may relate to your life in general. Then consider how they specifically relate to your approach to trading and investing.

The Goal Set Is Unrealistically or Even Impossibly High

Ron, who trades at home about once per week, tells me that he considers himself a "failure" because he has not been able to make money on more than two of the first 12 trades he makes online. Even though he does his due diligence before investing, his timing for entering positions has not been good. In addition, he is inadequately capitalized and ends up bailing out as soon as a stock drops a couple of points. And yet his unrealistic expectation is that he ought to be making a profit on every trade.

1. *Perfectionists cannot tolerate simply coming close to the goal.* They cannot tolerate anything less than hitting it on the nose. They leave little room for acknowledging and valuing gradual steps of successive approximation, or getting closer and closer to the goal with repeated practice. Coming close is the same as failing. This all-or-nothing thinking can lead to feelings of self-disgust, anger, regret, and make perfectionists blame themselves for the "failure."

2. *Perfectionists are not willing to be beginners.* They have little tolerance for the feeling of frustration that is natural to learning a new skill. They expect they ought to be able to perform perfectly from the very start. While they may realize this is irrational, they believe it nevertheless. If they can't learn a new skill immediately, they find some excuse for giving it up because they cannot tolerate feeling foolish and dependent. Perfectionists tend to avoid depending on others because they don't want to acknowledge their limits.

Unwilling to be beginners, they shy away from anything they have not already mastered. They don't like to be seen trying something new in public, where the potential for feeling embarrassment is even stronger. If they do let themselves try something new, they prefer to do so privately, where no one can witness their trial-and-error efforts. This helps explain, for example, why some who want to learn active trading at a day trading facility would never subject themselves to the imagined humiliation of learning in front of others.

Sometimes perfectionists rationalize their avoidance of trying anything new as a lack of interest. They would rather tell themselves and others they are simply "not interested" than admit their inability to risk vulnerable feelings of being a beginner. They need to believe that if they only had the interest, they could do anything well. And as long as they don't try new things, this belief is never put to the test.

3. *"Never enough" thinking often leads to procrastination.* When the perfectionist is willing to try something new, it may be only after long procrastination. Whatever initial excitement may have been aroused at the thought of trying something new is overcome by paralyzing fear of failure, possible humiliation, and feelings of shame.

Procrastination protects the perfectionist from the dread of the less-than-perfect result, which he or she views as failure. Fear of failure may also lead the perfectionist to procrastinate with more familiar tasks and projects, stifling creativity and holding the perfectionist back from what he or she most desires—achievement.

Procrastinators often rationalize their inability to face their fears of rejection and humiliation by all kinds of "good" excuses for not beginning a task. So, they not only avoid taking on threatening projects that may expose them to shame and humiliation, but avoid even the acknowledgment of the real reasons for their behavior. Because of this, it is necessary to first help procrastinators admit that, indeed, they are fearful of a catastrophic outcome. Once this fear can be acknowledged, it becomes possible to work more directly with catastrophic expectations and negative thinking.

4. *No matter how well perfectionists perform, they struggle to feel satisfied with the outcome. They feel an inner emptiness instead of the joy of accomplishment.* For example, Jason had only been trading at home part-time for a year. He had managed to make enough good trades to show a 30 percent profit. But he wasn't satisfied. He compared himself to other traders he talked to who were making hundreds of thousands of dollars per year.

Instead of letting himself feel good about beating the odds of losing the first year, all he could do was compare himself to experienced traders whom he considered the real "winners." He could not, therefore, allow himself to enjoy the good return on his trading that he had earned.

5. *Perfectionists are unable to savor the moment of accomplishment and unwilling to celebrate the event.* Upon returning from a trip to Europe and noticing the increase in cell phone usage, Michael does his due diligence on Nokia. After following the stock for a while, he decides to buy. Three months later, he has made a 60 percent return on his investment.

Not wanting to risk his profit, he decided to sell. Rather than allow himself to feel good about this trade, all he thought about was how he should have bought double the amount of shares. He worried that maybe it will keep going up and that he sold too soon. He also told me that it came too easy, that he didn't have to work hard enough for his gain. He didn't allow himself to enjoy the good trade he made. Because of this, he didn't use it to help build his sense of confidence for future trades.

This is the paradox of perfectionism: Perfectionists want things to be magically easy to accomplish, but at the same time they are mistrusting of themselves if they accomplish something too easily. Since they basically don't trust whatever talent they have, they are suspicious of anything that they don't have to work very hard to attain. This makes for a frustrating no-win situation—"If things come too easily, I won't value myself, yet I expect to be able to do everything expertly without much effort."

6. *The perfectionist often fears being found out as an impostor.* When he or she does temporarily measure up, the perfectionist only succeeds in pushing away the fear of failure for a while longer. This is part of the reason why the perfectionist feels so little true satisfaction and joy. Failure is always lurking just around the corner, with the next performance, promotion, or evaluation.

Fear of Being "Found Out"

This fear of failure is related to the perfectionist's often stated feeling of being a phony or feeling like an impostor. They feel they are deceiving others; that they are not as competent or worthy as they appear to be. Impostors know they will sooner or later be found out—it is only a matter of time. They almost wish it would be sooner so they could give up the anxiety-tinged charade.

For some perfectionistic online traders, one way this surfaces is the fear that steep losses and the deliberate attempt to cover them up will be discovered by others. Feelings of inadequacy and embarrassment block discussion when traders get in over their heads. Since the outcome in trading is very clear—making money or losing it—traders who exacerbate poor trades by borrowing on margin and getting further in debt may question their competence as a trader. They may feel like a phony, not a skilled trader or investor.

The fear of failure and being found out is so strong because the perfectionist lacks the inner self-worth that can sustain any type of criticism. To be less than perfect is to be fallible, to make mistakes. And when perfectionists make a mistake, they believe others will make the same harsh, rejecting judgments that they make toward themselves.

When the part of the perfectionists' self-concept that strongly identifies with this role of being perfect is confronted by the evidence that, to the contrary, they are fallible like everyone else, then following all-or nothing thinking, their inner critic believes that admitting mistakes means that they are not only less than perfect but incompetent and a phony. The reasoning goes like this: "If I think I am a perfectionist but really I am fallible, then I am a phony and my fallibility will be discovered and used to humiliate me. I'm really inadequate."

Perfectionists may also feel like impostors because they are able to create a surface picture of competence and control that covers their inner sense of confusion and turmoil. But as they achieve higher levels of responsibility, the fear of finally having their incompetence found out begins to crack the outer pretense of self-assurance.

The Driven Perfectionist and the "So What Have You Done for Me Lately?" Mentality

This type of thinking is generated both from within, as well as from the outward performance-oriented society.

Here are some examples of this pressure to perform without pause: Movie and TV stars who, no matter how many films or shows they have made, are "only as good as their last performance"; professional athletes quickly forgotten by the public if they don't stay on top; the author who may have had a best-seller two years ago but feels compelled to repeat his performance for his readers; the boss who makes it clear that the last big sale was great but, "Hey, that was two weeks ago, and what can you do for me today?"

The message is clear: "You're only as good as your last victory, sale, or performance. Don't stop—keep pushing for more." But this is heard and experienced by the perfectionist as, "You are only a good (lovable, worthwhile) person if you keep on performing. Don't stop now or you'll turn to dust." To stop performing is to diminish one's sense of self-worth, feel empty, and to have one's identity challenged to the core.

The competitive nature of our society sanctions this "what have you done for me lately?" mentality. It is never enough to set a record once or have one outstanding market performance year; we must do it repeatedly. And if we can't, sooner or later, we are sure to be viewed as nothing more than a vapor trail.

REDEFINING THE TERMS OF SATISFACTION

One aspect of perfection seeking that is not examined closely enough is the assumed connection between striving for perfect performance and the desire to feel satisfaction. We assume that the better we do something, the more satisfaction we will feel from doing it. While sometimes this is true, it is by no means a connection we can assume is *always* true.

An important step in giving up the pursuit of perfection is for us to break this long-held and unconsciously assumed connection. We must realize that it is possible to feel deep satisfaction with ourselves and our projects even when we don't perform perfectly. Because finding alternative routes to satisfaction is a key to letting go of perfectionistic standards, we will concentrate on tools to help us find these alternatives.

We experience satisfaction as a feeling of wholeness, completeness, pleasure, or integrity. It may come from many sources other than perfect performance: doing a job well, filling our inner emptiness, the finding of our true inner goodness and self-worth, winning the respect and admiration of others, or connecting with our own original perfect nature. Despite self-critical judgments of our performance, we continue to desire this satisfaction. Think about your answers to the following questions:

How much actual satisfaction do you get from the process of striving for perfection? And how much satisfaction do you derive from your actual accomplishments? When was the last time you experienced satisfaction because you actually measured up to your own perfectionistic expectation? For the sake of argument, let's say that you can actually remember when you last measured up to your standard and experienced a sense of satisfaction. Compared to the infinitely greater number of times you have felt nothing but frustration, self-torture, regret, and inadequacy, does it really seem worth the small chance of measuring up to subject yourself to all this turmoil? Aren't the odds of achieving satisfaction heavily stacked against you when you link satisfaction to perfection?

Can you imagine finding satisfaction in your projects and activities even when you do not perform perfectly? Try this simple visualization: Imagine a common situation in which you perform well but less than perfectly. See the actual outcome in your mind's eye and compare it to your image of the perfect performance. How different are the two? Are they so different that good enough performance should bring you any less satisfaction than some unrealistic state of perfection?

Now, using this same outcome, imagine feeling *very* satisfied with your performance, more than you would ordinarily allow yourself to feel. Notice that you have a choice as to how much satisfaction you feel over your performance.

Enjoying Less Than Perfect Performance

The connection between satisfaction (or pleasure) and perfection was made long ago, in childhood. For the most part we don't even think about it anymore. But the way we experience it is quite obvious: we feel less satisfaction and too much self-critical pessimism. The self-acceptance and satisfaction we could be enjoying is replaced by a self-critical sense of inadequacy. Instead of stroking ourselves gently with soothing gratification, we bat ourselves over the head for not being good enough.

For example, let's say your expectation of perfection involves how you play tennis. You have an image in mind as to what it would be like to play the perfect game. And you always end up feeling like you have fallen short, since your image of perfect tennis means committing no unforced errors. While you may occasionally play a match in which you have a few unforced errors, you may have never have played a match with none. Consequently, you have deprived yourself of feeling the amount of satisfaction with your performance that you would have felt had you lowered your expectation from perfection to excellence. More satisfaction might be possible if it were permissible to give yourself a healthy dose of good enough feeling for simply playing the best you could.

Your degree of satisfaction, then, is a matter of consciously giving yourself permission to feel more enjoyment and contentment with a less than perfect performance. How much satisfaction you feel about anything, including investing, is up to you. This can be reinforced by saying, "I will allow myself to feel a high degree of satisfaction with 10 or fewer unforced errors in any given match." The goal of

10 or fewer unforced errors can be defined as your standard of excellent performance. If you reach your goal, you will allow yourself to feel just as much satisfaction as if you had played with no errors.

You are going to be constrained in your ability to feel greater satisfaction by the restricting unconscious psychological programs of which you are unaware but that continue to exert powerful influence. And this is where the help of a good psychologist can be of added value to what you are able to accomplish on your own.

ASSIGNING GOOD-ENOUGH PERFORMANCE

In learning to break the connection between satisfaction and performance, it is helpful to keep a record of your degree of satisfaction in performing various activities. You can do this by recording various activities in which you assign a good enough performance rating to projects.

This exercise is helpful for two reasons. First, it encourages you to define and refine your expectations in realistic, attainable terms. Second, it helps you set up the conditions to give yourself approval and feel satisfaction upon achieving your goal. If you set your terms too high, you will see this clearly as you continue to keep your record. You can then lower your objectives accordingly.

This exercise forces you to realize the difference between perfect performance and good enough performance. It also allows you to feel satisfaction even when you don't measure up to good enough performance and even when you fall short of your goals and even when you don't think you will derive much satisfaction from an activity.

First, identify the activity. Then decide what you want your good enough performance to be. Put it in objective, measurable terms, if possible. After you have tackled the task, enter (as a percentage) how close you feel you came to achieving your good enough performance. And in the last column, estimate the degree of satisfaction (again as a percentage) that you derived from your performance of the task.

Working with this record form for a few weeks will help you think in terms of measurable performance until it becomes second nature. In this way, you are less likely to judge yourself as falling short simply because you don't feel like you have performed perfectly. It will require your subjective judgment in assigning a percentage score for how you measured up to your objective goals. And, of course, your assessment of how satisfying the activity was is also purely subjective.

What You May Gain

In working with this record form, you may discover the following:

- Performance is not always positively related to satisfaction.
- Performance in objective, measurable terms gives you something realistic to shoot for rather than an unreachable standard.
- You can equate good enough performance to excellence and need not be dependent upon the standards of others as to whether you have achieved excellence or not.
- Much more than you might think, it is possible to enjoy activities in which you don't measure up to perfection or even good enough performance.
- Most importantly, you can begin to see how much you control satisfaction and pleasure, regardless of the activity itself or the actual outcome of your performance.

"GOOD ENOUGH" AFFIRMATIONS

The following statements of affirmation should be repeated frequently during the day (either internally or out loud) as an aid in transforming perfectionistic thinking to excellence thinking. Affirmation statements put into positive words those beliefs that lend direction and support to a chosen goal. Obsessive-oriented perfectionists often do well with affirmations, because they tend to repeat various statements to themselves anyway in the effort to maintain self-control.

After reading the following list, choose one affirmation that feels right for you to focus on. Repeat it whenever you find yourself standing in line, driving, waiting for something, and other moments when your mind is not occupied. Sometimes, if you repeat it many times, you may find that the affirmation begins to repeat itself without any conscious effort on your part. Repeat the affirmation you choose for at least two or three days and then choose another one to focus on.

The value of these affirmations is that they may slowly begin to counter your unconscious, negatively programmed beliefs and help instill new, positive ones. Use these affirmations only in a constructive manner—do not become obsessed with any of them, keeping in mind they are only mental tools.

- Perfection is impossible; I will be satisfied with excellence.
- I am entitled to feel satisfaction without having to be the perfect investor.
- I will allow myself to feel deeper levels of satisfaction and pleasure.
- I will be open to and accept the feeling of being good enough.
- I will not judge others harshly for failing to live up to my standards.
- I will not make my self-worth depend on my performance.-
- I will note and neutralize as quickly as possible all critical self-talk.
- I will counter all critical self-talk with positive statements.
- I am a unique human being of value; my value can never be taken away.
- Since there is nobody in the world just like me, I need not compare myself to others to feel special.
- I need not compare my trading record with others to feel good.
- I am special simply because of my uniqueness.
- No matter how much I enjoy the profits I make from trading, I will not make my self-worth dependent upon always making more.
- Enjoying material comforts and possessions has nothing to do with my value as a human being.
- I am not less just because I might have less; I am not more just because I might have more.
- Momentary perfection comes as I settle into the present and accept myself as the best person I can be.
- I will continue to grow toward wholeness in every way possible.
- The pursuit of trading excellence will help me feel a sense of self-respect.
- I vow to give my best and most conscious effort to everything I do.
- When I fall short of good enough performance in trading, I will remember that I have still made my best effort.
- I will not feel guilty in investing or anything else unless I know that I haven't made my best effort.

CHALLENGING FALSE BELIEFS

One or more of the false beliefs presented here are commonly part of the self-talk that maintain perfectionistic thinking. Often they are unconscious and unchallenged by the perfectionist and therefore continue to exert considerable influence. In pointing out each falsely assumed belief, the point is to make them conscious and to fully acknowledge that they are not true and thus should be substituted with true counterbeliefs. In this way, we can begin to dismantle the assumptions which support perfectionism. In addition, you may want to pick an affirmation from those given earlier that supports a specific true counterbelief.

False belief #1: Perfectionism means following the rules to the letter, never deviating from what you're told.

Counterbelief: It's OK not to take things too literally; it's OK to think for yourself and find creative solutions without relying strictly on rules and regulations.

False belief #2: I will be punished if I don't always try to be perfect.

Counterbelief: I will be punishing myself if I keep trying to be perfect.

False belief #3: I ought to feel guilty if I don't perform perfectly.

Counterbelief: I need not feel guilty as long as I try my best.

False belief #4: Thinking like a perfectionist makes me more perfect.

Counterbelief: Thinking like a perfectionist makes me more miserable.

False belief #5: Being critical of others helps me feel superior to them.

Counterbelief: Being critical of others only reveals my own need to feel superior to them and my underlying insecurity that goes with it. Anybody can be critical.

False belief #6: People can be as perfect as smoothly running machines.

Counterbelief: People are more like machines that continually need to be adjusted, tuned, and periodically given complete overhauls.

False belief #7: Trying to keep things frozen in a state of stability will make for a more perfect life.

Counterbelief: Without change, there would be no room for growth and new possibility.

As we all sooner or later become painfully aware, the very nature of life is constant change. According to Eastern philosophy, it is the ability to skillfully surf the waves of this ongoing change that is viewed as being in the perfect flow of life. Do you let yourself become part of this perfect flow or do you struggle to swim upstream, against the flow? Healthy striving for excellence means using all of one's skills and talents to make creative adaptations to this ongoing flow—not struggling to fight the changing nature of life—or the securities market. So traders are fond of saying: "Don't fight the tape."

While stability and security are legitimate and powerful needs in our life, they are only one side of the coin. We must confront our fear of the other side of the coin—the side that represents the need for new stimulation, surprise, change, and even disruption, chaos, and transformation. And, of course, part of the excitement of online trading is that it never fails to deliver all of these conditions!

One way this acceptance of change is experienced by those striving for excellence is in their ability to enjoy the process of getting to the goal, not just focusing on the goal itself. The perfectionist tends to forget that it is the process of getting there that is what creative adaptations to life are all about—not just reaching some artificial goal, which is then quickly replaced by another goal, and then another.

FACING RISKS AND TAKING CHANCES

Taking risks requires what the perfectionist dreads the most—the fear of the unknown and of failure. So it is important to "put your head into the lion's mouth," directly to dare to take some risks that you know will challenge your image as a perfectionist. This means doing some things that you know you are not very good at, and letting it be OK to be a beginner. Allow yourself to be a vulnerable beginner with the attitude of *beginner's mind*, the mind of fresh appreciation, where everything is approached with keen interest, as if for the first time.

For example, try making a short-term trade if you've never done it before, cooking a simple meal if you never liked to cook, learning a new dance step, traveling to a distant city or foreign country that seems too far away and scary for you, or sitting down and writing a passionate letter, essay, or short story if you've never liked writing. It doesn't matter what you choose—the idea is to take a risk.

Along with trying risky activities that are new for you, try some activities that you know you like but have avoided because you don't think you do them well enough. Let yourself recapture the interest and excitement you had with these activities before you cut off your excitement by turning it into the fear of not being good enough.

Think about the number of activities and projects that you have started but never completed because of a fear of never being good enough. Go back to those dance lessons, learn that instrument, or take that language class. Give yourself a new chance, with an attitude of allowing for mistakes but enjoying it anyway. Approaching an activity with a new attitude, you may experience much more pleasure than you previously allowed yourself.

You must be willing to face your own embarrassment of not measuring up and your need to be in control at all times. The more you see that you can cope with being out of control and manage your embarrassment at knowing little or nothing about what you are doing, the more you will be ready to accept that good enough performance is, indeed, something worthy of feeling real satisfaction from. This understanding puts you squarely on the path toward transforming your perfectionism to the healthy pursuit of excellence.

The emotion of embarrassment is important in another way. The recognition of your uniqueness, instead of being a good reason to love yourself, is turned against yourself negatively in the form of embarrassment. If you are going to find "perfection in imperfection," as Zen encourages us to do, you have got to be at peace with your own uniqueness. This means overcoming your embarrassment of your individual differences.

Perfectionists have a deep fear and mistrust of their individual differences. While they want to stand above others and be recognized as superior to them, at the same time they fear standing out because it makes them feel different. For example, you might be embarrassed by a body part that is not perfectly proportioned, your voice, manner of speaking, or style of walking. Each of these examples may be experienced as making you different and therefore out of step with others—or it may be experienced as an expression of who you are that need not be altered for the sake of pleasing others. *One sign of healthy adult maturity is coming to accept, appreciate, and honor one's individual differences rather than be embarrassed by them.* This is taking the risk of allowing yourself to truly be yourself. To do so you must view your individual differences through the lens of an attitude called *appreciative mind*.

Appreciative Mind Versus Judging Mind

It is possible to transform judging your behavior, others' behavior, and the world in general, to a nonjudging appreciation of things just as they are. While a judging mind likes to focus on differences that lead to evaluating and comparing everything and everybody, the appreciative mind allows things to be left alone just as they are without comparison.

One way to work with the concept of the appreciative mind is to walk around for a day with one simple idea in mind: that everything you do and everything you see others doing is to be appreciated, just as it is. To appreciate something means to take pleasure in it or receive satisfaction from it and to honor and respect it. The way to appreciate your own behavior and that of others is to view it as perfect in its imperfection.

For one day, see everything that you do as just right in its imperfection. Begin to notice how you can switch your perception from judging and comparing to appreciating all behavior as uniquely perfect just as it is.

THE ELEMENTS OF ONLINE INVESTING EXCELLENCE

So far in this chapter we have presented ways of confronting the negative and self-defeating aspects of the perfectionistic mind. We have offered some tools for beginning to transform these self-defeating aspects into the more healthy characteristics of striving for excellence. We will now identify some of the elements of excellence that the perfectionist probably already possesses. The perfectionistic view of these qualities can be shaped into a more moderate form in realizing the good enough mentality. This is not an exhaustive list but only an indication of those elements that I believe are important in the pursuit of excellence. Following this list, we will indicate how the perfectionist's perspective may be altered toward excellence by utilizing these elements.

> *Knowledge.* Are you willing to acquire the basic and advanced knowledge of the discipline of investing through the reading, study, and experience that is necessary to thoroughly perform trading skills at a high level? Have you chosen an area in which you are capable of obtaining this knowledge? Or is this knowledge beyond your limits? Is this knowledge interesting and meaningful to you? Do you have a passion to learn it?

Compatibility. Does your wish to excel in online investing follow naturally from those skills and talents that you already possess? If not, is it an area in which you have a realistic possibility of learning at a high level, given your natural limitations? Are your temperament and personality compatible with the skills and talents necessary to perform at a high level? If others are involved in your trading situation, can you work with them well enough to do the job you desire at a high level?

Dedication. How much does it matter to you whether you excel or not? Are you willing to practice your trading skills as much as is required to reach a high level of proficiency? Are you, within reason, willing to sacrifice certain pleasures and diversions if necessary? Are you willing to hang in there without quitting even after repeated failures in falling short of your goals? Will you have what it takes to handle the loss of a chunk of your capital as part of the price of learning? Can you afford it?

Motivation. Are you sufficiently motivated to not allow yourself to be distracted by other interests? Are you, without being driven, strongly pulled toward reaching success? What makes it so important for you to excel in the online trading arena? What are your true motivations for caring about it? Do you have any ulterior motives that you don't like to admit?

Commitment. Is reaching excellence as an online trader a short-term goal for you? Or are you willing to be committed over the long term, refining your skills even after you reach your desired level of competence? What will you do when your attention is captured by another, equally interesting area to pursue? How much are you willing to dedicate of your life to truly becoming an expert over time? How much are you willing to change your habits if necessary? For example, are you willing to wake up at 5:30 A.M. PST each morning to prepare for the opening of the market at 6:30 A.M.?

Satisfaction. Do you derive satisfaction from incremental steps toward your goal of trading excellence? Do you know how to break your goal into various steps, each with a subgoal that brings you some enjoyment, pleasure, self-respect, and sense of well-being? Is there anything else you'd rather be doing than this particular chosen area of striving? Are you able to make it a dance toward excellence rather than a struggle that is all consuming? Do you really enjoy the life of the passionate online investor and trader? Is your enjoyment worth the price of the stress involved?

Moving from Perfectionism to Excellence

In transforming perfection to excellence, we take the previously selected elements of excellence and make the following alterations in
the perfectionist's attitude:

Knowledge and excellence. We move from knowledge that confirms
an air of superiority to knowledge that ensures adequate ground-
ing in the trading discipline; learning to use knowledge to gain confidence and to ground skills rather than using knowledge to feel superior to others or to boast about one's intelligence and learning;
learning to give up the narcissistic position of being the only one
who knows, who is entitled to special attention and treatment.

Compatibility and excellence. Learning to choose the pursuits that are
right for you, not just those that have status attached or reflect what
your parents and friends think you should do; finding the work
and projects that fit your personal style. From a viewpoint of "me
against the world" to "we're in it together." Learning how to cooperate and be compatible with others for one's own benefit as well as
for their benefit; going beyond gross forms of jealousy, envy, and
vindictiveness to feelings of interest in and joy for the triumphs of
others. From "there's only room at the top for one" to "there's room
enough for everyone."

Dedication and excellence. From conditional dedication based on easy
reward and low frustration to dedication based on personal integrity that demands one's best performance; moving beyond blaming
others when it isn't easy; not quitting after failures; tolerating second best, if necessary; making use of constructive criticism.

Motivation and excellence. From motivation by fear of failure to motivation derived from personal satisfaction and achievement; moving
from desperate performance to avoid shame to spirited, interested
engagement with reward in both the process and the goal; from
compulsively moving on without time to savor the achievement to
allowing oneself full satisfaction without devaluing one's accomplishment. Making room for celebration of success as a way to gain
nourishment for further challenges. The perfectionist's obsessive
tendency can be used positively to sustain motivation despite distractions competing for his attention.

Commitment and excellence. From commitment based on short-term
ego gratification to commitment based on strong investment in the
skill or work itself. From surface-level narcissistic gratification to a

deeper sense of right livelihood, or doing work that one enjoys that is consistent with one's morals, temperament, and personal beliefs and takes cares of one's personal needs; transcending short-term interest based on fad and fashion.

Satisfaction and excellence. From momentary relief based on temporarily fending off anxiety and the fear of failure to deeper satisfaction and contentment based on a sense of pride of accomplishment and enjoyment of the process of reaching it; from focus only on the goal to focus on enjoyment of the incremental steps toward the goal; from frustration and fragmentation to a sense of wholeness and completeness.

Are you willing to make these changes and to address the elements of excellence that may be lacking? If you are, you will be in a strong position to transform the "good enough is never enough" stance into, as Lao Tze put it, the wisdom of "he who knows when enough is enough will always have enough."

MORE TOOLS TOWARD EXCELLENCE

We will conclude this chapter with additional selected tools and ideas which may be helpful in striving for excellence:

1. *Restrict the amount of time you engage in perfectionistically driven activities.* Purposefully cut back in those areas that you know you devote large amounts of time to but where your performance does not seem to improve. There is a delicate balance between the commitment of time and energy needed to excel versus being compulsively overcommitted.

At a certain point, striving becomes self-defeating because it is possible to try too hard. You may spend too much time doing and redoing to get things perfect. Research on leadership suggests that a moderate amount of motivation (leading to moderate time investment) tends to be related to best performance.

2. *Always break large goals down into smaller subgoals.* As with end goals, try and put subgoals into objective, measurable terms. In this way, you can give yourself nourishment along the way toward your end goal. Breaking end goals into subgoals will also tend to reinforce enjoying the process of reaching your end goal.

For example, if your goal is to learn how to understand Level II quotes, subgoals might be to understand the flow of quotes in relation to the bid and ask prices; who the main market makers are and how they tend to behave; how to use time and sales information; how to predict the movement of the stock from the imbalance of orders to buy and sell; and how to put in bids that are between the quoted prices.

In determining subgoals, be careful not to set them at too high a level, or you will defeat the purpose of periodic self-nourishment. If you set the subgoals too low, you will not feel worthy of enjoying any satisfaction when the subgoal is met.

3. *Break the habit of being critical.* Refrain from criticizing others' performance, no matter how much you feel the desire to comment on their inadequacies and shortcomings. If you can break the habit of being critical of others, you will also tend to be less critical of yourself. You will begin to see that it is not necessary to continually compare yourself to others. This is not easy to do, since there is continual cultural reinforcement for playing this comparing game.

4. *Try journal writing to help you along the path of accomplishment.* Write about those projects and activities that matter to you, and compliment yourself when you reach subgoals and end goals. Let your journal be a record of your successes, so that you may return to it for support whenever you tackle a challenge that seems too big to handle. Reading about your successes will help give you the confidence to tackle larger and riskier projects. Use your well-practiced compulsivity in a positive way to ensure that you make entries in your journal regularly.

5. *Keep company with people who support your projects.* It will be much easier for you to reach your goal of excellence if you have others who value excellence in their own lives and who are willing and able to help support your efforts. Refrain from spending too much time around heavily critical people who are unable to appreciate your desire for excellence or who put you down out of their own envy, feelings of inadequacy, and perfectionism.

6. *Keep in mind the final determination of excellence is up to you.* The goal of excellence is not a matter of the outside world giving you approval or applause. While it is desirable and gratifying to receive approval and recognition from others, the real gratification comes only when you have accepted yourself at a deep enough level that you can view your own projects and very existence in this world as good enough. *The ultimate judge, jury, and trial reside within.*

There is no substitute for learning to love and accept yourself. All of the glitter from exciting market gains and recognition in the world cannot make you feel good enough if you are unwilling or unable to give to yourself what only you have the power to give. Without this acceptance you will always feel like more is never enough.

9

What "Investor's-Mind" Has to Offer Traders

There are some fundamental differences between short-term trading and long-term investing. The difference in time horizon has traditionally made for different styles of thinking and behavior. While we don't need to focus on these differences as they have conventionally been viewed, we will mention some of them in passing as reference to illustrate our points. And we can think of these differences as broadly defining what we may refer to respectively as *investor's-mind* and *trader's-mind*. Investor's-mind, then, is the mind-set traditionally associated with long-term investors, while *trader's-mind* will refer to the typical thinking of short-term traders.

What is becoming increasingly clear is how the technology of cybertrading and the heightened volatility of the market have forced us to question some of our long-held assumptions regarding these two mind-sets. Both the rules of the game (the advent of deep discount brokerages and of electronic trading) and the playing field itself (the exchanges, ECNs, after-hours trading) are obviously changing rapidly; this requires that our thinking keep pace.

As a result of these changes, some of the thinking of short-term traders may be usefully applied to the longer-term online investor. We will examine how this may be done in Chapter 10. But first, in this chapter, let's flip it around and ask what active traders can gain from investor's-mind. Does investor's-mind have anything to offer the trader?

To begin with, the popular notion of the short-term, and espe-cially the day trader, is rather narrow. When everyday investors hear about short-term trading, all they hear is how much it's like gambling. They hear that traders are being set up like unsuspecting sheep being led to slaughter; how they all are losing large amounts of money.

In addition, when it comes to day trading they don't under-stand how any money can be made scalping an eighth here and a six-teenth there. They don't know why anyone would possibly want to "burn tickets" by compulsively trading in and out of positions all day long, paying so much in commissions, along with short-term capital gains on whatever profit may remain. The public certainly doesn't view this kind of trading as having anything to do with a profession—unless you want to call it professional gambling.

Like almost any subject that is handled in a cursory manner by the media for its sensational news value, the story is not so simple or one-sided. And I say this making it clear that my bias is against scalping, fully aware of how difficult it is to consistently come out ahead in day trading. Indeed, what is presented in this chapter is ori-ented toward day traders and other short-term traders thinking more like investors, exactly *because* I understand the risks under-taken.

Yesterday, while visiting the local trading firm, I was told about one of the hypertraders on the floor who has been known to trade up to 500 times per day, or 250 round-trip tickets. The guy pays a gradu-ally lower commission rate the more he trades, from $20 per trade down to $8. Sometimes he'll make $9000 per day. When he subtracts the $4000 he pays in commission costs, he still has a net gain of $5000 for the day, before taxes.

Now, while large numbers of day traders have no particular in-terest in (and are not suited for) this kind of hypertrading, who's go-ing to argue with a guy able to earn $5000 for sitting at a computer terminal for a few frenzied hours hitting buy and sell keys on the keyboard? If this guy can consistently make large amounts of money, it makes sense to ask: at what point does the element of gam-bling decrease and the element of knowledge, instincts, and execu-tion increase? How long would he have to earn good income before we entertained the notion there was something else happening here besides gambling luck?

While, as we have already discussed, there most certainly is an element of gambling involved, that element can be reduced with thorough knowledge of the stock one is trading. In watching the movement of a stock very closely over a period of time, you can learn the patterns that tend to occur at certain periods of the trading day. And with experience on a Level II screen, you become reliably able to anticipate and predict very short-term movements more often than not.

My point is that day traders who have no idea about the company they are trading are at a distinct disadvantage compared to the traders who know their stock thoroughly. They have studied it day after day and traded it often enough to be confident of their moves in and out of it. For them, the element of gambling is going to be less than for the traders who couldn't care less what company is behind the stock symbol they are trading.

As a group, professional day traders appear to be maturing in their thinking. They are becoming more flexible and more knowledgeable in their approach to trading. They are borrowing some of the thinking of institutional money managers who are active traders. In the last two or three years, those who followed blindly the instructions to begin trading 1000 shares before they even knew what they were doing lost a lot of money. But they also generated a lot of revenue in commissions to the firms with which they were trading.

The movement is now away from pushing day traders to generate lots of commissions through trading. That is not where the money is now being made. After all, we've already reached the point where a sufficient account balance means free trading. The shift today is toward better education of traders before they are allowed to have a seat on the trading floor. And even those who choose to trade in the comfort of their own homes are interested in getting an education before they start risking their capital. Some seek out programs in day trading firms and then go back to their homes to apply what they have learned.

The short-sighted inadequacies of the past in allowing traders to begin trading with poor training and no supervision are trying to be corrected. And although the risks continue to be high for large numbers of day traders, the media does not tend to give the public the whole picture about the more positive direction the industry is moving.

Week-long courses cost $3000 and up. Some firms, like Online Trading Academy, require a second advanced course, also a week, that costs another $3000. This means you will have made an investment of at least $6000 before you are allowed to hit the trading floor and make your first trade. Obviously, your motivation has got to be pretty strong to hang in for two weeks of daily training plus the substantial costs involved.

DO YOUR HOMEWORK

Like long-term investors who follow the companies they invest in, smart short-term traders need to be aware of the news of the companies they are trading. While the momentum of a stock may be enough for scalpers to focus on, those who are doing swing trades of a few hours or position trades for a few days are basing their decisions on news regarding the stock. They need to be very tuned in to the nuances of the stocks they are trading, hoping to capitalize on the short-term effects of them.

When I went back to the trading floor, one thing that hadn't changed was the select group of stocks deemed most popular for trading. Interestingly, many professional day trading scalpers stay away from the very volatile stocks, like CMGI, Inktomi, and JDS Uniphase. They leave these to the "amateurs" at home (like me), who love these stocks.

For example, I sold CMGI a few days ago after holding it for only two weeks. (I say "only" with the long-term investor in mind, who will tell me he or she has food in his refrigerator older than that; conversely, the day trader looks at two weeks as an eternity, and might tell me, "Greenspan could drop dead any day—why take a chance by holding overnight?"). CMGI had a strong 60-point run-up in that two-week period and was approaching its 52-week high, which it ended up breaking through a few minutes after I sold it.

By the end of the session, due to a late sell-off, the stock closed 12 points lower than I had sold it for. I decided a 60 percent gain in two weeks was good enough for me. In addition, the NASDAQ had been on a great run for a month and I felt the pressure was building, that it had to release some steam. My decision looked pretty good, especially when the following day proved to be the day the top blew off so the pressure could escape, and all tech stocks took a thrashing. And then, the day after that, they began their climb to even further highs, with no breather until the first week in January 2000, when finally a bout of heavy selling ruined the party.

This stock (CMGI) simply moves too fast for me to consider trying to get a point or two here or there, especially given my not having a direct access execution system. And even with the advantage of an instant execution platform, most day traders have decided it moves too fast for them, too. They prefer a handful of technology stocks that offer high volume, good but not lightning-fast momentum, and a stability of the price spread of no more than one-sixteenth of a point. The big five that were most popular for trading continue to be Intel, Microsoft, Dell, Cisco, and, more recently, Applied Materials.

When the basic stable of trading stocks is limited to these five, traders can more easily become experts in one main stock. Then they can choose one other stock as a backup, or understudy trading stock, following this one as closely as they do their primary trading stock. This kind of close tracking of the primary trading stocks is similar, if not more intense, than what long-term investors do with their core portfolio. Actually, because they are counting on short-term news to move the stock, they need to be even more aware of the news than the longer-term investor, who does not need to be watching so closely when the stock is doing well.

Day traders need to spend time before the market opens and after it closes researching the stocks they are trading. They need to stay up on bulletin board news and opinion and anything happening with the industry the stock is in and how it may affect their particular stock. They need to be very tuned in to the nuances of the stocks they are trading, hoping to capitalize on the short-term movement.

My point then is simple: If you are going to be a disciplined short-term trader, you've got to be reading everything related to your one or two main stocks that you can get your eyes on, both online and in hard copy. You've got to know as much as any analyst following the company. Like an analyst, you should be able to stand up before a group and lecture on the stock, the company, and everything related to it. If you can't imagine doing that, you don't know it well enough. You need to know all about the sector the stock is in and how your stock compares to other stocks in that sector. This will help anticipate short-term moves for swing and position trades.

CONSIDER HOLDING POSITIONS LONGER

Experienced active traders know a lot about getting out of stocks quickly. The good ones have stop limits set, at least mentally, to exit a position when their stock has dropped to a specified level. They have learned to always be thinking about the downside risk of their positions. They do this kind of defensive thinking much better than intermediate- and longer-term investors, who think they don't really need to bother with it.

But what about day traders holding positions longer, rather than the knee-jerk reaction to sell when it goes down an eighth or a quarter? In other words, have active traders gone overboard when it comes to quickly exiting positions? This question, of course, goes to the heart of the whole method of grinding out fractional gains.

It all depends. If there is a lot of money on the line and say, 500 or 1000 shares, obviously to preserve capital, active traders are forced to exit positions quickly when their stock drops a fractional amount. They can't risk losing a chunk of their capital. If they have 1000 shares and the stock goes down a quarter point, they are down $250 plus commission costs. This, as every trader knows all too well, can happen *very* fast. It is the best argument for not trading in larger share lots until you become very experienced. But let's say they're only trading in lots of 100 or 200 shares. Then if the stock drops a quarter point and it only is worth $25, they will not feel so desperate to get out of their position. They can watch the stock a while, and give it a chance to come back to at least where they bought it.

I understand that it is tough to make much money when that quarter point doesn't mean more than $25. But if the object of the game is to preserve capital and carve out fractional gains, what's the matter with carving out a few hundred dollars per day with far less risk?

I will never end up a scalper because it simply is not compatible with my personality. And there is no compelling reason that I can see to try and fight my personality and natural trading approach. I have concluded the risk-reward ratio is not favorable for me to deal with the stress of scalping. Swing trading makes somewhat more sense to me but is still quite nerve-wracking, and position trading makes more sense still. But my own preference is for what most would label the intermediate term—a few weeks to a few months. Some call this "speculative" trading, viewing anything short of holding for the long-term as too risky. But speculation that is informed is clearly in a different category than wild gambling.

For example, if CMGI has one of its "incubator" Internet companies coming to market with an initial public offering, I know that the parent stock will rise when the new company becomes public. This is not really any risk—it will go up when one of its companies comes out. Buying CMGI for the short term then is informed specu lation and what the position trader specializes in. But to do this kind of position trading, you can't be phobic about holding a stock for days at a time.

I recently talked with a professional who had been involved in day trading for the last three years. She doesn't do much day trading now, preferring to be involved in helping educate new traders. But she still trades selected IPOs as soon as they hit the open market. While this tactic can be quite risky compared to getting in on the initial offering price and being assured a gain almost totally risk-free, for her it seemed less risky than what she had been previously doing as a day trader. She told me that when she learned day trading, she was a victim of being taught that she "must" trade in 1000-share lots to make any money. She said instead of making money, this approach cost her a lot of money—both in working capital and in commissions.

She told me that if she were to do it again, one thing she would do differently, in addition to trading fewer shares, is stay in her positions longer, not being in such a hurry to get out as soon as the stock dropped a fraction. This is counter to what most traders think. They tend to err on the side of not getting out fast enough, even though they are far better at exiting than longer-term investors. But this trader's opinion was that often her stock would come back the eighth or quarter within a couple of minutes. And if she hadn't had 1000 shares riding, she could have taken this chance and held on to it longer.

The Dating Game: "Can I Bring Her Home to Meet Mother?"

I talked with another professional trader who has been buying securities for many years and trading the last two years through direct access at a trading firm, and was now teaching an advanced class for day traders.

The analogy he used for day traders extending their positions beyond scalping for fractions was one of getting to know a new woman gradually. He said he needed to begin slowly by trading the stock for fractions, getting to know it day after day, but not holding it for very long. He likened this to having casual greetings and maybe chit-chat with an attractive woman where there was some interest but not really spending much time with her.

As he felt more comfortable, he held the stock for hours at a time, doing swing trading. This was the equivalent of showing interest and going on dates with a woman to really get to know her. If this dating worked out and he didn't lose any money holding his position for hours, sooner or later he would take the next step in the "relationship" and take the stock home with him overnight. This was the same for him as a couple deciding to finally spend the night together.

If he didn't end up with a losing position by holding her overnight (still liked her the next morning), he began to think maybe it wasn't just a fling. Maybe he could develop a longer-term arrangement with his new sweetheart stock. He would then consider holding the stock for weeks or months, in a steady (but not necessarily exclusive) dating relationship. If all went well, he might eventually marry the stock (as he had Microsoft) and never sell her no matter how badly she treated him; he took her for good or bad, 'til death do they part.

This trader/investor had developed a method of making the stock prove itself worthy of becoming a long-term hold. But the point here is he made room in his thinking and behavior to become not just a day trader but an investor as well. He borrowed something useful from investor's-mind to add to his armamentarium as a trader. While most men and women don't put the stocks that end up in their portfolio through the same kind of rigorous courting ritual as they do their potential love partners, it isn't a bad model or analogy for the day trader to consider.

BE A TRADER FOR ALL MARKETS

Smart, disciplined online traders need to be flexible in their trading style. Just as it is useful for a trader to have personality characteristics that balance both attention to detail, good concentration, discipline, and a dash of the risk-taking gambler, it is also useful to have a flexibility of approach to trading. This enables traders to meet the market under any conditions they might find it.

We can think of this flexibility as being like expert skiers who can ski well under any physical conditions. They can enjoy cross country or downhill, and varying degrees of difficulty. They can handle it when the snow is packed, when it is slushy, or when the slopes require caution rather than all-out downhill exuberance. And they know when it might be best to stay off the slopes altogether.

They can adjust their style to fit the type of snow they are skiing so that their performance does not suffer no matter what the conditions. While they may have a preference, they do not complain when the conditions happen not to meet their preference.

Likewise, flexible traders know when the market calls for grinding out fractions because that's all they're going to squeeze out of it. They can be comfortable doing day swing trades for a few hours or position trades for a few days or weeks. They will ideally even have some long-term positions to balance their portfolio and to balance their thinking.

Psychologically, it is much easier to think like an investor when you have some longer-term holds—in other words, when you know how it feels to hold a position over time without undue anxiety or worry. In an earlier chapter we mentioned being able to adjust our view of what began as a short-term position into a longer-term position—we called this *reframing* our view of the stock. Most investors find they are forced to change their thinking when a stock drops and they don't want to (but probably should) sell it. But wouldn't it give us a greater feeling of control to be able to choose to hold it for a longer term rather than be forced into this position by default? This, of course, is what investors do all the time.

In addition, flexible traders know when the market is telling them it is best to keep their powder dry and stay on the sidelines. As we all know, there are sharp, violent sell-offs at times that only traders wanting their heads handed to them on a platter would consider jumping into.

Smart traders know how to let the dust settle when things take a sharp down-turn. This allows them to increase the probability that there will not be further selling and they do not end up getting in the way of the proverbial falling knife. The greed of getting a good deal has to be balanced by the prudence of restraining oneself until it looks like a bottom has formed. This is why many traders say it is best to wait until the stock begins to come back up before considering taking a position—not while it is still falling.

Example of Flexible Thinking

In December of 1999, the technology sector had been on a very hot upward spiral for over a month, since the market had been consumed with interest rate fears, causing a sell-off in October. James Cramer, referring to this period, unequivocally called this market "the most powerful I have ever seen in my 20 years in the business." (*The Street.com*, Fox News Network, December 4, 1999).

I bought Nokia (NOK) the previous month, November, and watched it gain over 40 points in two weeks' time. Trying to stay aware of downside risk when the market seems like it can do no wrong, I had decided toward the close of the market a couple of days ago that I would put in a limit order to sell my shares and take a nice gain.

But, as is my wont, I always make the stock work to be sold. In other words, I make it go higher than I really think it will reach if I am to give up my shares. In this case, I was OK if it didn't sell because I knew there was a good chance this stock had a ways to go. But I knew I could buy it back if the technology bubble bursts in the next three weeks.

I set my limit order at 145 1/2, knowing there would have to be a nice run toward the close to reach my price. In addition, I purposely set it at a half, knowing it is tougher for the half point to be hit. It was a delicious, nonpressured feeling that I don't get to experience often enough. If it reached my price, great, I would take my healthy gain and be happy. And if it didn't, I would still be in the game the next day and make even more with a name I really like. In psychology, this is called an *approach-approach* situation because either way I choose, both end states are desirable.

Either way it went, I was going to feel content. So, of course, the stock starts moving up about five minutes before the close after trading in a rather narrow range for this stock most of the day. It makes it up to 145 1/4, just 1/4 short of reaching my limit to sell. When it hits 145 1/4, it begins to fade a little and finishes at 144 5/8, up almost 3 for the day. I had come within a quarter of a point of selling my shares.

The next morning, Nokia gaps up 9 1/2 points at the open, holds its opening price all day, and closes 17 3/8 points up for the day. I decide when I see the gap up that I will hold this stock for the longer term. Nothing like a 9 1/2 point gap up and 17 3/8 gain for the day to change your thinking! And if that's not enough, the stock comes back on Monday and goes up another 14 1/2 points. This one is too good to get rid of.

The reframing of my thinking was simply to see that if it drops, I'd let it drop and let it come back, rather than try and time the market perfectly, trading in and out of it. In other words, I simply shifted into investor's-mind from intermediate-term thinking, which tends to be my preferred time frame for holding positions. But, like most amateurs, I can be quite patient in holding certain losing positions for a long time just to get back to even.

I recently had my patience pay off in finally getting out of Seagate Technology, which I had held for two and half years. Of course, I lost the *opportunity cost* of that money being in another position and actually making a profit, rather than sitting on "dead" money. But there is a certain satisfaction, I must admit, in holding it until I got my initial capital back. And in fact, I ended up feeling so content just with getting out of it that it ends up feeling like a gain, even though it is only a psychological gain, not a monetary one. The psychological perspective that allows this reaction might be stated as, "Been down so long getting even feels like up."

Curiously, while I have had the patience to hold fund positions for years at a time, along with individual stocks that I was holding losing positions in, I have not been one to hold winning individual positions for more than a year or so. I have never had any interest in holding a Coke or a Disney for many years.

Truth be told, I don't even want to own a Coke or a Disney. Now that I have had a taste for the faster track, I must admit the old, solid companies seem too slow for me. But I didn't want to own them even before the whole Internet revolution.

When was the last time Coke or Disney gapped up 9 1/2 points in the morning? When you have that happen with a CMGI, JDSU, or watch any other "red hot" like Redback Networks or dozens of others make a run for the moon, it's tough to get excited by a two-point move on a good day by Disney.

CONSIDER TAX CONSEQUENCES

Many active traders seem to pay little attention to the tax consequences of their short-term gains. They believe that they can make enough money with day and short-term trading to make taxes on gains a nonissue. Long-term traders have always been concerned about capital gains, not wanting to hold stocks less than a year so they will not pay short-term gains on profits. This has always been part of their rationale for not considering more active trading. What can active traders gain from investor's-mind on this issue?

Depending on what state you live in and your gains from trading and anything else you do that brings in taxable income, you could be taxed as high as 30 to 40 percent between federal and state taxes. This means that you will keep only 60 percent of your profits and that is before you subtract your commission costs and other trading-related expenses.

One way for short-term active traders to trade free of capital gains concerns is to trade in a self-directed retirement account, such as a Keogh. I talk to many longer-term investors who, for whatever reason, simply have not considered this tactic. Obviously, those professional traders who are attempting to make their living from trading will not be able to avail themselves of this strategy. But there are hundreds of thousands of online traders who are fairly active, trading at least a few times per month or more. The size of this group will only grow, as the number of traders who are familiar with online trading and have the right technical tools for short-term trading increases.

It seems apparent that this is the direction we are moving in: more short-term traders utilizing varied short-term approaches and styles; more sophisticated trading tools, knowledge, and training; around-the-clock electronic markets; very low fee to free trading; and larger amounts of savings, retirement, and discretionary income that can be funneled into the market. And, most likely, greater volatility in price moves.

This suggests that larger numbers will become more active traders but choose to trade from a self-directed retirement account. The advantage of trading from a retirement account is that you don't have to consider short-term capital gains—because there are none.

The total worth of your portfolio when you finally retire and are ready to begin distributing it will be taxed as ordinary income at that time. The idea, of course, is that since you would be retired at that time, you will be in a lower tax bracket than you are now and therefore pay fewer taxes on the total value of your holdings. In addition, when you retire, you are not forced to begin to withdraw money from your retirement account.

If you have a Keogh, for example, it can be rolled over into an IRA until you are ready to begin distribution. Those who have independent, self-directed Keogh accounts lose the great benefit of having their contributions matched by their employer, as do those participating in 401-K company plans. But they do enjoy the freedom to trade individual stocks as they see fit. They are not subject to having someone put their money into one fund or another, often with little choice or variety.

Now, conventional conservative thinking was that you didn't want to take any foolish risks with retirement savings. This has been drummed into almost everyone's thinking about retirement investing. You wanted to diversify your assets by allocating some to a few growth and value funds, some to a bond fund, maybe a token international fund, and have a chunk in a money-mart fund. You certainly didn't want to risk losing your retirement capital by putting it into individual securities. This was the common thinking before the birth of the cybertrading revolution.

This is how many financial planners and accountants will advise you today—don't take undue risks with retirement money. But the stock market is too hot. There is too much to be made for us to invest by these conservative and out-of-date guidelines—guidelines and thinking that are pre-cyberinvesting savvy and pre-deep-discount brokerages. The whole game changes when you've got access to information. All the rules are rewritten when you pay almost nothing or when you get to trade commission-free. How can we not take more risk given the technology, the knowledge, and the know-how? And especially with the glut of baby-boomer savings that have helped create the greatest bull market in history? I mean, you can park your savings and retirement in bond funds or a nice, safe CD if you like.

Better yet, you can put a chunk into an index fund that tracks the S&P 500 and do pretty well. But you are still going to lose between 30 to 50 percent or more to the clever online traders who are gobbling up hot, leading-edge technology and Internet-related stocks as fast as they can be offered up. But you must be willing to handle the downside risk as well.

Remember, you don't need a whole portfolio of hot, but risky stocks. One or two that bring a great gain can more than make up for some of the positions that earn little or even go down. All it takes is one high flier to bring up one's total portfolio.

Yes, the risk goes up and you can get whacked if the whole technology sector takes an extended dive. But would you rather be taking that risk with an index fund, or Coke or Disney—none of which is a sure thing? Or would you like to take a chance with Internet and telecommunications stocks that can double and triple your investment? If you want to take the added risk, you better have the stomach to watch them dive 20 points in an hour or less without woopsing your cookies, as my mother would say.

All of this is to say, trading individual stocks in a retirement account means you can trade as much as you want, make the commission charges almost a nonissue, and not have to give a thought to paying short-term capital gains. In 1999, most of my trades were made in a Keogh account. Of course, I can still lose money. And, unlike a taxable account, I cannot write off losses against gains at any time. But this is a small consideration compared to not having to worry about capital gains. So, if I want to sell CMGI after a 60 percent gain in two weeks, I don't have to worry about paying the government a big chunk of my gain.

It won't be long before I am able to trade for free, not worry about paying any taxes on gains, and am using free sophisticated trading software to earn those gains. And this will be possible for ever-increasing numbers of online investors who also have a self-directed retirement account. Perhaps, like me, they will also have a separate taxable account, where they will have to be more considerate of short-term taxable gains. But in order to do it, longer-term investors have to borrow some of the thinking of traders. So let's move to Chapter 10 and see how we can do that.

10

What "Trader's-Mind" Has to Offer Investors

At no time in history has technology provided us the ease with which we could so effortlessly and cheaply make a stock trade as it has today. Part of the mentality that previously guided the long-term investor was dictated by having to go through stockbrokers and market makers, the "guardians at the gate." They were the only ones who had access to information and the means to actually make stock trades.

The cost of trading was prohibitively high for individual investors to think about frequent trading. How could you think about holding a stock for only a few weeks or a few days (let alone a few hours or minutes) when you were paying $150 to $200 or more to make a trade? How could you think about active trading when you had very limited information, and no access to quotes to even know where a stock was trading?

In the old days, if you wanted stock quotes, you had to literally sit in front of an overhead electronic ticker tape at your brokerage office, inhaling the stale second-hand cigar smoke from wealthy retired men. I can remember watching the ticker tape as a teenager when visiting my stepfather on the brokerage floor. He worked for many years at Bache, in the pre-Prudential days, when it was a whole different investing world than it is today.

The hierarchy of the game heavily favored traditional brokerages, like Bache, and their brokers, who dictated how much information would be shared with clients. If there was any churning of accounts to be done, they'd be the ones to do it—not you, the investor. You gave away your own decision-making power in favor of the greater knowledge, experience, and access to research information and execution possessed by your broker.

So, unless you were a trader on the floor of one of the exchanges or an institutional money manager, your opportunities to trade more than occasionally were very limited. And this almost dictated a buy-and-hold approach to investing.

Companies were viewed as slowly growing their revenues and (to use a term that wasn't in existence) their "bottom line" over many years, with the investor holding stock and profiting as the company slowly grew to maturity, full productivity, and prosperity. You looked forward to a nice annual dividend if all went well, and maybe an occasional stock split. You married a stock for good times and bad, in sickness and in health—often literally until you died.

In some ways, it was like becoming attached to the hometown baseball or football team, in that you identified with the company and rooted for its success. And when you left this earth, the stock was finally sold and the gains were distributed to your heirs. The obituary of a typical investor might have read: "He was a good husband, father, dutiful son, and a dedicated employee. He was a God-fearing man who went to church and a loyal member of his local Kiwanis Club. He was also an astute investor, a life-long holder of 200 shares of Standard Oil." It was a perfectly adequate model for the 1960s, 1970s, and even into the 1980s.

But we're in a new cybergame for a new millennium—and obviously the rules have changed. And anybody who doesn't see the changes as they are occurring and accommodate them will simply be left behind. The Wall Street parade will have passed them by. Instead of being on the forefront of the curve, they will be bringing up the rear.

As usual in the Age of Information, the key is being an early adopter. You've got to have access to the information, choose to pay attention to it, and then skillfully apply it. And, of course, you've got to have the capital to invest. One result for those who feel they have not gained their fair share of the pie has been an outbreak of a particularly virulent strain of envy, which we will address in Chapter 11.

How have these changes in the securities markets influenced the way investors look at their options today, in a cybermarket? What does *trader's-mind* (that is, the typical way traders tend to think) have to offer longer-term investors? How can longer-term investors improve their return by incorporating some of the thinking and methods of short-term traders? These are the questions we will address in this chapter, in addition to some related issues.

Let's state one generalization that is easily overlooked in a high-flying market: It is one thing to be able to make money in a great bull market as we saw in the 1990s. It is another thing to be a disciplined trader who can make money when the market is more choppy or takes a prolonged downturn, either as a major correction or an outright bear market. The concepts presented here are offered to help broaden our thinking, so we can perform under varied market conditions, not just in a hot market when almost anything you pick stands a good chance of going up.

Balance has been the watchword throughout our exploration: Balancing different aspects of personality and trading approach; balancing isolation and information overload; balancing fear and greed, intellect and emotion, euphoria and shock; and balancing trading excitement and disappointment. We also need to balance and utilize the complementary forms of self-control. And we do this while walking the razor's edge of excellence without falling into the perfection trap. Is performing all this too much to ask? Not for the serious disciplined online investor, it isn't!

That's what the whole concept of discipline is really aimed at—not becoming rigid robots, but staying on a steady path that is always trying to balance upside and downside, and staying with a preset plan, not being unduly influenced by what others are doing. And not losing sight that when the see-saw goes too far up, the dynamics of market psychology demand that, sooner or later, it come back down. But when it's heading for the moon, the wishful fantasy is that it will last forever. And when it is going down week after week, it is tough to remember it will recover.

SETTING EXIT LEVELS

Long-term investors often buy stocks—whether they be individual stocks or mutual funds—with little or no thought about what kind of return they are looking for. They may fantasize how much they'd like to make but don't really determine a set price or a strategy. Perhaps they like a company, know something about the products or management team, and buy the stock not only because they think it's a good investment, but because they like the idea of having a small piece of the company. As we said in Chapter 9, they tend to identify with the company. And the longer they hold the stock, the stronger becomes their identification with it.

The discipline they can borrow from *trader's-mind* is to have a specific goal in mind as to what amount of money or percentage gain they would like to see with each stock purchase. Day traders and other short-term traders are very clear when they go into a position what they want out of it. For the day trader, it might be 1/4 of a point and then out. For the swing day trader, it might be a full point and then out. For the position trader holding for a few days, it might be three or more points. All of these short-term traders have to be clear on the goal of their trade. What makes them effective as short-term traders is exercising the discipline to get out once they have reached their price.

At the same time, short-term traders are also much quicker to exit their positions when the stock falls to a certain preset level. They are aware of the need to set stop limits, so that they are automatically "stopped out" of a position when it drops to that point.

What intermediate speculators and long-term investors need to adopt from *trader's-mind* is this clarity regarding exiting their positions and setting downside limits in the way of stop losses.

Why is this important if you think you want to hold the stock for months or even years? Because without any idea where you want to sell, it is easy to "fall in love and marry" the stock and become complacent. The relationship is left open-ended, rather than seen as an investment where the object is to sell the position and end up with a tangible—not just paper—profit. Even when you say you want to let profits run, it still is good discipline to have a set point to take your profits and be satisfied.

When the relationship is left open-ended and there is no clear exit strategy in place, it is easy to overlook information that may signal that it is time to reevaluate your position. Sometimes this is because of a change in the fundamentals of the company. At other times, there is a change in the story of the company or the sector the company falls within.

When a whole sector that has been in favor with the Wall Street community and investors suddenly or gradually falls out of favor, those who are married to a company may misinterpret the new information. If they interpret it correctly, they may refuse to act on it. Other times, it is not just one sector but the trend of the market as a whole that shifts, and long-term investors simply are not mentally prepared to change their thinking to accommodate this change in the trend.

It is more difficult to act decisively on a change when one event signals the shift in sentiment than when a number of events occur gradually over time. For example, recalling the story I told about giving back my big gain in Pfizer: When the earnings report came in under the estimates because Viagra was not continuing to sell at the same level as when it first came out, the panic to exit the stock ended up being a shift in the stock story from which, nine months later, Pfizer has still not recovered. This one event was enough in itself to keep the stock from reigniting its previous momentum.

Because I didn't imagine the story could change so fast, I held on stubbornly rather than be one of those heading for the exits. Had I put in a stop limit order to protect my gains, I would never have had to make a mental shift in order to immediately jump out and protect my gains.

The issue here for long-term investors to consider is how they are going to cover themselves in these sudden shifts if they have not set a clear exit goal ahead of time. More disciplined investors solve this issue by having *trailing stops* that they up little by little as the stock rises in price.

Had I not been so complacent about Pfizer, that stop limit might have been set five points below the current price. Then, when a sudden shift in the stock story is ushered in by an earnings report that doesn't meet expectations and a free-fall begins, I don't have to rely on my mental agility to shift gears. If the stop is in place, the stock gets sold, and I can then sit back after the fact and try and figure out what happened.

Related to these sudden shifts, there is some thought that more violent corrections are being compressed into shorter periods of time. For example, the three-day correction in tech stocks in the first week of January 2000 was followed by the highest and second highest point gains by the NASDAQ. For anyone unable to react swiftly enough, the short window to seize the chance to get in on these stocks at a bargain would be missed.

Here, again, having stop losses in place would preserve a profit and set one up to then enter the stock at a drastically reduced price. But it is all happening so fast that investors are left frozen by the violent nature of the reversal and unprepared to spring into action before the window closes.

In a sense, long-term investors are flying on the high wire, risking investment capital, and yet having no safety net below them by having no stop limit orders to protect them should the stock drop quickly and violently. And, at the same time, they have no upper limit at which point they are ready to take their profit and not risk the chance that the stock is running out of steam.

What the long-term investor can borrow from trader's-mind is a closer, more disciplined attention to acceptable versus unacceptable risks. With that attention, precautionary measures to manage the unacceptable risk need to be taken and this means having clearly defined exit goals from all long-term positions. Institutional traders and fund money managers know their exit price, and so should you.

Levels of Support and Resistance

Related to considering exit points and having mental, if not actual, stop losses to protect profits and limit losses, the disciplined short-term trader is often more tuned in than the long-term investor to what are called the *support* and *resistance* levels of a stock.

Support means the level at which a falling stock's price will be met with buyers coming in to prop it up so that it does not fall further. The stock is deemed at the support price to be a good buy. Buyers are willing to jump in at this level. When you look at a chart of a stock, you can determine the level of support by noticing where it "bounces" off a price repeatedly.

There is usually more than one level of support, each signaling a more severe drop than the one above it. Stock charts indicate these support levels and are well worth paying attention to. If the long-term investor knows where the stock is supported, he or she may then use this information in considering entrance and exit points. When the stock breaks through its first support level, traders may use this information to consider getting out. They can see where the next support level will be. Often, breaking through the initial support means the stock will enter a free-fall before hitting the second level.

Not being aware of these fairly stable levels of support, long-term investors will tend to panic when the stock falls through the initial support level. They will then sell out of anxiety and even panic, having no idea why the stock is in a free-fall. The investor who is technically able to read the chart and determine these levels will not be surprised that a free-fall ensues when the stock breaks through its initial support level.

Long-term investors need to have this rudimentary information in helping them understand why a stock is falling so fast. Then they need not panic and end up selling at the bottom, which is often the second or third level of support.

Conversely, the concept of resistance is simply that a stock will tend to rise to a certain point and then have trouble breaking through a specific number. Some stocks will sit at their resistance point for days or even weeks or months before they break out and head higher. And sometimes they never will make it past a certain point, no matter how long you wait. You can watch it come right up to the number and then fall back; this will happen repeatedly, and when it does, it is viewed as the resistance point.

This, too, can be useful information for deciding a possible exit point. At the least, you have an idea why the stock refuses to go any higher when it hits this point. Although for those who do technical analysis the concepts of support and resistance are taken as a truism, large numbers of online investors do not know of them.

Sometimes these resistance points are whole numbers that mark a new decade, like 20, 30, or 40. This is why you see smart traders put in sell orders for something like 29 7/8 rather than 30. They know it is tougher to push the stock to the next whole number and they also know that less sophisticated investors are thinking in terms of whole and half numbers. Because there are more of them waiting in line to sell at this round price, let's say 30, they know it will be easier to hit the bid price of 29 7/8 or 29 13/16 than the round number. So, basically, you decide to cut in line in front of everyone waiting for 30.

You can easily verify this by watching the movement of a stock on Level I dynamic, updating quotes. Sometimes the price will hang around the whole number a long time, just under it, before breaking through. I have seen times when the price never has enough steam to break through. This can be viewed as a "miniresistance" and is often controlled, at least to some extent, by market makers. Of course, when the pressure of buy orders pushes the stock up, the market makers step out of the way and let it run its course.

A stock's resistance point is important to know for another reason. When you see a stock break out sharply above the resistance point, you don't want to be in a hurry to sell it, as it needs to be given some latitude to find the new resistance. When you watch quotes on a real-time "tick" graph that charts the movement from minute to minute, it is pretty clear after a while how these support and resistance numbers affect traders.

So, our main point here is that the concepts of support and resistance may be useful to longer-term investors, just as they are used by active traders, to help plot entrance and exit points, and to have a way to help make sense of a stock's movement.

Now, like anything else in the securities markets, the concepts of support and resistance will hold for much—but not all—of the action that takes place. There are limitations to all the charting concepts used by technicians, just as there are obvious limitations to the traditional fundamentals when applied to Internet companies.

No one—whether they were using technical or fundamental analysis, computer programs, phases of the moon (some were saying that the fact that the moon was 100,000 miles closer to the Earth on December 23, 1999, closer than it had been in 120 years, made for the surge) or anything else—could have predicted an astonishing 86 percent gain in the NASDAQ for the year of 1999. The normal valuations applied to Internet and selected high-technology stocks went out the window. Typical resistance points were blown through as if they never existed. The market showed us something toward the end of 1999 that no one had quite seen before. It left long-time Wall Street watchers and seasoned traders shaking their heads in disbelief.

Which all goes to prove what? *That the market has a mind of its own.* And sometimes it belies and perplexes even the most sophisticated computer programs that we can apply to it.

In Gestalt psychology, this is stated as the concept that "the whole is greater than the sum of its parts." As applied to the market, we can take this to mean that no one individual can possibly grasp all the pieces of the market puzzle at once. As we said, we are always being forced to make decisions on limited data. No one person or group can control the whole market (on second thought, maybe Alan Greenspan can). But the forces of individual traders, fund managers, large institutions with computer programs, foreign investors, short sellers, options investors—and every other human and material aspect of the market, through their respective complementary and opposing actions, together create an entity that is larger than the sum of all the individual parts.

All patterns that are used to predict future movement of a particular stock or the market as a whole are based on the notion that the past accurately predicts the future and that we can project these past patterns to predict the future. While this is more true in certain aspects of life, it just isn't true when it comes to the stock market. While the past patterns may be quite useful in making educated guesses about the future, there is no direct cause-and-effect relationship, much to the dismay of business school professors, economists, market historians, chart technicians, and analysts.

It is far easier to predict the individual behavior of people playing the market than it is to predict the short-term or long-term moves of the entire market itself. You know the stale qualifier that all brokerage companies include when they give the yearly return on investment of funds: "Past performance is no guarantee of future results." And, of course, sometimes past performance is a contraindicator of future results!

The Psychology of Market Maker "Head Fakes"

Active traders know that market makers for NASDAQ stocks like to play mental electronic games. Longer-term investors can save some emotional wear and tear by being aware of the head fake, so when they see it they will not react quite so instinctively and end up feeling duped.

The purpose of the head fake, as in basketball or football, is to make it look like the play is going one way when it is really going the other way. The fact that this goes on electronically is one argument for more casual investors not to being glued to the monitor all day, thus not having to negotiate and sustain the short-term abrupt movements that speed hearts up and clench stomachs into knots. And yet it is considered simply part of the game for traders, and can be exciting when the reversal move is in the direction that they're looking for, as I will indicate later in this chapter.

Sometimes, market makers will scare the hell out of traders and spook investors by taking a fast-moving Internet stock down 10 points or less in a matter of literally two minutes. The idea in doing this is to force what are thought of as the "weaker hands" (or the "scared money") into selling their shares, out of fear that they will lose whatever profit they may have accumulated. Or, to scare those who are watching a loss mount up tick by tick to bail out so as not to lose even more.

When a serious head fake is taking place, it can come out of nowhere. Things are looking nice and calm and then the stock jumps down violently and keeps moving straight down. No one steps in to buy, each tick is less than the one before it. It's a free-fall and each tick is costing a lot of people a lot of money.

I watched this occur during a few minutes' reversal a couple of days ago. Redback Networks, considered one of the "red hots," had been hovering around 134 or so since the open of the market. Suddenly, it starts sinking. In less than two minutes it is down over 10 points. At this point, finally some buyers come in and 10 minutes later, it had recovered all but two of the 10-point loss. Now, this was in the midst of the greatest surge in technology stocks in December that the market had ever seen, and especially the "red hot" Internet business-to-business and infrastructure stocks. This was a head fake that could scare anyone, no matter how experienced.

What makes this so scary is that by the time you realize what is happening, it is already too late to react. Unless you have direct access execution, you will be too slow to get in a sell order. The stock will have already dropped 10 points before you've pulled the trigger. And, ironically, this is one of those times where the limitations of the technology actually benefit the investor. Because by the time you've comprehended what's happening and decided to sell, entered an order, confirmed it, and sent it to your brokerage, the stock has already begun to come back up again. So, the slowness of the execution process may unwittingly give you the time to reconsider as to whether you want to react out of fear. As the stock begins changing direction, the anxiety dies down and the trade can be canceled or voided.

Now, in addition to the jarring head fake, here is what was so amazing about this particular day. Once Redback had recovered, not much was happening to it until about 45 minutes into the close of the market. It was still down for the day, and hadn't done much when all the other stocks in its universe had been doing well.

What happens? Well, the thing takes off like a rocket, the likes of which I can't remember ever seeing before in quite the same way. Redback begins climbing straight up with almost no selling for the entire time up to the close of the market. It leaps from 134 up 5, 10, 20, 30 points to just over 163 and then, just at the close, falls back to 162. All of this is in only 45 minutes! It was the prettiest move up on a real-time tick graph I can remember seeing. If, a few years ago, someone had told me I would end up describing a stock's movement on a chart as "pretty," I would have laughed and said they must have me confused with someone else. But this was a sight to behold. There is, indeed, a certain aesthetic elegance in watching a stock surge straight up on a graph without pause that can be appreciated only by those who indulge in this kind of investment minutiae.

PRICE MOMENTUM INVESTING

The preceding story of Redback shooting for the moon is an example of the power of price momentum. Traditionally, price momentum trading was the province of day traders, who, as we have mentioned, would jump in and out of fast-moving stocks without caring what the ticker symbol stood for or what the company did. But price momentum trading is no longer just for day traders. It has become quite the fashion. And online investors have contributed to the life of the investing party.

Bob Pisani, CNBC commentator on the floor of the New York Stock Exchange, in reflecting at the end of 1999 on the most significant events of the year, believed that the popularity of price momentum investing was the biggest investment story of the year. He ranked it to be even more important than the rise of ECNs, the explosion of popularity in IPOs, or even the astonishing performance of technology stocks for the year. His point was that mutual fund managers, hedge fund managers, and, most significantly for our purposes, individual online investors, had become more taken by the price momentum approach than by value investing or the buy-and-hold approach. Perhaps not so surprising that momentum investing would become popular when everything is going up!

Stocks like Redback and other fast-moving Internet infrastructure and business-to-business plays are not the only ones upon which Pisani was commenting. He made the point that in all sectors, not just technology high fliers, the move toward momentum investing had dramatically increased.

For the online investor who chooses to be a part of momentum investing, the requirement is to be able to jump in relatively quickly to what is moving and to see these plays as great until their steam runs out and then to move on. The change in thinking is that more trading in and out of positions is necessary, since by definition, momentum doesn't last forever. Another change in thinking is realizing that the traditional fundamentals that investors have typically used to make their decisions may have little or nothing to offer when it comes to a momentum play.

What long-term investors can borrow from trader's-mind, then, is the agility of mind and quickness of reaction to take a ride on fast-moving stocks without the traditional fears that have tended to block them from taking this kind of risk.

Toward the very last days of 1999, little old ladies who were used to safely stashing their money in bond funds were calling their brokers and demanding that they sell the funds and put the money to work in Internet stocks. This, of course, was seen as a telling indication that the frothy tech stock train was heading for a crash, that the market had reached its top. If price momentum investing continues to be popular, many of the tools we have discussed in this book will be useful to the investor who wants to risk at least part of his or her capital in these kinds of positions.

TRADING STAGES, RHYTHMS, AND CYCLICAL EVENTS

Investors who don't trade very often usually don't pay much attention to the rhythms of the trading session. They don't utilize some of the information that short-term traders take for granted and use daily to help time their trades. With this information, investors would not make some of the bad trades they make, like buying at the wrong times when they pay the highest prices or selling at times that almost guarantee them less than they could get at other times. Some of these rhythms are more crucial than others. Some of them are best learned with experience, not just being told. But all of them should become part of the common knowledge of the disciplined online investor.

Typical Stages of the Trading Session

Generally, active traders who are watching and trading the market all day tend to break the trading session into three broad divisions, each lasting about two hours. Both the first and last segments are characterized by heavier volume, while the middle two-hour period is relatively light. If we want to refine the stages a little more precisely, we can break down the trading day into five stages, each one having a particular event that characterizes it.

The first stage is what is called the *clearing* stage at the open of the market. It usually lasts about 20 minutes into the new trading session. It is during this time that the market makers on the NASDAQ and the specialists on the New York Stock Exchange must execute all the orders that have accumulated since the close of the market on the previous day. The opening of the market is usually a particularly volatile time, with strong volume—often the strongest volume of the day—and not considered a good time for inexperienced investors to try and trade.

One reason for this volatility is that the market makers have a distinct information advantage over the casual investor, who has no idea what kind of orders have accumulated overnight and are stacked up, waiting to be executed. Because of this, the unaware and naive investor can be caught in a "whipsaw" effect wherein he or she pays too much for a stock, not knowing what the market maker does: that the price will be brought down as soon as the accumulated orders have been executed.

In other words, the opening bid and ask prices may be set artificially high so that market makers can clear their slates of waiting orders, and then bring the stock back down. When you watch Level II quotes or even Level I quotes from premarket trading up until the time the market opens at 9:30 A.M. EST (6:30 A.M. PST), it is easy to see how bid prices are often inflated. This gives the impression that the stock has been bid up in premarket trading and that it is going to jump upon opening. Sometimes this is an accurate reading of what is happening. But often, it is not. Since the bid price has been artificially jacked up, the offer price gets inflated, too.

If you jump in to buy at this early point, you will often be paying too much for the stock, only to see it drop quickly within the first 20 minutes or so of the opening. So it is not the time to buy. But it can be a good time to sell, often representing the highest bid price of the day.

Short-term traders who hold positions overnight like to take advantage of these inflated opening prices. They may buy stock at the close, in hopes of seeing it "gap up" at the opening. They sell their positions before the market makers bring the stock back down. So, for experienced traders, the opening of the market can be a good time to sell stock. And it can be a good time for casual investors to sell a position as well, either by having a limit order in place, or by watching the action closely and then "hitting the bid" when they see a price they are happy to sell at.

Again, just to emphasize: the opening of the market is a terrible time for the casual investor to try and jump in to buy stock. Putting in a market order to buy at the opening is one of the most common and foolish mistakes that inexperienced or unknowledgable investors make. The simple rule here for investors is: Never try and buy any stock with a market order at the open. And, in this case, never really means *never!* You are guaranteed to pay the highest possible price the market maker can get you to pay and cursing yourself for your mistake an hour later.

The cliché in trading circles is that the first hour of the market is called the "amateur hour" because all the beginners make all the wrong moves for all the wrong reasons in this first hour. Investors need to sit back patiently and watch how the action unfolds. They need to see what the trend for the morning will be. It is usually unwise to try and buy anything during the first hour unless you are an experienced trader who knows how the market gets manipulated during this period.

The Reversal Stage

After the clearing stage, the next 10 minutes or so (9:50 to 10 A.M. EST, 6:50 to 7 A.M. PST) is called the "reversal." In this relatively brief period, whatever trend has been established over the first 20 minutes is reversed. Why does this occur? Because the market makers, who have been either predominately buying or selling from the open, now line up on the other end (that is, if they having been buying at the open, they begin selling) to make gains by taking the market in the other direction.

It is important for the casual online investor to remember that the market makers and specialists have no real interest to see the market go one way or the other. Their money comes from commissions, so all they want to do is make as many trades as possible, scalping whatever spread between the bid and the ask they can get away with, in addition to a small commission per trade. They are experts at knowing every possible way to take advantage of quick, short-lasting reversals in the trend and countertrend.

They are masters at getting the unknowing investor to pay the highest price to buy and take the lowest possible price to sell. They know how to move markets faster than you can possibly react. To verify this, simply watch a Level II quote screen on any fast-moving stock, like CMGI, Inktomi, JDS Uniphase, or any other of the so-called red-hots that have strong volume and volatile price changes.

For example, I recently observed JDS Uniphase being bid up eight points in the premarket. At the open the stock began rising, continuing up another three points. After about 15 minutes, it began a swift reversal that wiped away all of the 11 points it had been up. What happens to the people who think it's going to continue up and buy when it reaches its high of 11 points up? They get their head handed to them on a platter, that's what. This is why common knowledge suggests that you not get caught in this early trading action. Traders know it, and investors need to know it, too.

Some traders believe the reversal stage is a good time to jump in and buy. But unless you are following the action very closely, you will find it tough timing your entrance just right.

While it is never transparent to the trader or investor how much influence the market makers actually have in pushing the market versus responding to computer buy and sell programs or large orders from money managers and institutional traders, it is wise to be very careful in volatile stocks by always using limit orders to buy and sell.

I will almost never use a market order at *any* time of the day, as I am unwilling to be tossed around in the stormy sea of quickly moving numbers. No stock *ever* seems worth chasing at any price—either I will control the price I pay or I will not play the game—very simple. And if it doesn't hit my price one time, I know there will always be another opportunity. This is where the discipline of being able to wait patiently for your price comes into play.

The only time I will even consider a market order is when it is clear from Level II that there is plenty of stock to buy or sell at the price I am wanting and that trading is proceeding relatively slowly. Then and only then I may safely enter a market order and not risk surprise.

For those who favor limit orders as I do, one recent related development for your consideration: As of early 2000 there is at least one company, R. J. Thompson, a new start-up online brokerage (*rjt.com*), offering both market and limit orders at the price of $5. Up to now, investors have always had to pay slightly more for limit orders. Now that this is changing, there is little reason not to protect yourself and use limit orders for almost all trades.

Intelligent Trading Stage

From about 10 to 11:30 A.M. or 12 noon EST (7 to 8:30 or 9 A.M. PST), the market settles down and a predominant trading trend until the afternoon session tends to be established. It is during this period that much of the trading by professionals takes place and where the market movement is best for active traders. Investors should use this period of the trading session to enter and exit positions with a greater degree of probability that market makers do not have as much advantage over them in the way of information.

Economic reports that are not announced before the market opens usually come out during this period, as well as company news that may move an individual stock or an entire sector. Stocks tend to settle into a range that sometimes points to their trend for the day, although in a volatile market when news may be announced, the morning session trend may be thrown upside down by what happens in the afternoon session.

Mid-Day (Lunch) Stage

This occurs at 12 noon EST and 9 A.M. PST and lasts until about 1:15 P.M. EST (10:15 A.M. PST) on a day of good to heavy volume. On a slow day, the closing action may not begin until 2 P.M. EST (11 A.M. PST). Usually, on a typical day, this is the least active stage of trading for the day, where stocks tend to settle into a narrow and uneventful trading range. Day traders tend to take a break at this stage, not wanting to "burn tickets" (rack up commissions) by trying to scalp when the action is relatively light.

Investors should use this time to analyze the early session trend and plot possible afternoon positions. This is a good time to step away from the computer, stretch, or do something else so that you are not too caught up in the trading action. Investors should know that this is not the best time to enter the market, as it is best to get a sense of the closing stage action before jumping in.

The significant event that occurs at noon (PST) is that the bond market closes for the day. This can create added activity in the stock market in the few minutes leading up to noon, as bond traders begin adding or subtracting liquidity to the market. Investors should be aware of this, and be careful during this few minute period.

The other significant activity that takes place during the mid-day period is that institutional traders are given a mid-day report by their research teams that influences the trading action beginning at 1 to 1:15 P.M. EST (10 to 10:15 A.M. PST). Certain stocks are touted by the analysts, and this leads to renewed trading in these stocks by the institutional traders that may result in sharp spikes up in these particular securities. Sometimes the action at this time is ignited by programmed trades, which are large block trades that kick in automatically and that have been placed earlier in the morning.

The Closing Stage

This stage begins at about 2:15 P.M. EST (11:15 A.M. PST) and lasts until market close at 4 P.M. EST (1 P.M. PST). The close is further divided into the period from 2:15 P.M. until about 3:30 to 3:40 P.M. EST and then the rather frantic action that takes place in the last 20 minutes or so before the market closes.

Active trading takes place during the first part of this stage, often—but certainly not always—following the trend established in the morning. On a more volatile, news-driven day, the trend reverses in the afternoon and there may be a steady sell-off after the market has been up through the morning and mid-day. Or, there may be a shift in trend in the other direction, as buyers come in and prop up what has up to then been a sagging market. Obviously, making generalizations about what may typically occur at any given stage is tough to do.

The last 20 minutes or so is like the opening 20 minutes, a volatile time, a dash to the finish line, wherein stocks may rise quickly and then fall just before the close due to individual and institutional traders jockeying for position as they close out the day. Many fast-moving stocks that have been up for the day will have a sell-off in the last 10 or 15 minutes or so, as day traders exit their positions to lock in gains and go home "flat."

Market makers have the upper hand during this period, just as they do at the open, as they know what orders are on file to be executed at the close. They will attempt to bring the stock up if there is strong buying momentum and they expect the stock to open strong the next morning.

This is a period that the inexperienced investor should avoid like the plague. It is not the time for even more experienced investors to enter a position, no matter how anxious you are to buy the stock, unless you can time your buy literally five minutes or less before the close. Remember, with the growing awareness and availability of trading in the after-hours market, you will always have a chance to buy a stock if you believe you must have it due to an anticipated news release or for some other reason.

Because stocks can be easily manipulated during the last few minutes by market makers, it is best for online investors to know the trading patterns of a stock toward the close before participating at this time. I have sometimes found this a good time to enter low-ball offers to buy and see if they get taken, when a stock is selling off during this stage. But I do it only when there is reasonable probability that the price I get it at will set me up to already put me ahead by the next morning. In other words, I never buy at the close if I think the price is going to continue to fall in after-market or next morning trading.

Cyclical Events Affecting the Market

Besides the broad stages of the trading day, investors also ought to be aware of some of the cyclical events affecting the market. Active traders stay informed of these events because they know that the events can influence the market. They then time their trades with these events in mind. While the more casual online investor is not going to go through the trouble of learning the various events that may affect the market, at least a passing familiarity with them gives you more of a piece of the puzzle.

The market is a curious beast in some ways. As a psychologist, I find it fascinating how wild and panic-driven the traders can become when there is a powerful rally or correction occurring. There is a certain primitive, gut-wrenching drama that gets played out in the heat of buying and selling that clearly provides an exciting adrenaline rush for the participants. All you have to do to confirm this is to watch the guys gyrating in the bond market or witness the scene in the commodities pits.

Don't think for a minute that those who last in these scenes don't like the action. They thrive on it. But it probably won't last much longer. Instead of guys standing around frantically calling out bids and offers, it will all be done by computers.

Knowing that there is a payoff to the frantic action makes it more understandable how some of these guys can last through this process on a daily basis. Most people would no more want to work in the commodities pit than be forced to dig for coal in the pitch-black depths of a Kentucky coal mine.

While there is this element of unpredictable and frantic action that takes place when the market is moving, on the other hand, traders seem to love things to be rather predictable. While on the one hand, they love to make big bets with their own and other people's money and thus are by nature risk takers, they also have a conservative streak that wants political and economic events not to disturb their trading world.

There are a number of repeating events that traders keep track of and live by. This is one of the interesting aspects to me about professional traders: they love the wild action and they also are slaves to the same events week after week, month after month. In a sense, being a seasoned trader means knowing how to predict market movement based on having experienced these events so many times before. And yet, while it is similar, the market never quite unfolds in just the same way. This is, of course, part of what makes the more mundane aspects tolerable for them.

Economic Indicator Reports

There are a number of rather dry economic indicators that astute traders pay attention to, some more carefully than others. Again, investors should be aware of them because they may affect the movement of the market when they are released.

Here are some of the indicators: Consumer confidence, consumer price index, consumer credit, employment cost index, employment report, existing home sales, gross domestic product, National Association of Purchasing Managers (NAPM), new home sales, producer price index, retail sales, and others.

The indicators that affect traders most heavily tend to be the following: Consumer price index (CPI), released about the 13th of each month at 8:30 A.M. EST; the Employment Report, released the first Friday of the month at 8:30 A.M. EST for the prior month; the report from the National Association of Purchasing Managers, released on the first business day of the month at 10 A.M. EST for the prior month; and Retail Sales, released around the 13th of the month at 8:30 A.M. EST for the previous month.

These four reports are most crucial to short-term traders because if there are any surprises that suggest a strengthening or weakening of the economy, the bond market reacts, which then affects the S&P futures trading, which affects the stock market.

Most casual investors have come to understand how important the meetings of the Federal Reserve Board are because of their effect on all the securities markets. Although usually of lesser impact than Fed decisions, these main economic indicators are still worth knowing and considering for the online investor. This is where having CNBC on in the background is very useful, as they are sure to be focusing on any timely economic data.

Earnings Reports, Warnings, and Whispers

This is one of the predictable rituals played out four times per year in the market. Since earnings are considered by many to be the fundamental engine that drives stocks forward, earnings season is never far away from the minds of those who follow the markets closely.

Because different companies report earnings according to their individual business year, the ritual of earnings reports tends to get dragged out over at least a two-month period. And when it isn't yet time for actual earnings to be released, traders are paying close attention to any preannouncements that companies may make as to whether they will fall short, meet, or exceed their own projected numbers and the assessments of independent analysts who cover the company.

In addition to possible preannouncement earnings warnings by companies which can cause a stock to tumble, there is a further phenomenon being played out that relates to earnings. And that is the enterprise of those who guess what the "whisper" number may be. The whisper number is what analysts unofficially think the earnings will come in at, usually exceeding the stated numbers by the company. This is why a company can meet the expectations they had set and yet still watch their stock take a dive—they fall short of the whisper number that has been set by a number of analysts.

The whole enterprise related to earnings often appears strange and nonsensical to the uninitiated casual investor. He or she has a difficult time understanding how a stock can rise and fall simply because a company misses its earnings projections by a penny or two. How can it make such a difference? It's only one business quarter, anyhow, right? Why punish a stock when it measures up to expectations but falls short of a whisper number? This is where the psychology of the market plays such an important role. If investors pay a premium for high-falutin tech stocks, then they want their expectations not just met but exceeded.

The casual investor is further mystified by the importance of the conference call that is coupled with the earnings release. One of the ways you can tell that you've become a very serious online investor is when you have the interest to tune into the conference call of the companies you're following. They are available on broadcast web sites, as well as by telephone, and are played at varying times, so anyone with the interest can find a time to listen.

How, investors wonder, can you not measure up to the earnings number but be saved by a "good" conference call that is positive and upbeat, wherein the company presents reasons for falling short as well as an optimistic picture of the upcoming quarter?

Why do analysts hear one conference call and walk away positively, giving the stock a reprieve, and yet hear another call and walk away and punish the stock? Sometimes it appears to the casual online investor that analysts, underwriters, and institutional traders interpret information in whatever way will best help them and the companies for whom they work get an edge and make more profitable trades.

Investors further wonder how one company can have all their proverbial ducks in line—make the number, equal the whisper, and have a good conference call—and still see a sell-off the next morning, as traders have "bought on the rumor and sold on the news." Another company may skyrocket when it, as they say, "blows out" the earnings number. There was a period during the summer and early fall of 1999, for example, when every tech company that came through with good earnings immediately sold off in the after-market and the next morning. This was viewed by market commentators as an indication of the skitishness of the market at that time, and that traders were oriented toward locking in profits rather than taking greater risk.

Other Cyclical Events to Be Aware Of

The beginning and endings of months and quarters tend to be related to good or bad performance of the market. The beginning of months tends to be positive, while the end of a month can be choppy, as portfolio managers want their month-end portfolio to look good. So they tend to sell stocks that are underperforming the market.

In the same way, the end of quarters brings on the same kind of selling, as money managers want to lock in gains of their winners and dump their losers. The buying and selling at the end of a month by big fund managers is called "window dressing," and simply means they want to end the quarter (and the year) with what are considered the top-performing stocks at the time. They want to be able to show those they work for that they have positions in the popular stocks. So, for the long-term investor, you simply want to be aware of when this is taking place, as it may affect a stock you are considering buying.

Another event that may spook the market is what is called the "triple witching" Friday, which falls on the third Friday of the month at the end of each quarter. It is on this day that falls the quarterly expiration of index futures, index future options, and certain stock options. What this means is simply that on this day the market tends to be more volatile, as prices get manipulated both in the morning and afternoon related to these expirations. Again, simply knowing that this is occurring can help explain some of the swings that may be witnessed in the market on that day and caution investors to be careful with their trading.

Program trades (large block trades of shares that are set in motion by computer programs at certain prices and/or times of the day) are common at about 3:30 P.M. EST each day. When they say that the first hour of the market is ruled by amateurs and the last hour is ruled by professionals, one of the ways this is meant is that these block trades are set in motion. These can drastically affect the share price one way or the other on those stocks that are involved, since the blocks being traded are very large.

Often, periods leading up to and following certain holidays tend to be associated with specific market performance. For example, the week between Christmas and New Year's has been a positive time for the market, as has January, when certain pension funds begin adding liquidity to the market. As another example, the two or three days leading up to the July 4th holiday has also been viewed as an up time for the market.

Technology stocks tend to do well during certain periods when there are a lot of technology shows and conventions where new products are introduced. At the same time, conferences with underwriters and analysts are used to report any good news that may give a boost to the stock price.

When the casual investor takes the time to understand how many cycles and patterns are played out in the market on a predictable basis, the striking thing is still, with all these scheduled events and themes, how little anyone is able to truly predict the direction of the market at any particular time.

In other words, while these patterns may increase the probability that the market as a whole, or certain sectors, may move in a certain direction, there are always other variables that are unpredictable and that have just as much sway on the movement in stock prices.

11

The Tao of the Dow

Zen may be viewed as the inner art and wisdom of the Orient. It was rooted in China by Bodhidharma, who came from India in the sixth century, and was carried eastward into Japan by the twelfth century. Zen emerged as a distinctive school from the blending of one strain of Buddhism (Mayahana) with Chinese Taoist pragmatism five generations after Boddhidharma translated the essence of Buddhism to China.

Tao (pronounced "dow") is the term for the absolute. It is a poetic term layered with meaning. It can be interpreted most simply as a way, or path, for people to follow. Tao is viewed not as a metaphysical abstraction but the fundamental rhythm, flow, and force of the universe. Bodhidharma described enlightenment as entering the Tao. Lao Tzu, who formulated the philosophy of the Tao, described it this way:

> Tao is real, yet unnamable.
> It is original non-differentiation and invisible.
> Nevertheless, nothing in the universe can dominate it.
> If rulers and lords were able to abide by it, all
> things in the universe would yield to them naturally.
> To abide with Tao in the world is to be the same as
> mountain streams flowing to the rivers and the sea.*

---

* *The Way of Lao Tzu,* translated by Wing-Tsit Chan, New York: Bobbs-Merrill, 1963.

Tao is viewed as the unity behind all things. It is single, like an uncarved block before it has been split up into individual pieces or covered up with superficial adornment.

This final chapter must by necessity be no more than a brief mention of Eastern concepts, as our intention is to inquire as to what these concepts may have to offer the online investor. It therefore runs the risk of sounding like just another overly simplified, cutesy "the zen of this, the zen of that" rip-off that cheapens the meaning of these rich traditions.

With that concern in mind, let me briefly offer my credentials: I began studying Taoism and practicing a Japanese (Nichiren) form of Buddhist chanting meditation in high school. In college, I learned T'ai Chi Chuan, a Chinese slow-movement form of meditation.

I have logged thousands of hours on the meditation cushion over the last 30 years, including intensive retreats in the Buddhist forms of Zen and Vipassana meditation. During the 1980s, I attended intensive 4- and 10-day Vipassana silent meditation retreats in the California desert for eight years consecutively. I have been exposed to the philosophies and methods of Zen, Theravadan, Tibetan, Taoist, Sufi, and Hindu teachings.

Over a decade ago, I did a month-long pilgrimage of Buddhist and Hindu temples in India and Nepal, including a week with the Tibetan monks at His Holiness the Dalai Lama's residence in the high mountains of Dharamsala, India. And, closer to home, over the last quarter century I have presented papers at conferences, given workshops, and published dozens of professional articles and one book on the integration of Western psychotherapy and Eastern thinking.

I state this background simply to attest to my theoretical and experiential knowledge of what I am writing about. I would not venture to introduce these ideas in such a cursory fashion in a book on cybertrading if I didn't believe there may be some value in doing so.

Let us ask, then: After explaining these concepts, what might we take from them to help us when watching and trading the market? Can we possibly find the Tao in the Dow? Can the game be anything more than beating the market and making money? That is what we will address in this final chapter.

The Zen habit of self-searching through meditation to realize one's own true nature, with insistence on self-discipline and simplicity of living, ultimately won the support of the ruling classes in

Japan and the profound respect of all levels of philosophical thought in the Orient.

Zen has been described as a teaching without scriptures, beyond words and letters, that points to the essence of one's highest mind and a seeing directly into one's truest nature. That is why Zen masters often answer questions with silence or simple acts, pointing to something ineffable. That said, there are indeed scriptures and plenty of books that have tried to capture the flavor of Zen thinking and practice. But most of these materials point the reader toward meditation practice as the doorway to experiential understanding.

Zen spirit has come to mean not only peace and understanding, but devotion to art and work. To begin to understand the meaning of Zen, according to teachers, is to begin a rich unfolding of contentment and insight in our lives. It is to appreciate the expression of innate beauty and the intangible charm of incompleteness. And it is to understand the meaning of the present moment in our lives and how we may sink deeply into this moment in all its richness and simplicity, even when faced with unpleasant emotions such as fear.

> **Buddha told a parable in a story:**
> A man traveling across a field encountered a tiger. He fled, the tiger after him. Coming to a precipice, he caught hold of the root of a wild vine and swung himself down over the edge. The tiger sniffed at him from above. Trembling, the man looked down to where, far below, another tiger was waiting to eat him. Only the vine sustained him. Two mice, one white and one black, started to gnaw away at the vine. The man saw a luscious strawberry near him. Grasping the vine with one hand, he plucked the strawberry with the other. How sweet it tasted!*

Zen carries many meanings, none of them entirely definable. If they are defined, they are not truly Zen. This is what confounds the Western mind, looking, as it does, for a neat and packaged definition to pin down the meaning. "Just tell me the real meaning of Zen." But Zen refuses to do this.

Related to this, for over a decade I have had personalized license plates that read: *zen mind*. Quite often, someone will see the plates, be curious, and come up to me and ask, "What does this mean? What is Zen mind?" And I will usually say something like: "It means the universal mind that is all minds, the highest nature of

---

* *Zen Flesh, Zen Bones,* compiled by Paul Reps, New York: Doubleday, 1958.

your own mind." And they might smile at me, nod as if they understand, and mutter, "Oh, I see, that's cool."

Or, if they are a bit bolder (and older), they may ask, "Do *you* have a Zen mind?" And I might respond: "Of course I do, don't you?" and then smile. Or maybe: "Sometimes I do and sometimes I don't, sometimes I will and sometimes I won't," and then smile smugly, knowing this is a very Zen-like answer.

Or, when I'm in a playful mood, I might answer: "Do you think an agency as conscientious as the DMV would have dared issue me these special plates if I didn't? After the eye exam, they brought in a Zen master to rigorously test me and I passed with flying colors." Straight face, no smile. This is not what they are expecting to hear.

Everything up to this point has been money-focused: How to use speedy cable modems or direct access connections, how to get the jump on the other guy so that we can make a faster trade and make more profit; how to preserve our capital, balance our thinking and emotions, exercise self-control—all in hopes of making high returns.

But is there any goal beyond being a good, disciplined online trader, beyond making money? Money in the service of what? A house in the country or a boat in the marina? More vacations? Private schools for our children? No worries about money? How much of our contentment in life is dependent on amassing material wealth? How much money do we need to be content in this short life and how much of our precious time do we want to spend making it? What does it mean to live a prosperous life? Here is one meaning of prosperity as a Zen master views it:

> A rich man asked Sengai to write something about the continued prosperity of his family so that it might be treasured from generation to generation.
>
> Sengai obtained a large sheet of paper and wrote: "Father dies, son dies, grandson dies."
>
> The rich man became angry. "I asked you to write something for the benefit of my family! Why do you make such a joke of this?"
>
> "No joke is intended," explained Sengai. "If before you yourself die your son should die, this would grieve you greatly. If your grandson should pass away before your son, both of you would be broken-hearted. If your family, generation and generation, passes away in the order I have named, it will be the natural course of life. I call this real prosperity.*

---

* *Zen Flesh, Zen Bones.*

Zen would have us reflect upon the simple things in life, especially the natural world, for an appreciation of the beauty and perfection inherent in things just as they are. Remember I suggested earlier walking outside during the trading session for periodic breaks? I walk in my backyard garden and listen to the waterfall. Sometimes I skim the leaves out of the small pond that the water cascades into. I look at the stone Buddha statue sitting next to the waterfall and use the lush garden setting to clear my head of the quotes on the monitor, the talking heads on CNBC, and the Wall Street money-is-everything mentality.

I close my eyes and meditate on the sound of the water falling into the pond. And sometimes, Zen-like phrases come to mind:

Searching between a rock and a hard place
to find the Tao in the Dow
even my 15-year-old nephew knows
it isn't hiding in Alcoa

Fortunes come and go in lickity 2 for 1 split mind moments
oh look! there goes JDS Uniphase blasting off to the second
uniphase of the moon

Riding high in the saddle on Redback Networks,
I enter the consulting room smiling.

Zen would remind us that no matter how successful we are as traders and investors, ultimately the most important thing we can do is to know our own deepest essence. It would instruct us to ask, just as we are feeling excited, skillful, and prosperous after a winning trade, "Who is it who feels giddy with satisfaction over making some money?" "Who is it who lets his whole attitude and demeanor for the day be conditioned by a rise or fall in the Dow or the NASDAQ?"

Looking for a rise in the Tao this morning,
the shimmering vibration of the hummingbird to my left
reminds me not to look any further.

The search for one's Buddha nature in Zen means the same as finding one's own deepest self-nature. It is to find the essence of who we are behind the online trading that we do. Can we possibly find our own highest nature through the process of online trading? Or, to state it another way: Can online trading teach us something about ourselves that takes us beyond ourselves to something larger?

Zen inquiry asks us to penetrate who we are behind our actions and behind our usual pretensions and identifications. More self-inquiry: "Who is it who is so frightened at losing his capital?" "Who is it getting so excited when Redback climbs 30 points in 40 minutes?" "Who is it who is feeling greedy after holding for so long, wanting just a little bit higher price for Dell before selling?"

Zen suggests that we stay flexible in our self-concept of who we think we are. In the same way we have said we need to be able to shift our mental gears quickly when a stock story changes, a sector changes, or the psychology of the market as a whole changes, we need to stay fluid in how we go about constructing our identities.

We should not allow ourselves to get too locked in to any one approach to investing, any one method, tool, opinion, or behavior. While a disciplined approach is useful to keep us on track, Zen would suggest we learn when to drop the discipline and accept what is new in this moment, what is right in front of us and calling for a response.

Rigid personality types can't handle Zen spontaneity. It threatens their compulsive routines. And yet, Zen monks are as orderly, precise, and predictable in their daily routines as the most neurotic, compulsively disciplined people you could find! But the distinction is, they do it from a radically different mental state. They are not performing their rituals out of anxiety, as the compulsive is. They are very present with each precise movement—not at all leaning into the future. And because they are so present-centered, they are free to respond with spontaneity to the demands of the moment.

An example of overly rigid discipline would be not having the flexibility to flow with the market when many technology stocks took off for an unprecedented ride toward the end of 1999. If we are too stuck in one approach, say value investing, or too caught in our doubting of what we see happening, we would not be able to shift gears and adapt to the market just as we find it. As we said in Chapter 10, the window to adjust to the violent changes seems to be getting smaller, as violent ups and downs are compressed into shorter periods of time.

Some continued to argue against having positions in telecommunications or Internet business-to-business stocks on fundamental or technical grounds. They worried about parabolic upward curves that they believed would collapse on themselves and interest rates that were three months into the future—all the while missing out on what the market was telling them.

They said things like, "The bubble won't last, everyone will end up losing when the correction begins. It's far too speculative, the bubble will burst." And how could it not burst after being up 86 percent for the year? The tide finally turned with at least three very ugly days of brutal sell-off during the first week of January 2000. But their ideological thinking stopped them from participating as this sector surged upward. Their fears prevented them from taking calculated, hedged, and reasonable risks that could have been very profitable.

While Wall Street tends to live in the future, with one eye on the next quarter's earnings warnings and one foot always out the door, ready to sell, Zen might question whether this attitude of worry and apprehension is really going to be the best approach. Zen would coax us to find a way through or around the "wall of worry" that the market is always having to climb. It would remind us that if we have constructed our view of the market as being composed of a wall of worry, then we will always find something to worry about, and therefore, a wall that needs scaling. So, the Zen master might give us a *koan*, or riddle, that can't be solved through the intellect but only by a breakthrough realization: "Ah, how do you realize your Buddha nature when you climb wall of worry?"

As we have made clear, the online investor needs to muster all the rational thought he or she can so as not to be overwhelmed by the power of emotions such as fear and greed. The fast pace of the market, as we have said, almost begs us to leap to action before we may be ready, and always with limited information. If we are to hug the emotional flatline, we need to temper these strong emotions with the strength of clear thinking. Thought allows us to hold back from impulsive reactivity. It creates the mental space necessary to act from conviction after due consideration, not from the anxiety of the moment being dictated by the herd mentality.

The strengthening and application of rational thought encouraged by cognitive psychology, however, is viewed with suspicion in Zen. In fact, Zen offers methods for cutting off thoughts at their roots, just as if they were tenacious weeds. It focuses more on attaining a state beyond thought and warns us not to take our thoughts as being "really" real. This is why I suggested the exercise of shuttling back and forth from the data on the screen to your inner world, always monitoring how your thoughts and fantasies are affecting your decision making.

Again: Most day traders and serious online investors have no idea how much time they are lost in fantasy while watching the market.

Now, fantasies themselves about the market are not necessarily a problem. In fact, they can be used to help motivate us to stay on a disciplined path of research and inquiry, and help fuel a growing passion for the market that sustains us during rough periods of loss. But Zen warns us that we far too easily hold *traces* of thought from the past that we become obsessed with and which distort the present:

> Tanzen and Ekido were once traveling together down a muddy road. A heavy rain was still falling.
>
> Coming around a bend, they met a lovely woman in a silk kimono and sash, unable to cross the intersection.
>
> "Come on, girl," said Tanzan at once. Lifting her in his arms, he carried her over the mud.
>
> Ekido did not speak again until that night when they reached a lodging temple. Then he could no longer restrain himself. "We monks don't go near females," he told Tanzan, "especially not young and lovely ones. It is dangerous. Why did you do that?"
>
> "I left the girl there," said Tanzan. "Are you still carrying her?"*

These past traces of thought may be derived from previous experiences trading the same stock or with a different stock but in the same situation. Of course, we want to remember our past outcomes so as not to repeat mistakes, or to remember past actions that worked so we may repeat them. But we need to be careful not to let the past mistakes unnecessarily frighten us so that we freeze and are unable to take the action demanded that is before us now, in this new but similar situation.

It is when we are not paying close attention that images arise. What I mean by this is that when we are fully present and paying attention, there is no gap for the mind to create thoughts or images. See what happens when you pay close attention to the changing quotes on your screen or to graphs of the movement of stock in real time. The mind, totally present with the moment to moment changing numbers, does not need to create fantasies about the future or get lost in reverie about the past.

QUOTES: MORE THAN MEETS THE EYE

Watching dynamically streaming and updating quotes, then, can be of benefit in helping us to learn to be more present-centered with our attention. While we are trying to calculate the best time to enter a

---

* *Zen Flesh, Zen Bones.*

trade or to sell a position, we will be more consumed with positive or negative thoughts and images than when we are totally focused on simply watching the quotes come and go. In this way, even though it is not our intention, watching real-time quotes may be used as an attention-training device, not just as a source of data. Be careful before you think that those who sit around watching quotes for long periods are "wasting" their time.

As with anything in life that we get involved in, there are worlds within worlds that begin to surface as you watch quotes changing. And believe me, had I not experienced it myself, I would never have believed such a mundane, passive, and "boring" activity could bring up the welter of thoughts, images, and feelings that it did. Anybody can experience a little anxiety watching if you have money on the line. I'm talking more about all the images and associated thoughts that bubble up when you do it for a while. But the key is to know when to walk away, take a break, and not to get trapped into feeling that you're going to miss something important if you're not sitting there all session long. *Don't get strangled by the tape.*

For those of you who resist watching quotes at all because you can't stand the anxiety of watching your money go up or down from minute to minute, at least experiment with it. It is useful to gain the emotional distance of being able to watch quotes for a while without being emotionally attached, even if you don't do much trading. Of course, it is especially useful for those who are more active online investors to be able to do this.

For example, I wrote much of this book with quotes flickering on a screen (a Java applet) behind my writing page. Every few minutes, when I wanted to see what was happening with my stocks, I would simply bring this quote screen forward. If I got too involved in watching a stock moving, I temporarily lost my focus on the writing. Because the market was moving so fast during the last two months of my writing, there were a lot of exciting times with stocks I owned making parabolic moves upward. It made my writing flow more easily—which would not have been the case had the market been going down in the same fashion.

Besides using the quotes as an attention-training device, they are also useful as a simple way to grasp the Buddhist notion of the impermanence of all things. We fight this impermanence with the quotes. We fight it while watching an updating portfolio manager that ticks off the changing value of our stocks. We resist it the same way we do seeing our bodies aging, or anything else in our lives that we can't stand to see change. That's what the Buddhists mean by the suffering we experience when we refuse to accept impermanence in our lives.

Watching our capital change from minute to minute, hour to hour, day to day, month to month is a minidrama representative of the other kinds of changes that take place in our lives. There is nothing quite like having made a healthy profit on paper, enjoying it, fantasizing how you will spend it—and then watching it abruptly evaporate in a violent sell-off—to bring home the notion of impermanence, is there? It can send us into a disorienting spin and tangle our stomachs into knots. So, the Zen master might ask, "Ah yes, how you find your Buddha nature in time of sell-off panic?"

Recall from our earlier discussion the concept of slouching toward the future. It is when we feel we must respond to the quotes—that is, we must use them to hurry and execute a trade—that they are going to be tinged with the anxiety of moving us forward in time. And, as we said, it is the perception of our *leaning into the future* that creates the tension that we feel.

When there is no demand to do anything and we can just sit back and calmly observe the quotes coming and going, it is then that we have the chance to use them as a way to melt into the present without the urgency to do anything. The quotes are what they are—just flickering numbers—nothing more. They lose the quality of anxiety we attach to them when we take them to mean our changing financial condition.

So, our task is to learn how to sink so deeply into the present moment that we refuse to let the tendency to feel the tension between the now moment and the next, upcoming moment, be filled with *leaning*. If you are going to spend much time watching updating quotes, you might as well derive some benefit besides just the information of prices, volume, time, and sales. Play with the real-time process and see what you can learn about yourself from it. But be sure to try it when you feel absolutely no interest in or urgency to do any trading. It is at these times that it is most easy to let go of the tension of leaning.

GAINING PERSPECTIVE ON MONEY

If you hang around day traders at all, one of the things you hear them echo is that losing money in the market is a "good thing." When I went to the first international day trading conference, which happened to

be held in my area in the fall of 1999, I heard this repeated by present-
ers: "You've got to learn how to lose money." Upon hearing this, it
was easy to think they were just being pessimistic. But what they were
trying to say by this is that you need to learn how to lose without it
knocking you out of the game. You need to be able to handle a loss that
may rip your guts out emotionally and not let this make you quit trading, even if it makes you gun-shy for a while.

In this way, they see losing as necessary and positive, so that
they may learn the lessons of loss and be able to sustain themselves
psychologically to keep moving forward in their learning curve.

Of course, because almost all day traders lose significant
amounts in learning how to do short-term trading, this "losing is
good" belief might be just a rationalization (good excuse) to make
losing more palatable. I mean, if they could learn the lesson without having to lose *too much*, I'm sure they would prefer this, no?
Perhaps this is another example of cognitive dissonance, the concept we presented earlier: If I tell myself losing is good and necessary for learning, it doesn't hurt so much and I am more able to handle the financial loss and the blow to my ego. I am less likely to give
up in failure.

One of the things that sustaining a loss can do is broaden your perspective about the place of money in your life. I have found that having
some losing positions over a long time no longer seems like such a big
deal, as it did many years ago when I first began trading individual
stocks. But it makes sense to say that one should never be risking
amounts of money that, if lost, would deprive one of a single meal.

Some would say your losses should never deprive you of any
sleep. But that is asking for a lot. Because sooner or later, the mistakes we make in timing, judgment, execution, or just bad luck can
lead to some losses that very well may keep us awake at night. To the
degree that any difficulty falling asleep can be used to analyze our
mistakes so we are not so quick to repeat them, a little insomnia, as
one of my teachers used to say, is nothing to lose sleep over.

Here's an example of one that caused me to sleep fitfully. It was
the third straight day of massive selling in early January after they
ripped the apron off the mother of all tech rallies. I happen to have
added to my position in Lucent Technologies about an hour before
news was released that, for the first time ever, they would fall short
of their first quarter earnings.

I spent the afternoon in my office seeing patients and did not find
out that something was drastically wrong until I called in for phone

quotes in the late afternoon. I couldn't believe what I was hearing. I told my wife, who works in the office suite with me, that I thought it had to be a misquote. Other stocks I own move 20 or more points up or down but not Lucent. When I finally got online at home and discovered the earnings warning, I was momentarily shocked. For a while that evening, I noticed I was not paying attention to the outer world, just my thoughts about the miserable day with the market.

I couldn't believe my bad luck to have bought more shares just before this news was released. And yet there was really no possible way I could have known of it. It was not as if I had made a bad judgment in buying, as the stock had gone down along with everything else that day and it looked like a decent buy. What looked like a nice potential gain turned out to be a big loss. It would have been bad enough to have the stock drop 20 points from where I left it when I went to the office with just the shares I already owned. But what added insult to injury was that I had had the misfortune and terrible timing to buy *more* just before it tanked in after-hours trading! It seemed like a cruel hoax.

Talk about not sleeping at night. Between Lucent and my other fast-moving tech stocks all suffering gigantic losses, it was probably the worst day of net worth loss for me in the market that I can remember. I am much more invested now than I was back in the crash of 1987 or other major corrections since then. But that's the game: If you're gonna play, you have to take the bad luck with the good. So, the Zen master might ask, "How do you become illuminated at moment when you learn Lucent dropped 20 points?"

Attachment to our money and fear of losing it makes it tough to take reasonable risks with our trades. I am much more willing to invest large amounts of money in stocks than I am gambling it away in Las Vegas. I simply will not let myself look at chips as "just chips." I am always aware of exactly how much each chip is worth and therefore am never willing to adopt the gambler's mentality of taking big risks. I will take risks with stocks but not at the craps table, even when I am rolling the dice and on a hot streak. So, I usually end up making money for everyone around me by hitting a lot of numbers but don't end up with much for myself, despite holding the dice for 15 or 20 minutes when on a good roll.

This attachment to the implied value of the money and my not being willing to unduly risk it became very clear when I was at a Monte Carlo night party. This is where they have all the games of a real casino but it's just play. I found myself holding back from betting the $100 chips at the craps table, *even when it was play money* and the denominations meant nothing—they were all equally worthless. I didn't want to lose my play money too quickly and be out of the game. I was trying to preserve my capital, practicing good money management, just like a good investor. This attachment to the value of denominations on the chips, though, does not make me a good enough gambler to ever strike it big in Vegas. I can easily live with that.

When we think about our relationship to gain and loss in general, not just with money, is gain always positive? Is loss always negative? When we reflect on past experiences, is it ever true that what we thought at the time was a gain was actually a loss and that what we thought was loss turned out to be a gain? I certainly have had this shift in the way I evaluated the initial "loss" when later, I saw how losing something was actually necessary to open up the possibility for a future gain.

Craving, Clinging, and Attachment

Buddhists talk about the process of *craving* and *clinging*. Craving comes from our relationship to feeling; feeling is the condition for craving. Craving is also translated as "unquenchable thirst." Craving is the movement of desire to seek out and sustain the pleasurable contacts with sense objects and to avoid the unpleasant or to make them end. Craving may be to have something or become someone or something or the craving to make something end.

When we crave something, we lose our sense of authority, giving power to that which we crave. We have a restlessness of appetite and think there's never enough, that just one more thing is needed to satisfy us—whether it be one more mental state, one more experience, one more orgasm, or one more big trading gain. This becomes a basic hunger and can color our daily world so that no matter what we have, it feels like it's just never enough.

When craving becomes intense, it becomes clinging. The way it becomes strong enough to become clinging is when fixed positions are taken about how the world is. Clinging, or attachment to these positions, helps us define a sense of identity, of what we believe in and what matters to us. It also involves our holding onto our values of right and wrong and what we think about how the world is and how it should be.

While, from a psychological point of view, all of this is necessary as part of the normal development of individual personality and character, Zen takes a different stance. It proposes that we not become too rigidly attached to any person, place, or thing. Zen is interested in personal enlightenment and the enlightenment of all other beings. Psychology is interested in shaping our character and finding and creating a healthy balance between our own personal needs and the needs of others.

Now let us look at one result when we are not satisfied with what we have and instead want what the other has. Here's a psychological and social artifact of the great bull market we have enjoyed.

A SIGN OF THE TIMES: WINDFALL PROFITS ENVY

In the same way some short-term traders in a trading room who do well are envied by other competitive traders who are not doing as well, long-term investors who have been fortunate enough to make large gains from the bull market become the easy target of envy.

We can think of envy as the painful or resentful awareness of an advantage enjoyed by another joined with the desire to possess the same advantage. Or, to put it in everyday lingo: "you've got it and I want it and I can't stand you for having it when I don't!"

Those who end up feeling envy may be unable to invest as much capital, don't choose the right stocks, or aren't willing to take the same degree of risk as those who do very well. Some aren't going to be as savvy as others and are unwilling to invest in individual stocks rather than mutual funds. Most don't have the resources to hire personal money managers to watch over their portfolio or are unwilling or unsuited to a good job of managing it themselves. But whatever the cause, the result, from the top of the investing hierarchy (or investing food chain) down to the bottom, is the same: The *prosperity* enjoyed by some creates a *disparity* suffered by others.

And, lo and behold, from the murky depths of this disparity and our baser instincts oozes forth from the slime the Green Monster of Envy.

When we feel envious of someone for something they have, it is easy to make a further association and judge ourselves as less than them—less successful, less intelligent, less beautiful, or whatever. We're not talking about being envious of just possessions here. Possessions are bad enough to long for, as we all know from our own experience. We're talking about nothing less than what it takes to obtain these possessions—the coin of the realm, the medium of exchange that determines the haves from the have-nots, the winners from the losers.

The desire for the other person's money is envy in its most raw form, isn't it? Perhaps the only thing that even comes close is the desire to possess his or her alluring sexual partner. But when you've got that person's money, you've got a better chance of winning his or her partner or can attract an equally desirable one, if you wish.

When we feel we *are* less because we *have* less, it's then common to think or say critical and disparaging things about how those we envy obtained what they have. We may gossip behind their back. Or if the envy is very strong and we can't contain it, we may say something directly to them or indirectly in the form of a snide remark. This makes it easier for us handle that they have something desirable that we want but don't have.

All of this comparing to, feeling less than, criticizing, and trying to even the score is so our ego doesn't suffer what psychologists call *narcissistic injury*. It may be done consciously and intentionally or unconsciously, just slipping out. The problem is that we end up equating what the other person has that we don't with our sense of self-worth.

It's an old story: If you have a much larger and more extravagant house than I do, a much fancier car, are able to enjoy travel to exotic places, wear more expensive clothes, and have many playthings that make life more stimulating and enriching, somehow I end up twisting my thinking and take this to mean that you a more valuable person.

I don't simply say you must be having more fun in life than I am, which may or may not be true, as we all know or know of rich but unhappy people. Or say you must be suffering less from the harsh realities of life, which is probably true. If I stayed with this, I would be on reasonably firm ground. But I take it further—and this next step is the psychological kiss of death. I actually convince myself that all this stuff makes you a more worthy and valuable human being. And if you happen to be famous, in addition to your stuff, well, that's just more than I can handle! "You've got it, and I want it." That's the tune of envy.

Most of us try to fight this kind of thinking and emotional reactivity. We do our best to realize that the measure of who we are as human beings transcends our material wealth and lifestyle. And a part of us really does believe it.

Perhaps we strive to live a good, ethical, and caring life, giving something back to others in some form. We realize that doing so brings us self-respect and the respect of others, dignity, and a measure of contentment. We rationally understand that money is useful as a tool to satisfy our material needs and wants and that it can buy us the time and freedom to do those things in life that we really want to do.

We try not to overly identify with our money and material stuff, knowing that our core sense of self must transcend *everything* with which we identify. If not, who will we be when everything is lost in a fire or when it is taken away from us? As we asked in an earlier chapter, who will we be when we lose a chunk of our investment capital?

We try to keep perspective by remembering all those who are lower on the materialistic food chain than we are. But there is no denying that everywhere we look, we are bombarded by every conceivable toy to help us through life and that we live in the most materialistic culture in the world. We are socialized from our earliest years to value money and all the great comforts, luxuries, cultural appreciation, good health care, and love and friendship that it can buy.

You think money can't buy love? Well, maybe in the sense that it can't force someone to open up his or her heart to you in that special way we call "love." But it sure can pay your entrance fee into the social hierarchy that allows you to meet charming, beautiful, and cultured men and women who are looking to live a nice, comfortable lifestyle, and want, as they say, "the best of everything." You say you don't have enough money to get through the guarded gates? "Well, sorry Charlie, you may be a wonderful person deep inside but on the surface, you're not quite what I'm looking for."

Money can't buy you friends? Of course it can—just ask anyone who had money and the friends that went with it and then lost the money and noticed friends didn't quite show the same interest. It happens all the time. Disgraceful and undignified people buy their way into prestigious private country clubs, exclusive gated communities, and high-powered social and political groups all the time. "Membership has its privileges." And money buys membership.

So, all of this is to say that it's tough not to feel envy when we see what others have. We imagine life being more happy and care-free *if only* we had the wealth of the other. Wouldn't it be nice, we tell ourselves, to never have to worry about money? To never have to think about how the bills will be paid? To have the freedom to see something we want and not have to think twice about whether we can afford it? To never have arguments with loved ones around the topic of money? To think to yourself and be able to exclaim to the world, "Money is no object"? Most people answer this simply, "yes."

I've now heard this envy phenomenon enough in varying forms both inside the consulting room from clients and outside in casual conversation with acquaintances to have given it a label: *windfall profits envy.*

A "windfall" is a sudden or unexpected gain. During the course of the last couple of years specifically (and over the last decade more generally), the gains for many have indeed been rather sudden and/or unexpected, certainly higher and faster than most ever imagined. Predictably, this has resulted in a euphoric sense of well-being for those fortunate to have partaken in the bull market festivities. But it is the seething envy felt by those who are left out or who compare themselves to those who have done better that we wish to point out here.

There is something different about the way people talk about those who have made a lot of money in the stock market. They seem to put it in a different mental category than when someone receives an inheritance. And while envy is a common emotion to experience when someone has something—any material possession or situation—and we want it, there is an especially sharp envious reaction to finding out that friends, acquaintances, business associates, or even strangers have made a killing in the market. The shorter the period of time it took to make the money and the greater the gain, the stronger the envious reaction.

Rather than muster up the emotion of sympathetic joy, or the identification with the other as we feel joy for their prosperity, instead, it is easy to want to make excuses or to disparage them. We can't stand that those who start off with the greatest resources end up making the most from their investments.

It is not always the case that only the wealthy may partake; growing numbers of those from the middle income bracket have taken risks and done very well in the market. But more often than not, the rich are still getting richer at a faster pace than those of modest means are getting comfortable. All of this is, of course, relative to what you've got and what you want. But here are a couple of examples at the higher end of the scale, both from my clinical psychotherapy practice.

Two Examples of Windfall Profits Envy

Ron has come to see me on and off for over a decade. He is a bright, capable, verbal, and opinionated mid-thirties computer programmer who writes custom software and who runs his own consulting business. He makes an excellent income but has never been able to manage his finances well enough to get free of debt.

Ron is an outspoken, self-absorbed workaholic who loves what he does and takes pride in his code-writing skills. Over the years, I have helped him mature from a rather insensitive, awkward, and judgmental man who disdained most social interaction and felt contempt for others into a man who could slowly step outside the insulated bubble of his work and allow himself to fall in love and marry. While he has had few interests outside his work and technology-related gadgetry, he is beginning to find meaning and pleasure in other facets of life that previously held little interest for him.

His brother, a few years younger than Ron, was also educated in computer programming. His brother got a very lucky break a few years ago and was hired by one of the big Silicon Valley Internet companies just as it was beginning to take off. He received stock options that, in an incredibly short time, became very valuable and made him wealthy beyond anyone's wildest expectations. Nothing moves faster than the valuation locomotive of the Internet express; Ron's brother was fortunate enough to climb aboard at the beginning of the line and is taking a swift ride with no end in sight.

Now, it was one thing for Ron to try and contain his feelings of envy in watching his brother have this windfall drop in his lap by being in the right place at the right time. It was especially tough for him to take that his brother never really had to work all that hard to build a successful consulting business, as Ron did. All he did was join the right company. Since Ron had the computer skills that could have just as easily filled the position that his brother was offered, this made the sting of his brother's windfall even more difficult to handle.

When he heard about his brother's stock options, Ron did his best to feel sympathetic joy for his brother's good fortune. At the same time, Ron wondered why he had to work so hard, still be in debt over many years, and shoulder the stress of running his own business, while his brother had stepped into financial heaven. Where was the fairness to it all? Didn't he deserve to step into a great situation like his brother?

So Ron was doing his best to contain his envy. But when he found out that his brother was going to receive a year-end bonus of $4 million, the mercury reading of his envy burst through the thermometer. He estimates his brother's net worth to be at least $40 million. The prosperity of one leads to the disparity experienced by the other—and boy, did he feel the disparity. His brother hasn't even had to actively manage a portfolio of securities. He just has to do his best to keep the stock price of his company going through the roof and his heart beating until he gets to cash in on all of his good fortune.

Comparing Apples to Oranges

A second example of windfall profits envy may be somewhat less transparent and dramatic. But it illustrates how easy it is to get stuck comparing ourselves to the person who is making more and living higher off the hog than we are. This seems to be a natural (socially learned) human bias: to focus more on the person who is above us on the financial and social pecking order than the one below us. Our desires keep us looking upward, if not always moving forward

If you are surrounded by people living lavishly with every convenience and plaything that money can buy, it is easier to get caught up in feeling envy than it is to feel grateful for what you have. To stay in touch with our own good fortune, we have to hang around (or at least visit) scenes where large numbers of people have much less than we do. It always works, at least for a while, until we leave the scene, come back to the land of lavish abundance, and then become unaware again.

In any case, this patient is about 40 and, like Ron, making a very good living as an attorney. He has put money into the stock market and has made a decent return. And he has enough in savings to make anyone feel secure. But he happens to have as clients people who are making very high returns from their investments. He compares himself to them and falls woefully short of the multimillions that they have been able to amass from their investments in the stock market and other holdings. And he ends up depressed and then ruminates about it.

He thinks he ought to be playing in the same league as they are. He has not been able to maintain the necessary and real boundary between himself and them, forgetting that he is serving them as clients, not on an even par with them. He walks around depressed for days at a time when he compares himself to them. Because he views himself as an entrepreneur, not just a contracts attorney, he believes he ought to be able to accomplish what they have accomplished.

This is similar to saying that because I may work with someone in psychotherapy who is far richer than I am, I ought to be able to earn the same as they do. The fact that we serve people in a business or professional relationship has little to do with how we compare to them in financial or social status. But like the example just given, when these are the people you are relating to on a daily basis, it is easy to blur the boundary and start thinking you ought to be where they are.

Pay attention to how you react to the good fortune of others, gained from the stock market or any other way. Notice in what forms envy may arise for you. You can be sure there will be plenty of opportunities to notice these thoughts and feelings bubble up. Expect to feel envy at least occasionally, as long as you are surrounded by the glittering toys that others have and that you would like.

See if you can remember that you are not any less of a valuable person than someone who is more wealthy than you are. But the trick is to do this without having to put the other guy down. And as you notice yourself comparing to others, identify with their good fortune and try to muster up the good feeling you imagine they must be feeling. The green monster of envy can be quite painful. But it is one of those emotions that we choose to indulge in and one that, with a little practice, can be transformed into sympathetic joy, or at least a healthy form of neutral disinterest.

EVERY MOMENT AT JUST THE RIGHT TIME

When we learn to live with our attention centered in the present, more and more of what the world presents to us can feel just right to us. More and more of what the stock market presents to us we can learn to accept with a measure of equanimity. To *present* something is to "bring it forth for consideration." What our life presents to us can feel just right for what we need, even if it is unpleasant or painful. We begin to sense the meaning of the Zen phrase that "every moment occurs at just the right time."

To be in this Tao, or perfect flow of life, requires a surrendering to the present, to what presents itself for our consideration. Whether it be a trade that goes bad, a market that goes against us, a quick opening to make a profitable trade, or even losing capital that we don't think we can afford to lose—all of these we learn to accept as part of the bigger picture of what really matters in our lives.

To face our anxiety and apprehension directly and begin to let go of the perpetual need to be threatened by leaning into the future is the first step to settling more gracefully into the present. And this present then becomes pregnant with possibilities that may lead to trading and investing excellence.

My hope is that this book has been helpful in increasing your awareness of yourself as an investor and your psychological dynamics as they relate to online investing. And I hope you are now more aware of some basics on the nature of the market from a psychological perspective. If you now have a greater appreciation for my slogan, "Mind moves the market," then I have succeeded in my task.

As we become more adept at accepting what life (and the market) bring forth for our consideration, may we gain the strength, courage, knowledge, and experience to more successfully manage our own investments and to use the profits wisely to help shape the course of our lives.

REFERENCES

Chan, Wing-Tsit, trans. *The Way of Lao Tsu*. New York: Bobbs-Merrill, 1963.

Hendlin, S. J. *The Discriminating Mind: A Guide to Deepening Insight and Clarifying Outlook*. London: Unwin Hyman, 1989.

Hendlin, S. J. *When Good Enough Is Never Enough: Escaping the Perfection Trap*. New York: Tarcher/Putnam, 1992.

Reps, Paul. *Zen Flesh, Zen Bones*. New York: Doubleday, 1958.

Shapiro, D. H. and J. Austin. *Control Therapy: An Integrated Approach to Psychotherapy, Health, and Healing*. New York: Wiley, 1998.

INDEX